CLAREN[...]

Michael Harrison

CLARENCE

Was He Jack The Ripper?

by

Michael Harrison

DRAKE PUBLISHERS INC   NEW YORK

© Michael Harrison, 1972

Published in 1974 by
Drake Publishers Inc
381 Park Avenue South
New York, N.Y. 10016

Printed in Great Britain

Library of Congress Cataloging in Publication Data

Harrison, Michael.
    Clarence: Was he Jack the Ripper?

    1. Whitechapel murders, 1888. 2. Albert
Victor, Duke of Clarence and Avondale, 1864-1892.
I. Title.
HV6535.G4H28   364.1'523'0924   73-15968
ISBN 0-87739-581-5

Contents

Endpapers: Whitechapel in the 1880s, showing the locations of the murders committed by Jack the Ripper.

Acknowledgments

In the preparation of any non-fiction work, the Author is necessarily indebted to many others for help.

First of all, my further acknowledgment of what seems to be a perpetual debt: the conscientious, professional assistance that any author may expect to receive from those too-often forgotten supports of the writer—the research and reference staffs of our public and private libraries. In this case, they are the staffs of the British Museum, the Westminster Public Libraries at St Martin's Street (Central Reference), Buckingham Palace Road (Westminster Collection) and Marylebone Road, and the Mile End and Whitechapel Road branches of the Tower Hamlets Public Libraries: to all of them, for past and present help, my many thanks.

For permission to quote from their works: Sir Philip Magnus-Allcroft, Bart, ('Philip Magnus'), for permission to quote from his *King Edward the Seventh*; Mrs Georgina Battiscombe, for permission to quote from her *Queen Alexandra*; to Mr Rupert Croft-Cooke, for permission to quote from his *Feasting with Panthers*; and to Mr Colin Wilson, for permission to quote from his article on Jack the Ripper in *The Leicester Chronicle*. And to their several publishers, respectively: John Murray, Constable & Co. Ltd, W. H. Allen & Co. Ltd and F. Hewitt & Son (1927) Ltd, of Leicester. For permission to quote from the late Dr T. E. Stowell's article in *The Criminologist*, thanks to Mr Nigel Morland

and The Forensic Publishing Co. Ltd, respectively Editor and Publishers of that famous journal. To all my sincere thanks.

My special thanks to my old friend Stephen Plomer, formerly of the Royal Hussars (Prince of Wales's Own), who introduced me to Lieutenant-colonel P. H. G. Bengough, the present commanding officer of this historic and distinguished regiment, and Major R. Archer-Shee, in charge of the Royal Hussars' Home Headquarters at Winchester. These two officers made me welcome both at Winchester and at Tidworth, opened their records to me, and gave me much valuable information concerning the military career of Prince Eddy. To them and to the other officers who received me, my warmest thanks.

I should like, too, to record my deep sense of obligation to a gentleman from a different profession: Dr James Harper, of Harley-street, the present Medical Director of St Andrew's Hospital, Northampton. For Dr Harper's professional assistance in enabling me to define, with accuracy, certain conditions of morbid psychology, as well as for his help in supplying me with valuable information relative to one of the central characters in this true story, I am most grateful.

I should like also to acknowledge, with fraternal thanks, that general willingness of fellow-authors to encourage one with suggestions, tips, the collection of apposite material, etc. I have already mentioned Colin Wilson's kindness in letting me quote from his article in *The Leicester Chronicle*; but his willing assistance did not end there. Despite an abnormally heavy writing commitment, he has still found time to give me valuable hints, and to point out directions in which my research might well find profit. He is not the only author to have shewn that selfless interest in another's work: to both Aubrey Noakes and John Montgomery, each a busily active writer, I also tender my thanks for generous and consistently forthcoming encouragement and practical help.

Let us candidly admit that there is . . .
nothing more difficult than to refuse yourself *anything*, when all men would grant
you *everything*.

Bossuet

Book I *Childhood*

1. Born before his time

PRINCE ALBERT VICTOR CHRISTIAN EDWARD OF WALES—'Eddy'
to all his family—was born at Frogmore House, Windsor, in
the bitter winter of 1863-4, which, with his mother's greatly
disturbed emotional state, may well have contributed to the
fact that he was born two months before full-term.

For his mother, the young and beautiful Alexandra, Princess
of Wales, it had been a bitter winter in more ways than one:
Christmas itself had been spent at Osborne House, in the Isle
of Wight, which the widowed Queen Victoria's necrophile
obsession with her dead husband had turned into a sort of
ghost-trap for the spirit of the departed—and even, one began
shudderingly to fear, for his resurrected physical presence.

Already the professional charlatans with a vested interest in
the supernatural had made their entry into Victoria's life, feed-
ing her credulity even as they battened on her wealth. The bedchamber in which 'He' (always spelt with a capital H) had died
was not, by the Queen's command, *left* exactly as it had been at
the time of his death, but *kept* exactly as it had been in the Consort's lifetime: the bed made afresh each day, the frilled night-
shirt laid out each night on the starched pillow, the hot water
for shaving brought up each morning, the soapdishes kept
charged with his favourite soap, the towels daily crisp-white on
the towel-horse. Even the chamber-pot, scoured with boiling
water each morning, with all the other chamber-pots in the

3

great house, was carefully taken out of its bedside cupboard every night and placed beneath the dead Prince's bed.

So the bedroom and dressing-room of the Prince Consort were to ape a living use for forty years, until, as almost the first act of King Edward VII as king, he ordered the trappings of this grim charade to be swept away, and fresh air, in both senses of the word, permitted to cleanse the rooms of their aberrant mortuary character. But that was not until 1901, and, in the meanwhile, the shadow of the dead hung—and was for decades to hang—exceedingly heavy over Osborne and over all who accepted the chilling hospitality of the Queen.

Christmas was an especially wearisome time at Osborne, for because the Consort had loved Christmas so much, adding to it those sentimental German warmths which, with Dickens's good public-relations work, effectually succeeded in Teutonifying the traditional British Christmas, the Queen was more than ever reminded of her 'perfect' Albert. There was, indeed, nothing in the Christmas observances—snapdragon, Christmas trees, presents beneath the tree, carols, roast chestnuts—which did not remind her of the paragon who had gone, and whom, despite all reason, she intended to resurrect by the force of passionate imagination alone.

The young Princess of Wales, still only nineteen, was chilled by the ghostly atmosphere with which her mother-in-law's obsession had charged every room and corridor of the great Italianate house. Alexandra—'Alix'—came from a land where ghosts were, and are still, taken *au grand sérieux*; where the ancient communion with the family dead maintained the old customs—the meals laid out for the wandering spirits, the curious ceremonies at tumulus and carved stone and bog-tomb to pacify the rebellious shades of the long-ago dead. As a daughter of the royal house of Denmark, she knew the old tales; knew of the old superstitions; acknowledged, if you will, that the dead are never *quite* dead, and that prudent people never begrudge the small, traditionally proven acts by which the dead may be kept, if not exactly friendly, then at least powerless to wreak harm.

But in Victoria's stage-managed pretence that her dead husband was still a member of the household there was something so primitive that one was reminded of the elaborate domestic furnishings of Egyptian and Etruscan tombs: as elaborate an attempt to keep the dead 'alive'—and as patently useless.

That Christmas of 1863 was the first that Alix had passed in England; it was also the first that she had passed as the wife of the Heir Apparent. She had married on the previous 10th March. Being in the middle of Lent, the date chosen shocked both High Churchmen and Low; but Queen Victoria rebuked both for their objections:

'The objection rests merely on fancy or prejudice and one in this case based on no very elevated view of one of God's holiest ordinances ... [The Queen] would be very glad of an opportunity of breaking through a custom *only* in use among the *higher classes* and which she can't help considering as very Catholic ... Marriage is a solemn holy act *not* to be classed with amusements.'

And accordingly, with the Queen, in deepest mourning, looking on from the privacy of 'Catherine of Aragon's closet'—a balcony room overlooking St George's Chapel—Albert Edward, Prince of Wales, was united in marriage with Princess Alexandra of Denmark, on the day that the Queen had fixed. The charm and beauty of the bride won all hearts—and for once, this is no journalists' cliché, but an exact truth. Nobody seemed able to resist the fascination of this exquisite creature, whose beauty and charm were such that not until he was over forty did her adoring son, George, discover the truth that he confided to his wife, that 'Motherdear is the most selfish person I have ever known'. And even so, this discovery made no difference: Motherdear continued to fascinate him until the moment of her death.

The night of her arrival in England—the crowd in London so thick and so enthusiastically unruly that the Life Guards had to beat back the people with the flats of their sabres—she went upstairs to where the Queen sat weeping in an enjoyable self-pity. 'Dear gentle Alix knocked at the door, peeped in, and came and knelt before me with the sweet loving expression that spoke volumes. I was much moved and kissed her again and again.'

It is curious that, in all the thousands of words of description that Alix's peculiar fascination has evoked over the past century and more, not even the most percipient observer has thought to compare her charm with that of the cat: yet in her physical grace, allied with an almost animal activity; in her unawareness of her beauty yet willingness to use it on all possible occasions to achieve her own ends; in her shallow affectionate nature, so that she loved all without loving even one to excess; in her laughing contempt for the intellectual and his pretensions; even in the notably asexual character of her warmheartedness; she was perhaps the most delightfully feline person ever to have be-witched others into making life as easy for her as they knew how. She was feline in her possessive love of her children; feline in her contemptuous non-jealousy of her husband's tom-cat prowlings (though she would spit and even unsheath her claws if the other lady-cats overstepped the limits of her private domain); feline in her resentment of the least criticism; feline, most of all, in her refusal to let others threaten her comfort: no-one could quarrel with her, though she could—and did—quarrel with others.

In 'that fierce light which beats upon a throne'; in that watchful atmosphere in which socialist and non-socialist repub-licans and mere gossip-mongers looked for the slightest sign of infidelity or even indiscretion; no one hinted of a lover, though all the world would have forgiven her taking one, even had she done so only to be revenged on her polygamous husband. Because there was no lover. In the cynical second half of the nineteenth century, 'smart society' was willing to believe that Oliver Montagu's devotion to his Princess was what it appeared to be, and what indeed it was: a devotion as affectionately Platonic and as romantically non-sexual as any hymned in the improbable verses of some twelfth-century *trouvère*. She was at

6

her happiest in that happiest of all feline conditions: looking enchanting with her well-licked young around her; too beautiful to be seduced, but too beautiful not to be adored.

A week's honeymoon was all that the exigencies of State affairs could allow the twenty-two-year-old Prince and the nineteen-year-old Princess. State policy also dictated the choice of place: Osborne. The Queen was not there, but the dead Albert decidedly was. The ghostly atmosphere must have chilled the spirits even of a boisterous nineteen-year-old.

No-one seems yet to have decided whether or not she was in love with her husband; but human beings when young can contrive excellent substitutes for passion out of the opportunity that propinquity gives to normal animal spirits, and in those first happy months it must have seemed to both that each was very much in love with the other. Bertie was already losing his figure—before his death in 1861, the Prince Consort had already rebuked his son for his obvious addiction to an excess of rich food—but he was pleasant-looking, and he joined with his young wife in all those outdoor exercises in which he, as well as she, excelled. She was a fearless—even a reckless—horsewoman (a skill shared with all the other really dominant women of her day), and while too tender-hearted to join in the wholesale killings whose mastery earned her husband the title of sportsman, she was active in other outdoor pursuits, long after his weight and premature old age had cut him off from all exercises save those of the gun, the table and the adulterous bed.

Like a cat, Alexandra was born to enjoy herself; she had, too, the cat's capacity to find pleasure in simple as well as in complicated circumstances, the cat's joyous ability to amuse itself with a wind-blown scrap of paper, as well as the cat's taken pleasure in hours-long waits for the pigeon which, the cat really knows well, will never fall into its claws.

There is a point that none of Alexandra's biographers has taken up: *the need for her always to have been fascinating.* Alix was not only an interloper in an international royal family almost exclusively German and German-orientated, but she was also an unwelcome and resented interloper. The position, no less than the paraded character, of the enchanting Alix will never be properly understood until it is appreciated that, but for her power to fascinate, she would have been at first neglected, then set aside, then banished—if not literally, then still in a severely practical sense. The German relatives of the living Queen and of the dead Consort (who had been Victoria's cousin) mostly disliked Alix; not perhaps from personal reasons—since they, too, found her charm irresistible when they actually met her— but out of loyalty to their caste and new-found nationalism. Though Alix's family was like all the other royal families of Europe—including that of Russia—strongly Teutonic or at least importantly Teutonized, the Danish royal family was, in sentiment at any rate, not only chauvinistically Danish but, because of that, emotionally anti-German.

Ignoring the Queen's preoccupation, both with her dead husband and with the management of her son and daughter-in-law, Alix had set out to enjoy herself in her marriage. Brought up in a household which, though royal, enjoyed an income of only £800 a year, and where such rare new dresses as came the girls' way had to be made by the women of the household, Alix took an unconcealed pleasure in finding herself the châtelaine of two—to her—grand mansions, one in London and one in a Norfolk whose bleak landscapes, so like those of her native Denmark, she found homely and welcoming.

But over her determined search for happiness hung the shadow of domestic and national tragedy. In 1853, the 'Great Powers'—Britain, France, Russia, Prussia, Austria, and Sweden —solemnly ratified the Protocol of London, drawn up on 8th May in the previous year. It can be argued that this was one of the most important treaties in modern history, and that when Prussia broke it in 1863, and Britain stood aside, every political change since, from the collapse of the Austrian Empire to the Bolshevik Revolution, from the downfall of the British Empire to the Chinese attempt to take-over East Africa, was made not only possible but inevitable.

The Protocol of London 'guaranteed' the indivisibility of a

Denmark which included the Duchies of Schleswig and Holstein, incidentally nominating Prince Christian, Alix's father, as heir to the Danish throne.

In the year that Alix married Bertie, the Prussians, by methods with which the world has become only too tragically familiar since, began to put pressure on the Danes. The intimate connections between the Prussian and the British courts —Queen Victoria's eldest daughter had married the Prussian Crown Prince; but this was the least important of the many links that bound Victoria to her German family—encouraged Bismarck to risk the consequences of defying the provisions of the Protocol of London; he was *sure* that Britain would not lift a finger to preserve either the integrity of Denmark in particular or a respect for treaties in general. He was right. The Prussians invaded Holstein a week after Alix's first baby was born; by mid-February, 1864, the whole of Schleswig, with the exception of the Danish fortress of Dybboel, had fallen. It was in the shadow of this early *Blitzkrieg*, and in the despair engendered by Queen Victoria's pro-German attitude and the British Government's dishonest determination to be neutral at the cost even of honour and—perhaps more important—of the world's respect, that Eddy was born.

Alix's father had become King of Denmark in November, 1863; in December—that December which was to be spent so drearily at Osborne—Prussia had declared war on Denmark. The Princess of Wales's spirits had not been raised by her compulsory observance, at Windsor, of the anniversary of the Prince Consort's death on 14th December. Though the news from Denmark continued to get worse, Alix was happy to escape the nearer intimations of mortality, and to be alone, once more, with her husband at Frogmore.

6th January—'Old Christmas'—was being celebrated by skating to a band on the frozen surface of Frogmore lake; and for Twelfth Night, Alix gave a large children's party, in whose traditional games and customs she could now take her wonted pleasure, seeing that the Queen's chilling presence was no longer at hand to stop the fun.

Frogmore.

On the following day, in high spirits, Prince and Princess decided to go over to Virginia Water and see the skating there. Lady Macclesfield, in view of Alix's condition, ventured a protest, but both Bertie and Alix made light of the Lady-in-Waiting's fears, and well wrapped in sables, Alix sat in a sleigh-chair until the short winter's day had faded to its frosty night. Only a few minutes after Alix had returned to Frogmore House, Lady Macclesfield, whom thirteen successful lyings-in had made an expert in pregnancy, recognized the symptoms in Alix of impending childbirth.

No doctor, no midwife, was present, nor (as protocol demanded in those days) was the Secretary of State for the Home Department, to attest to the legality of the child. Lady Macclesfield sent a maidservant running to Windsor for flannel from Caleys, the drapers. The local physician, Dr Brown, summoned by a panting footman, arrived posthaste on horseback: a fortunate call for the doctor, who gained a quite unexpected knighthood from the happy accident of his having been the only medical man within call. Lady Macclesfield acted as nurse—'As long as I see your face I am happy', said Alix, reposing complete confidence in her Lady-in-Waiting. At nine o'clock on 8th January, 1864, 'Her Royal Highness the Princess of Wales', *The Times* formally reported, 'was safely delivered of a son'. Though the boy, two months premature, weighed only three and three-quarter pounds, he seemed, as he was to prove, strong and healthy. In the absence of the Home Secretary, Lord Granville, the Lord Chamberlain, who was present as a guest, signed for the legality of a birth which was to give a future heir to the Throne.

Lady Macclesfield, after all was over, looked into the Princess's room, to see that nothing was amiss. She was touched to see husband and wife—still hardly more than children—clasped in each other's arms, the tears of mutual love and shared relief running down their fresh young cheeks.

It was the six-year-old Princess Beatrice, the Queen's youngest daughter, who told Alix what her first-born was to be called: 'Albert Victor Christian Edward,' said the child; 'that's what Mama's decided to call him.'

Alix, understandably affronted that her son should have been named without her having been consulted, and that her first intimation of this *fait accompli* should have come, moreover, from the lips of a six-year-old child, immediately did what she was always to do until her husband's death in 1910: complained to him, and then sat back to see him take up the quarrel on her behalf.

He was still only twenty-three, but his wife could always nerve him for conflicts with that Mama of whom historians will go on perpetuating the myth that her eldest son was terrified of her. He was not, but he had a proper reverence for his mother, and a then not uncommon reluctance to oppose her; Alix saw to it that this reluctance was never permitted to stand in the way of his defence of her 'rights'. In this fashion, Alix got what she wanted, usually, whilst avoiding the odium of having quarrelled with dearest Mama.

'I felt rather annoyed', Bertie wrote indignantly to the Queen, 'when Beatrice told Lady Macclesfield that you had settled what our little boy was to be called before I had spoken to you about it.' Not at all deceived by the personal tone of the protest into thinking that her son was alone responsible for the letter, Queen Victoria was adamant on this issue. She made a half-grudging apology for having 'overlooked' a consultation with the parents in the matter of the Heir-but-one's names, but excused herself complacently by explaining that the naming of the child was a national—or, to be more precise, a dynastic—affair, and not, as Bertie and Alix understandably thought, a highly personal and inevitably parental one. Further, the Queen pointed out, she wished that every king destined to sit henceforth on the throne of Great Britain and Ireland should bear the name Albert. Bertie and Alix must have listened to this wildly impracticable plan in wonder, seeing the generations of the future governed by monarchs distinguishable only by the number after their name. Knowing their way about the genealogies of Europe, they might have remembered the man who brought the Moravians to England at the end of the seventeenth century, Prince Henry LXXIII of Reuss.

The Queen was to return to this theme time and again before her death, but Bertie always managed to avoid the total commitment to call himself Albert the First on the death of his mother. One has the feeling that the Queen knew from the beginning that her son never would call himself King Albert, but this depressing conviction did not prevent her, over more than four decades, from trying to extract from him a promise that he would.

Having got her own way in the matter of the child's names, the Queen found the young people's rebellion not hard to overlook. All that she did to shew her disapproval of their opposition to her choice of names for the baby was to attend the christening wearing shabby mourning—'my poor, sad dress'—and to confide complacently to her daughter, the Crown Princess of Prussia, that 'the poor baby roared all through the ceremony, which none of you did. Alix looked very ill, thin and unhappy, she is sadly gone off.'

But Alix, who was unhappy because in the matter of the choice of names she had been bested, had already planned her revenge. In her own mind, she had determined that the boy should be called Edward, and not Albert; and she made the most effective start towards getting her own way by calling her son Eddy—the name that, despite all that the Queen could do, he bore throughout his short life.

In boxing parlance, if the Queen had won the first round on points, Alix had won the second with a knock-out blow.

But though Alix had won in her first serious contest with the Queen, the victory did not deceive her into thinking that she had won for all time; and the Queen's assumption of super-parental rights over her grandson warned Alix that she would have to exercise something more than the normal maternal watchfulness over her boy if she were to retain possession of him. Queen Victoria's early and open attempts to 'take over' aroused all that possessive spirit in Alix which was her most developed characteristic. From the christening onwards, Eddy was

'Motherdear's boy'—and, with his iron selfishness displayed behind the façade of willowy physical grace, languishing brown eyes and soft curly hair, Eddy was to look every inch a 'Motherdear's boy' until white marble and a wreath of immortelles covered the mortal remains of that epicene beauty.

The Queen knew that she had lost; and though 'Mama' —like most other people—was helpless to assert her will or even to complain in the actual presence of Alix, Mama could be indignant enough the moment that she was freed from the thrall of Alix's dominating charm.

What obsessed the Queen was the fear that she had lost her opportunity of 'managing' the baby Prince. Not as sure of herself as she used to be when Albert was there to back her up, the Queen affected to be anxious for Alix, when, in fact, she was anxious for her own future as a mother-in-law whose 'natural rights' looked to be in danger of being set aside by a wilful, selfish daughter-in-law.

In March, 1864—two months after Eddy's birth—the Queen wrote to her cousin King Leopold of the Belgians, who was staying in England, asking him to intervene, and to see that Bertie paid more attention to, and took better care of, his young wife, whose 'altered appearance is the observation of everyone'. Urging Leopold not to 'mince the matter, but speak strongly and frighten Bertie', the Queen then came to the real matter of her approach to Leopold. She wished to assert her 'rights' over her son's child and any future children: '. . . Bertie should understand what a strong right I have to *interfere* in the management of the child or children; that he should never do anything about the child without consulting me'.

Again and again Victoria returns to the theme of Bertie's neglect of his wife; and this has often been accepted as proof of Queen Victoria's tenderness towards Alix. The Queen did indeed feel much tenderness towards her daughter-in-law, but it was not this tenderness that prompted the Queen's concern, at this time, that Bertie should spend more time at home. With Bertie away, the Queen might well despair of coming between Alix and her children, of asserting those rights over their upbringing and education of which she had written to Leopold.

The point that all the biographers, in their consideration of this 'struggle for power' between Queen and Princess of Wales, may have failed to recognize is simply that Alexandra, though the member of a royal family and brought up as the daughter of a man destined to be king, never developed a 'royal mentality'. She had been brought up in modest—almost humble—circumstances, where learning was neglected and the girls sat down to sewing-bees rather than to lectures on political theory.

Prince Christian's preoccupation had been with what he considered to be his children's happiness, physical and mental. They all did gymnastic exercises under his supervision; they scampered about the shabby, poorly furnished house with scant respect for decoration or decorum; they learnt to play the piano, because they liked to sing; they learnt to ride and to shoot, and to despise the pretensions of the rich and grand. Their father did not take them to Court because the King was living with a seedy mistress whom Prince Christian did not wish his wife and children to meet. Anything less 'royal' than Alexandra or her family it would be hard to imagine; and so Queen Victoria's reasoned (and reasonable) plea that a royal child was *not* like any other child fell on deaf ears—a phrase which, in Alexandra's case, was becoming literally true, her deafness being a hereditary defect.

For a royal child is not, unhappily for it, like any other child. He or she—but particularly he—must be trained from earliest childhood to assume the duties of his or her rank. A royal child must learn more and know more than others; a royal child must be trained in the concealment of, and eventual domination of, his natural emotions. A royal child must learn the hard discipline of concealing his boredom with public ceremonies, however often repeated; he must know how to affect interest in a municipal gas-works as well as in a national opera-house; he must be as pleasant with Mr Mayor as with the Lord High Chancellor. He must learn to be, not all things to all men, but consistently one man to all: self-disciplined, pleasantly human, universally sympathetic and completely without observable prejudice towards either his own or another ruler's subjects. To achieve this perfection of conduct is no easy task; it cannot begin to be learnt too early, and the only chance that the tutors have of training their pupil in the way that he should go is to impress upon him, right from the beginning of his life, that it is his duty to be trained up to the standard of knowledge and self-abnegation that royalty imposes on royal persons.

This training had not been a part of Alix's upbringing; her mother had taught her what little she knew, and any criticism of her mother's system had aroused in Princess Louise's affectionate, dutiful daughter a quick and warm resentment. Apart from Danish, Alix spoke English, French and German: she spoke them all fluently but with a strong accent, and she wrote them all badly, disdaining the help of a dictionary to correct her spelling. 'They can understand what I mean all right—and that's all that matters . . .'

By the time that Eddy was eight, and had a little brother, George, aged seven, the 'non-system' by which Alix brought up her children had become so unalterably established that the Queen found them, in her own phrase, 'as wild as hawks', and complained that 'they are such ill-bred, ill-trained children that I can't fancy them at all'.

The younger surviving son, George, was fated to become a good and in many ways a great king; certainly, though the beginning of his reign held out no such promise, a most beloved king (as anyone who remembers his death and funeral will concede). By serious application, sprung from a deep sense of duty, he sought to make up many of the deficiencies of his early education; but even this serious-minded, duty-dedicated man never really mastered a foreign language—at least, not up to anything like normal royal standards. As for Eddy, not even the dedicated patience of even the most patient and dedicated of tutors could reconcile him to the necessity of learning; Mother-dear had set no store by it, in the days when he and his brothers and sisters ('rampaging little girls', as Lady Geraldine Somerset contemptuously called them) went howling like hysterical banshees along the corridors of Sandringham or Marlborough House, unchecked by parent or servant—certainly not by Alexandra, who was already, at twenty-six, so deaf that their howls could not worry her; not by Bertie, who had already begun to live his parallel bachelor-life; not by the servants, who liked the wild, affectionate children, from whom that streak of cruelty was missing which had been the one great blemish on the youth of their father. It is never recorded that either Prince Eddy or Prince George kicked or punched his valet or threw the contents of an unlit lamp's oil-reservoir over a servant.

No matter how Bertie had been brought up, Alix would have applied her non-system to her children, if she could. Bertie's dislike of his father's inhuman educational system made it all the more easy, of course, for Alix to have her own way. She would surely have agreed with Dr Voisin, Bertie's French-master, who had warned Bertie's tutor, Gibbs, who was conscientiously applying the Prince Consort's rigid educational system in the spirit as well as in the letter: 'You will wear him out early! Make him climb trees! Run! Leap! Row! Ride! . . . In many things savages are much better educated than we are.' If, Voisin had suggested, Bertie were left more to guide and direct himself, he would turn out far better. 'He has', Voisin added, 'the moral sentiments in a high degree—for instance, such a love of truth that he is ready to be a witness against himself. His account of any incident is not biassed by his personal interest in it.'

That this compliment was true and not the mere idle flattery of a court-servant is shewn by the frank way in which, when taxed by his father with having slept with the strumpet, Nellie Clifden, Bertie confessed to the 'sin'.

Alix would have taken Voisin's sentiments to heart: if it came to a choice between a system that demanded six hours study a day on six days of the week and a non-system which permitted children to grow up with their healthy natural sentiments uncorrupted, as Alix would have seen it, then let them grow up Voisin's way: at least they would grow up like human beings.

However, even Alix's children had to have *some* education, and since their mother would not have considered their leaving home for a boarding-school, she agreed, albeit grudgingly, to the appointment of a tutor. Accordingly, in 1871, Bertie appointed a thirty-two-year-old clergyman, John Neale Dalton, to be tutor to the two princes, Eddy, seven, and George, six. It is usually said that Dalton, a brilliant scholar, but a man of no family and no influence, gained his important appointment, because Queen Victoria had once heard him preach, and had been vastly impressed with the unpatronaged young parson.

It was, in fact, Gibbs, Bertie's tutor, who brought Dalton to the notice of the Prince of Wales and his wife. All things considered, Bertie and Alix might have made a far worse choice. Dalton was young, and his affection for his young pupils seems to have been untainted by any regard for personal advancement (even though considerable advancement *was* Dalton's reward for his service). What Dalton could do, he did; but of his limitations he became early and unhappily aware: he could teach the younger son, Prince George, but knocking even the most primal facts into the obstinately resistive mind of Prince Eddy was a task which often brought Mr Dalton to a sense of hopeless failure.

2. *The Education of a Prince*

Whatever Dalton managed to teach obedient little George and disdainful Eddy, all instruction had to be given under the jealously watchful eye of Motherdear, whose confidence in her priority over even such priorities as learning was such that she would not hesitate to interrupt a lesson to take the children off to a picnic—Dalton, of course, coming too.

In considering the difficulties that this worthy man encountered in trying to teach the rudiments to Eddy and George, too little account has been taken of the emotional atmosphere in which Dalton took up his duties. The I-could-eat-you-up love of Alix for the two boys—indeed, for all her children (even the 24-hour-old Prince John, whose death she never ceased to mourn)—could not offset the dangerously disturbing effects of the emotional hypertension that surrounded them. It was not a happy household; even though the children were spared the parental anger which is too often the sign of the parents' emotional tensions. Bertie had no inner resources of imagination or self-communing to enable him to enjoy the quieter hours of life; the picture of his sitting, slippered, before a fire in his own home would have been frighteningly repellent to him. He had to be entertained, amused, saved from the boredom which perpetually threatened his shallow mind, and escape from which was the dominant dynamic of his life.

Queen Victoria had already expressed her disquiet over 'the

most unhealthy life' that her son and daughter-in-law were leading, and this in the first year of their marriage. Society had responded to the promise of a gay, brilliant court offered by the opening-up of Marlborough House. The Queen had retired 'into her grief' with the death of the Prince Consort in 1861; but the raffish smart set which was now turning up at the Marlborough House luncheons, dinners and balls would never have been invited to any ceremony by the Queen, even if she had not retired into a very private life.

It is difficult to say whether Alexandra was aware of the immense social gulf which divided the status of so many of her guests from that of the guests who might be expected to receive a command from the Queen. Many years later, it became an accepted fact of English social life that many a man or woman might confidently aspire to an invitation from Marlborough House who would hope vainly ever to be received by their Queen. It is certainly exaggerating the state of affairs to liken the Marlborough House court to a sump, draining away that near-on-déclassé element which, though making up much of the Society of the day, was unacceptable as company to the Fount of Honour. For all the Queen's fears that her son's too-easy standards were letting some very curious fish into the social pond, she might have reflected that her son's acceptance of many people with imperfect claims to royal approval spared the Queen a host of unnecessary enemies.

Alexandra joined with her husband to do the honours in the non-stop gaiety of Marlborough House, first because her youth responded to the excitement and the glamour of those occasions on which, always, it is literally true that she was the observed of all observers, and, second, because she knew that only by keeping her Bertie constantly amused could she hope to keep him at home.

It is doubtful that she was much concerned with Bertie's popularity, which was already beginning to suffer through the adverse comment that neglect of his wife had inspired; the popular critics taking particular exception to his having gone 'pleasure-seeking' whilst his wife was ill of a grave rheumatic condition following the birth of her second son, George, on 3rd June, 1865; a condition which lasted for several weeks, gave rise to great and widespread anxiety, and which left the Princess with a permanently stiffened knee. Once again her child had been born prematurely, but once again the child was born healthy and strong.

Bertie's unpopularity, indeed, might have been altogether eclipsed had *he* not had the doubtful good fortune to fall ill of typhoid, the disease which had carried off his father at the early age of forty-two. For twenty years now, medical science had known what caused typhoid fever, but, so far, had not produced the cure. If natural self-healing power could not pull a patient through typhoid, there was still precious little that even the most expensive of fashionable physicians could do, save, by opiates, to alleviate the patient's sufferings. With a powerful and skilful public-relations campaign, conducted with an expertise of which a modern Madison Avenue practitioner might well feel proud, the British press used the typhoid to restore the flagging popularity of 'our Prince'.

In April, 1871, the Princess of Wales had given birth, again prematurely, to her third son; again there was no nurse, no midwife, no doctor and no layette. But this time the premature birth did not bring a strong, healthy child into the world: Alexander John Charles Albert lived just long enough to be christened. It was a death which profoundly affected not only wife but errant husband as well. The Princess's Lady-in-Waiting, Mrs Stonor, records how the anguished Bertie, tears running down his cheeks, laid the tiny body of his day-old son in the coffin, afterwards arranging the white satin pall and the white flowers above. This, the only child of theirs not to survive infancy, acquired an astonishing and disturbing reality for the parents; on 6th April, 1882, the day on which the dead boy would have been celebrating his eleventh birthday, the still desolate mother wrote to Prince George, reminding him that 'it is sad to think that nothing remains on earth to remind us of him but his little grave'.

But physically, Alix had marvellous recuperative powers; a

visit to Wiesbaden in August, 1867, after the birth of her first daughter, Louise, and the resultant rheumatic fever, had taken some of the stiffness out of her affected knee, and her deafness —first markedly noticeable following the illness—had grown no worse.

The journey to Wiesbaden had been made by way of Holland, the royal yacht *Osborne* taking the party—Bertie, Alix, the two young Princes and their infant sister, the complete Wales household and twenty-five servants—to that still enchanting 'Venice of the North', Dordrecht, where Alix's broadmindedness shocked Sir William Knollys: she not only encouraged *Osborne*'s sailors to sing on a *Sunday*, but laughed when Sir William tried to indicate the nature of some of the songs. 'Let them sing!' she said.

In 1868 the Prince and Princess of Wales visited Ireland. Bombing time for London by the Irish—which was to last over twenty-five years—had begun with the blowing-up of Clerkenwell Prison in 1867. Before it ended—when a split in the 'patriot' faction set both sides bombing each other, rather than the British—many a notable building was dynamited. As early as 1868 the Queen was nervous of the wisdom of a projected visit to Ireland by the Prince of Wales. She was even less convinced of the wisdom of the Prince's taking his wife with him. But Alix thought otherwise, and so, not altogether surprisingly, did the Prime Minister, Disraeli, who shrewdly reasoned that, though an Irish bullet or bomb might threaten the Prince, not even the most rabid anti-British would harm anyone so enchanting as the Princess. Alix wrote to the Queen, pleading to be permitted to accompany Bertie. 'All this I have not told my Bertie as I did not like to say anything about my private feelings for him . . . In these times now I think one gets to feel more anxious about those one loves most in the world and it makes me always feel anxious when we are obliged to be separated for a while but in this case I confess I almost shudder to think of the possibility of his going alone, and I should feel DREADFULLY disappointed if anything really were to prevent my going with him. I feel like a sort of call and wish to go.'

It was the letter from which this is quoted which finally persuaded the Queen to listen to Disraeli's request and permit the Princess to accompany the Prince to Ireland. It is an interesting letter, since it reveals so much. It is full of genuine affection for Bertie, but already—even though the Princess is still only twenty-four—it reads rather like the letter of a loving mother than of a loving wife—and perhaps that is why it inspired so complete a response in Queen Victoria: the subtle argument that both women loved in exactly the same way?

So on 15th April, the Prince and Princess of Wales landed at Kingstown. *The Times* correctly reported the visit as 'The Danish Conquest of Ireland'.

Ireland, in the next fifty years, was to give some very different receptions to visiting English royalty; but nothing could have exceeded the warmth of the welcome for the ethereal beauty dressed in green Irish poplin, with shamrocks in her white chip bonnet. But, as Georgina Battiscombe so acutely observes, in her *Queen Alexandra*, Alexandra 'would seem to have been exactly the person to fit happily into an Irish background, with her spontaneous gaiety, her informality, her lack of logic, her love of horses, and, be it said, her want of method and her hopeless and incurable unpunctuality. She would have found herself perfectly at home in that country where the clock has no significance. As a Dane, too, she was better equipped than the average English person to sympathize with the outlook of a small, defeated nation, brooding bitterly over its wrongs.'

This is well said; for it not only records Alix's triumphant 'conquest' of the Irish, it goes far to giving an explanation of the victory. Alix, in fact, was 'one of them'—and both she and the Irish (and Disraeli too) knew it.

When Lady Abercorn wrote that the success of the Irish visit had 'exceeded even the fondest hopes', one wonders whether or not Lady Abercorn valued at its proper worth the extraordinary, even if perfectly spontaneous, tact which enabled Alexandra to create, for herself, an atmosphere of completely uncritical friendliness.

After the visit, Sir William Knollys could assure the Queen

that 'the Princess of Wales has returned to London without being in the least the worse for her visit to Ireland—rather the contrary'.

On this occasion the children did not accompany their parents. Alix was prepared to face bullet or bombs with her husband, but she was persuaded that to expose the country's *two* heirs to assassination was unwise. But almost everywhere else Bertie and Alix went, the children came too. The Queen disapproved; the Queen even went so far as to forbid Alix to take the children—mostly on the grounds that they were too young to be subjected to the discomfort and even the hazards of travel. But Bertie was always able (even if one suspects that he was not always willing) to take up the defence of Alix's pleas to have the children with her—and in the end it was always Alix who won.

The Queen was particularly opposed to Alix's taking the royal children with her to Denmark. The Queen disapproved of King Christian and Queen Louise, not on moral grounds—they were as respectable as the Queen herself, and there was no Danish equivalent of a John Brown around to provoke unkind comment—but because her daughter-in-law's support of her parents could be always only at the cost of offending those Danes' 'ancient, inveterate enemies', the Prussians, one of whom Queen Victoria's eldest daughter had become.

Bertie was not anxious, either, to develop the Danish connection—but his were very different reasons: whether at Fredensborg or Bernstorff, he was bored, as they used to say, to extinction. There were no pretty girls, no fast men, no gambling, no racing, no smart gossip—nothing but the most drearily respectable middle-class entertainment—in the most drearily respectable middle-class milieu in the world.

But a guilty conscience could always make Bertie a most valiant champion of his wife; and he was prepared to plead with his mother even for the right to take his children to a place where, he knew, he would suffer only boredom.

'You can therefore imagine', he told the Queen, 'how hurt and pained (Alexandra) has been by your accusing her of being "very selfish" and "unreasonable", in fact, risking her own child's life. None of us are perfect—she may have her faults—but she certainly is not selfish—and her whole life is wrapt up in her children—and it seems hard that because she wishes (with a natural mother's pride) to take her eldest children with her to her parents' home every difficulty should be thrown in her way, and enough to mar the prospect of her journey, and when Vicky and Alice come here nearly every year with their children (and I maintain that ours are quite as strong as theirs) it seems rather inconsistent not to accord to the one what is accorded to the others.'

The Queen gave in; by this time, she was learning—arrogant as she was—how useless it was to seek to dominate Alix, who had so willing a champion as Bertie to blow up a 'simple suggestion' into a *casus belli*.

A visit to Paris, where Bertie and Alix were imperially received by Napoleon III and his beautiful Eugénie, preceded the visit to Denmark, to which the children had been sent in advance. Christmas was spent at Fredensborg. The children returned to England with their mother, while Bertie went on to Hamburg, Berlin, Vienna and the still unwesternized cities of an Egypt in the glittering sunset of her Oriental day; then on to Greece, of which Alix's brother, 'Willi', was King, and again to Paris on the way back to England and the children, and once again to the social whirl of which not only Queen Victoria disapproved. As Alix was once again pregnant, Bertie proposed that they should rent the Duke of Devonshire's house at Chiswick; but the Queen expressed her mistrust of the proposal: 'There is great fear lest you should have gay parties at Chiswick instead of going there to pass the Sunday, a day which is rightly considered of rest, quietly for your repose with your dear children.'

Bertie arrived back to find himself caught up in 'that disgusting Mordaunt Case', which had come before the courts on 30th April, 1869.*

* A detailed account of this most notorious of Victorian *causes célèbres* will be found in my *Painful Details*; London, Max Parrish, 1962.

Eddy was just six when his Papa became involved in the first *public* scandal of his scandal-haunted life.

A few days after the birth of his first child, Sir Charles Mordaunt went into his wife's bedroom, at her request. Lady Mordaunt sent the nurse to fetch the child; and then, with the nurse as witness, made this extraordinary statement:

'Charlie, I want to tell you something. I have been dreadfully wicked, and I have done very wrong. I have been unfaithful to you. I have committed misconduct with Lord Cole, and with Sir Frederick Johnstone, and with other people as well. One of them was the Prince of Wales. It is Lord Cole', she added, 'who is the father of my baby.'

Thus began the long and costly Mordaunt Case, which was before the courts, on and off, for six years; a case to which Poe's lines, 'much of madness and more of sin, and horror the soul of the plot', seem most aptly to apply. There was every folly; there was disloyalty; there was venereal disease and—as Lady Mordaunt's family spent thousands in trying to prove—there was probably madness.

It was the indiscreet practice of the Prince of Wales to pay social calls on young married women, and to spend a considerable time with them alone, after the footman had been instructed not to disturb the *tête-à-tête*. What made the indiscretion even more noticeable was that His Royal Highness neglected to cultivate the acquaintance of the ladies' husbands—or even to express a wish to meet them.

Bertie had written a number of letters to Lady Mordaunt, and though these, when produced, seemed unexceptionable, everybody still asked why he should write letters at all.

In practice, the Prince could not have been compelled to appear as witness in a court of law; and it says much for Bertie's courage that, though ordered by the Queen not to appear, he still volunteered to enter the witness-box and there to give evidence on oath.

It must be noted that the court treated their royal witness with remarkable tenderness.

'Only one more question with which to trouble your Royal

Highness. Has there ever been any improper familiarity or criminal act between yourself and Lady Mordaunt?'

The brief answer came clear and firm in that tense hush.

'There has not,' said the Prince.

It was not until 1875 that the courts finally decided that Lady Mordaunt had committed adultery with the Lord Viscount Cole. Cole and Johnstone were particular friends of Bertie. Johnstone, a great patron of the Turf, was to offend him years later, and thus forfeit an old friendship, but at the time of the Mordaunt Case, these three, all married men, lived what was virtually a carefree bachelor life.

Opinion, for all that the Prince was cheered as he left the Divorce Court, was hardening against him; and in the following year appeared the first of those bitter lampoons which were published, every Christmas, in a popular annual publication.

The first of these yearly attacks, entitled *The Coming K——*, was a clever parody on the then immensely popular *Idylls of the King*. 'The brochure', says Sir Sidney Lee, in his life of King Edward VII, 'purported boldly to draw the veil from the private life of the Prince and his comrades, and to suggest his unfitness for the succession to the throne.'

Throughout the initial hearings of the Mordaunt Case, Alix made her attitude clear for all the world to see. It was on her advice that Bertie defied the Queen's command to stay away from the witness-box—'Dear Alix has entirely taken the same view in the matter that I have and quite sees that it is an absolute necessity for me to appear in court, should I be called', he wrote to his mother—and by her own decision, she and Bertie presented at least the appearance of unity and confidence to a society only too eager to accept and exploit the least signs of guilt and shame. On the night of the Prince of Wales's examination in court, Alix and Bertie dined with the Gladstones. Gladstone's daughter Lucy noted that 'the Princess looked lovely but *very* sad when she was not exerting herself'. The public, however, never saw her looking even the least sad, and when she entered the royal box at the opera, the audience rose and cheered—hissing her husband when he appeared.

It was as well, then, that 'my naughty little man'—as Alix called Bertie in a letter to Bertie's sister, Louise—went down with typhoid in November, 1871, after the death of the day-old Prince John in the previous April and after a sentimental visit to the Passion Play at Oberammergau, where the first signs of Alix's later religious loyalties were first apparent.

Bertie caught his typhoid at Lord Londesborough's house, near Scarborough. After the house-party, several others, including two servants, were taken ill, but they soon recovered. Not so Bertie. Once more the decisive hand of Alix is seen. On her own authority, she sent for a brilliant but till then 'unknown' physician, William Gull, who was almost certainly brought to her attention by Gibbs.

To please the Queen, Alix consented to call in, as second opinion, Sir William Jenner, described by Alix's Lady-in-Waiting and beloved friend ('my dear little Mac') as 'a mean time-server and a dismal croaker'. It was William Gull who eventually pulled the Prince through, but it was not until the following Spring that he could pronounce his royal patient completely recovered.

Aware of the hostile public opinion that the Prince's pleasure-seeking and supposed neglect of his wife had inspired in every rank of British society, the moulders of opinion adroitly seized this literally God-sent illness in order to reverse existing prejudices and to restore the popularity that Bertie had, not so long ago, enjoyed. It is impossible to one who has observed the mechanism of opinion-moulding at work not to recognize the well-proven gambits and ploys: the sine-wave pattern of the bulletins, in which hope-raising is followed by the cautious warning (intended to sound more alarming than its words would suggest); the 'sudden grave relapse'; the summoning of the Queen to the patient's bedside; the news that the eighteen-year-old haemophiliac Prince Leopold (himself doomed to an early death) had pleaded to be permitted to join his brother, but had been refused ('on the considered advice of His Royal Highness's physicians'); the birthday permitted to pass without any rejoicing; then the grave relapse and the Queen's rush to

Sandringham with every available member of the Royal Family summoned to attend the bedside of the 'dying' Prince . . . And so to the Service of Thanksgiving at St Paul's Cathedral, which, though greatly abhorrent to Queen Victoria—'It seems to me to be making too much of *an outward show* of the most solemn and sacred feelings of one's heart'—was, nevertheless, what the public wanted to mark the absolution of the Prince from guilt and his restoration to the public favour.

On Gull's having diagnosed the Prince's illness as typhoid fever, Eddy and George were sent down to Osborne in the care of their nurse, Mary Black ('My good Mary' of Alix's letters) and Mr Dalton, who may have felt a disloyal but human satisfaction in knowing that his first efforts to instil the rudiments of learning would not be obstacled by the presence of Mother-dear.

One of the most industrious letter-writers of a letter-writing age, Alix maintained constant communication with Osborne, writing almost daily to Dalton, Nanny Black (later Mrs Blackburn) and the two boys, neither of whom could read or write—Alix 'wrote for them' when writing was necessary:

EDDY'S VERSE FOR PAPA'S BIRTHDAY

9th November, 1869

> Day of pleasure,
> Brightly dawning,
> Take the gift
> On this sweet morning.
> Our best hopes
> And wishes blending,
> Must yield joy
> That's never ending.

This is, of course, in Alix's handwriting. On the back of the sheet, in the same hand, is a shorter poem, 'from' Prince George.

Dalton must have felt relieved that he had the two boys to himself in the sheltered atmosphere of Osborne, where the gossip of the outer world was little likely to reach them. He assiduously applied himself to his task of instructing his pupils, but he was soon confessing that he found it a far harder task than he had expected. It is fair to Dalton to say that he did his best, as an honourable as well as an intelligent tutor; and it is probably correct to say that no other tutor in England could have done much better with such unpromising educational material. Yet, eight years later, we find poor Dalton having honestly but regretfully to report to the Prince of Wales that while, as cadets on the training-ship *Britannia*, Prince George had done well and 'earned golden opinions', Prince Eddy 'fails, not in one or two subjects, but in all'. Dalton confesses that he can find no other causes to which to attribute this distressing backwardness than 'the abnormally dormant condition of his mind', a dormancy which prevented Eddy's fixing 'his attention to any given subject for more than a few minutes consecutively'.

Yet, as is evident from the few letters of Eddy which have survived, Dalton taught him not only to write but also to spell. In all the holograph letters of Eddy's that I have seen, I have noticed only one misspelling—'Darby' for 'Derby'—and a solitary lapse into phonetic spelling may, I feel, be excused. But what is puzzling is how to reconcile Dalton's gloomy references to the 'abnormally dormant condition' of Eddy's mind with the alert, almost sprightly tone of his correspondence—a tone, too, which seems to reflect, in its entire lack of affectation and pretentiousness, a healthy and essentially masculine mind.

It is possible to argue—and both Bertie and Alix did passionately argue—that Eddy's 'abnormally dormant condition of mind' was no more than a fairly common type of arrested development, out of which, given time, Eddy would eventually 'snap'. What may be the explanation of Eddy's inability to take an interest in certain subjects is simply Dalton's inability to make them interesting. Perhaps we need not go hunting for more complex explanations—Eddy was as bored with certain subjects as his father was bored with certain people; and neither Bertie nor Alix was prepared to listen sympathetically to

Dalton's plea that they should put pressure on Eddy to make a little more effort to learn.

Bertie remembered, with some complacency, that Papa had complained to Bertie's sister, Alice (Princess Frederick William of Prussia) that 'Bertie's propensity is indescribable laziness. I never in my life met such a thorough and cunning lazybones.' In passing on Papa's strictures, Alice had let Bertie see what Papa gave as the reasons for his uneasiness: '. . . It does grieve me when it is my own son, and when one considers that he might be called upon at any moment to take over the reins of government in a country where the sun never sets (*sic*) . . .'

Now it is more than unlikely that Bertie, save perhaps in his adolescence, ever doubted his ability to take over, at a moment's notice, the reins of government. In fact, though he did have more than the normal wait for kingship, he had far less than the usual training, and yet he shewed himself, when he did mount the throne, an exceptionally capable king. Perhaps (as Rupert Brooke says of women), thoughts went blowing through him wiser than his own.

Alix, of course, had a laughing contempt for the adiposities of learning; she had proved triumphantly how it was possible to deal with all the complications of life with the minimum of educational baggage. But even Queen Victoria later sprang to the defence of Eddy in reminding Bertie that he had been not very bright as a child, the flattering implication being that the dull child had become a not-so-dull man.

The difference between Gibbs and Dalton as royal tutors is that the latter, confessing that he was—in his own opinion, of course—making no headway in his task of educating Prince Eddy, was not regarded, even by the Queen, as having failed; while the former, complacently conscious of having carried through (and, indeed, officiously 'improved upon') the Prince Consort's Plan of Education, was regarded, by both the Prince Consort and the Queen as having failed altogether. As the Queen wrote to her eldest daughter: 'Poor Mr Gibbs certainly failed during the last 2 years entirely, incredibly, and did Bertie no good.'

31

Once committed to plain-speaking, Dalton became obsessed with the pleasure that a licensed freedom of speech gave him, and in his reports to the Prince of Wales this good but dull man returns again and again to the impossibility of getting Eddy to co-operate in the business of educating himself. A disturbing 'psychiatric' note creeps into the tone of the reports as Dalton begins to take on some of the literary tricks of the writer on morbid psychology: '(He) sits listless and vacant, and ... wastes as much time in doing nothing, as he ever wasted ... This weakness of brain, this feebleness and lack of power to grasp almost anything put before him, is manifested also in his hours of recreation and social intercourse. It is a fault of nature ...'

That these gloomy criticisms fundamentally contradict all which is stated or implied in the 1,500 solid pages of Dalton's *The Cruise of H.M.S. Bacchante* is an important fact that, so far, no biographer of Eddy has noted.

Bertie duly and dutifully reported to the Queen what Dalton had to say, expressing his hopeful view that, by association with his brighter younger brother, Eddy would eventually get into the habit of brightness. 'The older they get,' he wrote to Queen Victoria on 22nd May, 1880, 'the more difficult we see is the problem of their education, and it gives us many an anxious thought and care.'

Yet it is clear that neither parents nor grandmother were really anxious, and for the good reason that Dalton's fears were that he would be unable to teach Eddy *what the parents could not possibly regard as important.* This is the true explanation of what seems, at first view, to be the insufferable complacency of the Royal Family in respect of Dalton's misgivings about Eddy. They *knew* what Eddy should learn; were confident that they did not need Dalton or anyone else to teach these important things; and that, with what Dalton could impart in the way of basics, added to what they themselves were, in fact, teaching the boy, Eddy would get by—as his father and some other royalties of a little further back had got by.

One of the few surviving letters from Motherdear to her elder

32

son, sent at Christmas 1871 when the Princes were staying at Osborne, is worth quoting. It is obvious that young Eddy's letters to which she refers were written for him:

'My own darling little Eddy,

Mama sends a thousand thanks for all the very nice little letters, and is so glad to hear from Mr Dalton that Eddy is a good little boy. Mama is so glad dear little Eddy has been going on praying God for dear Papa's recovery and the Almighty God has *heard* our prayers, and darling Papa is going to be quite well again and very soon we hope you may all come home again to see dear Papa once more! Mama is so glad her little Chicks will spend a happy and merry Christmas with dear Grandmama, and Mama sends you each a little Christmas card with many good wishes for Christmas and the New Year, which I hope will begin brightly and happily for all of us, and that my little Eddy will try and become a very good obedient boy. Remember me kindly to Mr Dalton with many thanks for all his letters, kiss Grandma's hand, and give my love to Uncle Leo and Aunt Beatrice.

Ever your loving
Mama Alix.'

Alix's *obiter dicta*, in her artless, often carelessly punctuated letters or in her equally artless and unpunctuated conversation, plainly reveal what *she* thought education should be. 'I think a child is always best looked after under its mother's eye' is a most revealing expression of opinion, and readily explains why Eddy felt no particular attraction towards learning in its more academic milieux. In an age when even the gentlest of schoolmasters and tutors had habituated their scholastic disciplines to the use of the rod, this traditional dynamic was removed from the educational pattern devised for Alix's boys: 'If children are too strictly or perhaps too severely treated,' the Prince of Wales wrote to his mother, 'they get shy and only fear those whom they ought to love.' Between them, Bertie and

Alix must have created the most enjoyable educational back-ground that any Victorian child could ever have hoped to enjoy.

At all times, the boys' parents—but particularly Alix—were more concerned with what our ancestors used to call 'the moral qualities' than with mere learning as such. Not until Eddy was nineteen did Alix shew any response to the reports of Eddy's *academic* failures; until then—and, indeed, after—she constantly stresses the need for good social behaviour. 'Above all, *don't ever quarrel* with your brother'; 'Mind that you in particular do not quarrel with or irritate your brother': this is a favourite theme in Motherdear's letters to Prince George; and she writes to Dalton (for whose character she had always the highest regard) to do his best to correct 'all those little failings [which] tell so much against them', in particular 'that *horrid* habit of always squabbling'.

It is possible that 'the inattention' that Prince Eddy shewed at lesson-time had a purely physical cause; one which, while perceived only by Sir Henry Ponsonby, who remarked that Eddy 'cannot apply himself for any length of time', may well be the explanation of that inability. 'I perceive', noted Sir Henry, 'that he is a little deaf.' Georgina Battiscombe has taken the point, tracing the possible connection between Eddy's 'slowness' and the deafness noted by Ponsonby. It would be interesting to know how loudly or softly Dalton spoke; his son Hugh's boom irritated Queen Victoria: 'Who is that very noisy child?' she enquired in understandable disgust; she did not live to hear that boom at its ripest development.

In her progressive deafness, Alix found that she was gradually reducing the circle of her friends to those whose voices she could most plainly hear—Charlotte Knollys ('the inevitable Char-lotte') was one—and it may well be that the well-attested social successes of Prince Eddy may have had a direct connection with the audibility or otherwise of the people he met. (In pur-suit of this hypothesis, it ought to be remarked that he got on particularly well with Australians, whose voice-pitch may have suited his ear, and that his conversations with Australians were conducted in what was then a country free from much industrial noise.)

There is another suggestion which comes to mind: is it possible that Eddy suffered, in addition to his hereditary deafness, from another hereditary weakness—epilepsy—which had manifested itself in his father's generation and was to manifest itself in his brother George's son, John? I do not suggest that Eddy suffered from the more serious form of epilepsy, with its characteristic seizures, but from that much milder form whose syndrome is so easily missed, even by competent physicians, that its presence often goes undetected, sometimes for many years, sometimes for the sufferers' entire life. This milder form, *petit mal*, has associations with migraine (another almost completely unexamined malfunctioning of ... what?), both responding with encouraging results to treatment by luminal and similar drugs. *Petit mal* in its classic form is characterized by the outward appearance of 'abstraction', this 'abstraction' reflecting the dissociation which, for the patient, is breaking down the familiar and reassuring co-ordination between his perceptions and the world perceived. In an attack of *petit mal*, the distressed sufferer is so concerned, in his alarm, with restoring normal association between his persona and the outer world that he 'withdraws'. To one untrained in detecting this condition—of which, irrationally, the average patient is *ashamed*—this characteristic 'withdrawal' of *petit mal* seems merely the bored inattention of one in whom interest just cannot be aroused.

Eddy may well have suffered from *petit mal*; added to his deafness, this could have rendered him the least promising of pupils.

Petit mal, so often associated with puberty, often goes with the end of adolescence; and though it may return, it does not normally do so until much later in life. If it was *petit mal* which accounted for Eddy's 'abnormally dormant condition' as a youth, then the passing of this condition at the end of his adolescence may well explain the brisk healthiness of the mind reflected in his later letters.

But, as the Princess of Wales wrote to Dalton, what really

counted in education was the development of *character*: 'One thing I must ask you, especially now that I am away, to pay great attention to their being obedient and obeying the moment they are told. Also let them be civil to everybody, high and low, and not get grand now they are by themselves, and please take particular care they are not toadied [to] by the keepers or any of those around them.'

3. Eddy at sea

The two Princes joined the training-ship *Britannia* in 1877, two months later than had been planned, because in the summer of that year Eddy had been stricken with what had now come to be seemingly an hereditary complaint among the males of the Royal Family: typhoid.

Gull—now Sir William Gull, Bart.—nursed the son, as he had successfully nursed the father, through this dangerous illness. Since his having cured the Prince of Wales in 1871, Gull had increased both in social importance and in influence over the Royal Family. In 1872, in recognition of his skill in having rescued the Prince of Wales from what seemed to the world like certain death, Gull had been created a baronet, and in the same year appointed Physician Extraordinary to the Queen. Under his care, Eddy made a complete recovery from an illness which had killed his grandfather and very nearly killed his father.

If Eddy, unknown to Dalton, was suffering from some condition like *petit mal*, this would explain away many of the apparent contradictions evident in the correspondence between the tutor and his charges' parents. It might also explain the presence of Sir William Gull in the Royal Household. Gull was a shrewd diagnostician who specialized in paraplegia, diseases of the spinal cord and abscess of the brain (rather than typhoid!), and his presence seems to point to the possibility of an abnormal physical condition. If the parents knew the real cause of their elder son's 'slowness', then they would (as they did) ignore Dalton's complaints and protests, knowing that nothing could be done *at present*, but that, if Gull's prognosis were correct, 'the trouble would clear itself up as soon as His Royal Highness ended boyhood'.

The Prince of Wales, complaining that Eddy was lacking in 'manliness and self-reliance', wished him to go to a public school—it is interesting to note that he had Wellington, the army school, in mind, and not, as one might have thought, Eton—but against this plan Dalton argued strongly and, as it turned out, persuasively.

Dalton's argument rested on one proposition: that it was impossible to separate the brothers, and if—because he was intended for a naval career—Prince George must go to *Britannia*, then Prince Eddy must accompany his younger brother, whether or not a naval career were planned for the elder. As Dalton explained, the brothers were devoted to each other, and in George's presence Eddy did at least make some effort to emulate the younger's respectable proficiency in his school exercises.

There is a passage of Sir Philip Magnus's, dealing with this period of Eddy's life, which has been misread:

'Arguing that a public school would, in any case, have exposed a weakness which had been more or less "masked" in *Britannia*, Dalton advised that a private tutor would be a fatal mistake owing to lack of stimulating competition . . .'

All that Sir Philip means, in this passage, by a 'masked weakness' is Prince Eddy's inability to learn; it does *not* refer, as some people have thought, to some vicious tendency which had already made itself manifest by the time that Eddy was ripe—in years at least—for a public school.

So it was decided that it should be *Britannia* for both the boys, even though it became apparent that the 'bright' one, George, was almost as far behind in his studies as was his 'dull' brother. The standards of the Navy entrance examinations had to be considerably lowered in order to allow even Prince George to

become one of *Britannia*'s cadets, 'cramming' after entrance
being trusted to bring both the princes up to normal educational
level.

The Prince of Wales took his two sons down to Portsmouth
by train, but in no very benevolent mood. 'I hear', Sir Henry
Ponsonby recorded, 'that the Prince of Wales snubbed Prince
Eddy uncommonly.'

Dalton continued as the Princes' tutor, and somehow Eddy
was pushed through the two-year *Britannia* course without
being exposed to too much humiliation. There must have been
plenty of covering-up, of course; but there cannot have been
too much—the other cadets would not have extended all *that*
tolerance to a duffer, even though he were a future Heir to the
Throne. Prince George, happily for him, liked naval life, and
in after years it was his great regret that a naval career had
been denied to him through the accident of his being called
to be King.

Eddy was thirteen when he joined *Britannia*, George, twelve.
In 1879, when they came to the end of their cadet-training
course, they were, respectively, fifteen and fourteen. It seems
impossible that, in the free-spoken world of public-schoolboys,
their loose-living Papa's scandalous life should not at least have
been hinted at by some of the other cadets.

Republican and politically unattached anti-royalist journalists continued the tradition of *The Black Book of the Aristocracy*,
which, 'exposing' the alleged parasitism of the Royal Family,
the Church and the Law, ran into edition after edition all
through the first three-quarters of the century. It was followed
by many other similarly inspired publications. *Reynold's Newspaper* built up its 300,000 circulation on a regular offering of
scandal about, and attacks upon, the Royal Family. There were
dozens of smaller magazines, from *Tomahawk* to *Town Talk*,
which exploited a common human tendency to parade the
frailties of the great. Gladstone told Lord Granville that he had
seen *What Does She Do With It?* advertised on the walls of the
railway-station at Birkenhead: a fact which may surprise those
who believe that 'permissiveness' in attacking the Royal Family

openly came in with the student society of bare feet and long hair.

That the Princes' deep affection for their father never altered, despite what they must have heard about the Prince of Wales's peccadilloes, seems certain, but we do not need to respect what we are compelled to love—rather, it is often the case that our love is commanded by those for whom we feel the least respect; and certainly, their father's exhortations to be 'good'—especially when, later, Eddy's own impulses were beginning to put him in scandalous rivalry to his father—must have taken on aspects of the ludicrous, even though both princes were not notably possessed of a keen sense of the ridiculous.

The question of a public school for Eddy again came up in 1879, when, the two years of *Britannia* training over, new decisions had to be taken.

What Dalton did not realize was that his success as a tutor was estimated by the Prince and Princess of Wales by very different yardsticks from those that he employed. He thought that his job was mainly to *teach*, rather than *bring up*, the princes; Eddy's parents thought that if Dalton managed to contrive it that Eddy passed off as a normal boy during his period of 'slowness', then Dalton had brilliantly succeeded.

Dalton might have realized this by the lack of reproach which came his way when, it having been decided that the two princes should join *H.M.S. Bacchante* as cadets in training for midshipmen, Prince George, no less than Prince Eddy, was found to be as far behind his contemporaries as he had been on joining *Britannia*.

As Dalton wrote in the preface to his *The Cruise of Her Majesty's Ship "Bacchante", 1879–1882:* 'When H.R.H. the Prince of Wales resolved to send his sons to sea it was chiefly with a view to the mental and moral training which they would receive as midshipmen in Her Majesty's Navy.'

Perhaps it was the awareness of a secret that he could not share with others which spiked the Prince of Wales's anger, but though always a 'constitutionally minded' Heir to the

Throne, a normal intrusion of politicians into the business of getting the princes off to sea irritated him to a point beyond ordinary discretion. There was no reason why the Prince of Wales's proposal that the two boys should cruise in one ship should not have been discussed at a Cabinet meeting. Perhaps there was some personal prejudice on the Prince of Wales's part against the man who brought the matter before Disraeli, the Prime Minister. The First Lord of the Admiralty was W. H. Smith, who played his cards so well that within ten years of his becoming Tory Member of Parliament for Westminster, he was a Cabinet Minister—an elevation, as someone spitefully said, possibly not unconnected with the fact that his bookshops handled Disraeli's novels.

Smith 'recommended' that the princes, far from being permitted to travel together, should cruise on different warships, two of which should accordingly be commissioned from the Admiralty.

His interference angered the Prince of Wales. Disraeli was summoned, and made to listen to language so strong that even the pliant Dizzy was hard put to it to maintain his respectful smile. He apologized for Smith's attitude, and gave his assurance that no more would be heard of the matter; the two Princes should travel on the same ship.

It was said that Dalton had urged the separation of the boys; but this statement appears to contradict the urgings of Dalton, in several letters, that the boys should not be parted. Whether or not it was Dalton's fault that a suggestion of separation had been put forward, Dalton tendered his resignation as tutor. The resignation was not accepted; and on 17th September, with the higher rank of 'Governor', Dalton embarked in *Bacchante* for the first of the three voyages that he was to make with his young charges.

With what Sir Philip Magnus calls 'a handpicked complement of officers and tutors', *H.M.S. Bacchante*, Captain Lord George Scott, R.N., sailed for the Mediterranean.

Bacchante was a new ship, representing in her design the transition between sail and steam. Equipped with engines of 5,250 indicated horsepower, she was cruiser-rigged, and used her sails turn-and-turn about with her steam engines. Her armament also shared past and present traditions: fourteen $4\frac{1}{2}$-ton muzzle-loading guns, each capable of discharging a 150-lb projectile, side by side with the latest Whitehead torpedoes and Nordenfeldt machine-guns. She had gone through extensive trials at sea before being commissioned to take the two princes to the Mediterranean and the Caribbean. As a precaution against typhoid, cholera and other water-borne diseases, 'during her commission, every drop of fresh water used on board was condensed'—or, as we say today, distilled; and it is true that, save for what Dalton calls 'a trifling ailment' which affected Eddy in Australia, on the second cruise, the two princes enjoyed remarkably good health.

The tutors were entered on the ship's complement as supernumeraries, but Dalton was entered as Chaplain (Acting) R.N., an honour of which he was most proud. When *Bacchante* was commissioned on 15th July, 1879, she bore nine midshipmen and six cadets (afterwards midshipmen). Among the six cadets were H.R.H. Prince Albert Victor C. Edward and H.R.H. Prince George Frederick E. Albert.

It was not until four years after the termination of *Bacchante*'s last cruise that Dalton published his account, 'compiled from the private journals, letters, and note-books of Prince Albert Victor and Prince George of Wales, with additions by John N. Dalton'.*

This large book, in two volumes, was offered to the public as a 'single' narrative made by fusing the two separate journals kept by Eddy and George, Dalton acting as the sub-editor who had made one narrative out of two. Dalton also permitted himself to add explanatory notes—sometimes quite lengthy—but his intrusion into the conjoint narrative is always marked by the interpolations being enclosed within square brackets.

In 1893, the year after Prince Eddy's death, John Murray published *His Royal Highness the Duke of Clarence and Avondale, A*

* *The Cruise of Her Majesty's Ship "Bacchante" 1879–1882;* London: Macmillan & Co., 1886.

Memoir (*Written by Authority*), by James Edmund Vincent. As Vincent explains in the preface to his book that it 'was not undertaken without the express authority of the Prince of Wales', one will hardly expect the author seriously to challenge the authenticity of Dalton's claim that his book was compiled from the writings of the two princes.

The trouble with Mr Vincent is that he argues too earnestly to prove a point which, were it generally acceptable, would need no arguing at all. But even in the most toadying of literature, it would be hard to find anything as unconvincing as this:

'Mr Dalton—an able young clergyman who had attracted the Queen's notice by a brilliant discourse—has so many merits as a writer and as a man, that he will forgive, and even welcome, the assertion that in some points of literary skill one, at least, of his pupils excelled his master. Here, for example, is a nervous sentence conveying in a few lines a vivid and appreciative impression of a scene which clearly photographed itself on the mind:—

"Now come forward on the foc'sle again, which is the coolest place, as there is not a breath of wind stirring, and see the whales spouting in the distance on both sides of the ship; they might almost be taken for sail on the horizon; they are all going South." This is precisely the sort of passage which a dishonest tutor would have altered, by way of showing the range of his pupils' attainments, by inserting an allusion to "that Leviathan," by quoting the line which describes the scene

"Where the wallowing monster spouted his foam-fountains in the sea."

'But here there is no such attempt at ornament; there is simply a terse sentence conjuring up a spectacle of life at sea on the 15th of April, 1880, in a manner realistic, impressive and graphic in its very simplicity.'

In fact, the proposition that the book was written by the princes, and not by Dalton, is ludicrous. Who, for instance, would believe that *any* boys of seventeen and sixteen, however 'brainy', writing separately or as a literary team, would—or, indeed, *could*—produce a paragraph like this:

'This afternoon we went with Lady Augustus (Loftus) to the Destitute Children's Home at Randwick, of which Prince Alfred laid the foundation stone. We saw 600 poor little boys and girls, who had a holiday that day. They all looked clean and tolerably healthy, but some bore marks of the affliction that comes of their parents' sins. "Iste grex quid commeruit?" (1 Chron. xxi. 17.)

Nor, indeed, is credulity easily tempted into being by reading (under date, 5th August, 1881) a long passage on the mining industry of New South Wales, which includes these observations:

'Between 1870 and 1883 the total increase in the British coal production was upwards of 53,000,000 tons—an increase nearly equal to three times the present production of France, fully equalling the present annual production of Germany, thirteen times the annual production of Russia, and about eight times the production of Austria. Enormous, however, as this increase is, it has been exceeded by that which has within the same period taken place in the United States. In the latter country, the quantity of coal produced in 1870 was 32,750,000 tons; and in 1882, 87,500,000 tons, an increase of about 55,000,000 tons, or over 170 per cent.'

Indeed, the book abounds in such passages, which seem to have been lifted, with no acknowledgment to the authors, from the pages of the world's blue books or economic and financial reviews. What makes such passages even more suspect is that they are not enclosed within the square brackets which are the signs of Mr Dalton's interpolation, but are offered to the reader as the verbatim notes of two boys, one of whom has been represented by Dalton as being almost half-witted.

As an example of a 'fine passage', Vincent gives this:

'There are yet, even in clearest blaze of sunshine, scenes full of ghosts—the ghosts of gallant sailors and soldiers. Truly here

> "The spirits of our fathers
>   Might start from every wave;
> For the deck it was their field of fame,
>   And ocean was their grave"—

start, and ask us, their sons, "What have you done for these islands which we won for you with precious blood?" And what could we answer? We have misused them, till, at the present moment, ashamed of the slavery of the past, and too ignorant and helpless to govern them as a dependency of an overburdened colonial bureau in London, now that slavery is gone, we are half-minded to throw them away again and "give them up", no matter much to whom. But was it for this that these islands [of the British West Indies] were taken and retaken, till every gully and every foot of the ocean bed holds the skeleton of an Englishman? Was it for this that these seas were reddened with the blood of our own forefathers year after year? Did all these gallant souls go down to Hades in vain, and leave nothing for the Englishman but the sad and proud memory of their useless valour?'

Vincent, in quoting this passage, remarks that 'truly the writer of these words, whether he was Prince Albert Victor or Prince George, had been educated in the right way, and had drunk in the spirit of patriotism'. Yet even Vincent admits that there were many who did not believe that the two Princes had a hand in the work's production. To what other conclusion any unprejudiced person could possibly have come it is difficult to imagine.

It would be easy, then, to regard the journal as acceptable only as a valid account of the voyage: where the ship went, on which dates, and what the princes did, aboard and ashore, written from first to last by Dalton. Yet it would be incorrect to classify the work as the production of Dalton, and of Dalton alone. Hidden away in the seemingly endless passages of statistics or rather woolly Radical philosophizing are the princes' own reactions to what were evidently exciting experiences that both of them found stimulating, completely enjoyable and most memorable. One has to seek the persona of each Prince—and the search is no easy one. Yet, because the lively personalities of the two princes have not been effaced by drowning in the turgid mass of Dalton's descriptive matter, they are to be discovered.

For the first of *Bacchante*'s three cruises—to the Mediterranean and the West Indies—the princes had the best of all send-offs. It was an August of blazing heat, and Cowes Week had never been more brilliant. There are no 'social occasions' today, but the Victorian age was full of them; and of all these occasions none was more socially important than Cowes Week. *Bacchante* lay off Cowes, and so the princes were bidden Godspeed, as it were, by all the socially prominent in Great Britain.

As soon as Eddy and George had joined their ship, *Bacchante* was visited by all the royalty present: the Prince and Princess of Wales, with the Princesses Louise, Victoria and Maud of Wales (later Queen Maud of Norway), and by their Royal Highnesses the Duke and Duchess of Edinburgh and the Duke and Duchess of Connaught. *Bacchante* herself was dressed with masthead flags in honour of the Duke of Edinburgh's birthday.

The cruiser lay in Cowes Roads for the duration of the Regatta Week. There followed an experimental cruise, from 11th to 26th August. In all the pre-voyage time, Motherdear had the opportunity of seeing her sons, before taking them to Denmark to see their grandparents and other relatives. They returned to the ship on 17th September; on the 19th their father bade farewell to the boys; and on 25th September, *Bacchante* set sail—literally.

On the morning of 6th October, 1879, they sighted Gibraltar; by the afternoon of that same day, Eddy and George had landed and were exploring the Rock in the vicinity of the harbour. The stay was brief; before the day was out, *Bacchante* had sailed for Port Mahon, Minorca. Palermo was reached on 22nd October, and here the boys first experienced separation, the Captain taking Eddy ashore to climb Monte Pellegrino, but ordering George to remain aboard. Messina was the furthest east that the ship touched; on 31st October, *Bacchante* turned back towards Gibraltar, where the princes were nobly entertained by the Governor, Lord Napier of Magdala. Both excellent riders from childhood, the boys were made temporary members of the Royal Calpe Hunt, and went bounding off across the bleak south Spanish terrain after a Spanish fox. The journal refers to these days, when the boys were made much of by Lord and Lady Napier, as 'very happy', and whoever wrote the verdict, one may be sure that it was a sincere expression of the boys' joint feelings. On 15th November, *Bacchante* sailed from Gibraltar for Teneriffe. The Princes' globe-trotting had begun in earnest.

If the princes had a royal send-off—in both the literal and metaphorical senses of the word—there was also a great deal of malice busying itself to do them harm. The journal, under date 7th October, 1879, has this:

'Got our letters and newspapers, and heard for the first time, to our surprise, from England of the "Mutiny" and disturbance on board the *Bacchante*.'

Mildly as this is expressed (by Dalton's sub-editing, of course) Vincent is correct when he says that the princes were 'both amused and annoyed to find that some purely fictitious story concerning an imaginary mutiny on the *Bacchante* had been spread abroad'.

But such rumour-promoting recurred in a much more serious way when, in Australia on *Bacchante*'s second cruise, it was reported that Eddy had been assassinated. It is well to bear in mind that most of the main sub-oceanic cables had already been laid by 1880, and that all the main cities of the British Empire

47

were in direct and immediate telegraphic communication with London. This meant, of course, that denials could be quickly made in order to scotch a rumour; it also meant that a rumour could gain world-wide currency—especially if it were of a highly sensational nature—before the correction could be put out.

That rumour should busy itself with the adults of the Royal Family is understandable, and, perhaps, not unexpected. It could hardly have been otherwise that tongues should have wagged about Queen Victoria's John Brown; though the malice of jealousy shewed a little more imagination when it attributed the Princess of Wales's permanently stiffened knee to a gonorrhoeal synovitis, due to her having been infected with this disease by her wayward husband.

But what is new in this calumniating activity is the deliberate attempt to involve the Royal Children in the muck-raking. Although inspired by malice, it may be explained by the fact that the private lives of adult republicans were often as loose as those of the royal reprobates whom the columnists were attacking. The republicans might have felt themselves a little too vulnerable in claiming that only royalty misbehaved itself. It was safer to start on the children.

On paper, at any rate, the provisions for the Princes' education seemed adequate, and under Dr Dalton, as tutor-in-chief, specialized instruction was given by a number of the warship's officers. The first lieutenant, the Hon. A. G. Curzon-Howe, taught the Princes seamanship, the gunnery lieutenant, Mr C. H. Adair, instructed them in gunnery, naval instruction was imparted by Mr J. W. Lawless, Navigating Instructor, and the Assistant-paymaster, Mr G. A. F. C. Sceales, tried to teach them French.

Bacchante was well equipped to make the gunnery lieutenant's task easy, for the ship was not only provided with the latest armament, but had what was then the most advanced form of electrical fire-control. Doubtless, for Eddy and George, as for every other boy of their age, firearms were more fascinating than a foreign language.

48

Bacchante was evidently a happy ship; even allowing for the fact that the ship's complement must have been chosen with considerable care, it is remarkable that *Bacchante*, on reaching Australia, lost only one man by desertion, whilst from one of the escorting warships no fewer than *sixty-four* of the crew 'jumped ship'. Rather surprisingly the journal explains that the men are hardly to be blamed, seeing the much higher profits their labour could command in Australia.

Now, leaving aside the fact that Dalton was commissioned, or conceived himself to be commissioned, to write a book in praise of his two charges, it is impossible not to accept the overwhelming evidence of the Princes' freedom from many of the prejudices which, one might have thought, would have been inherent in their upbringing.

It is not astonishing that they liked Americans—their father did, too. On Teneriffe, the princes were happy to be taken around the island by 'the American gentleman', Mr B. Renshaw. But the princes' unaffected pleasure evident in meeting ordinary people—not only Americans—comes unaltered through the dense cotton-wool of Dalton's reporting.

On the second voyage, on their first night on Australian soil, they went up-country from Albany, Western Australia, to the farm of a Mr and Mrs Young, who 'gave us a hearty welcome'. They were to stay in a small shanty attached to the farm, and obviously the simple life appealed to the princes. 'There are two pails of fresh milk set out for us, which some drink neat and others prefer to take mixed with a little whisky before turning in. Some fall asleep at once, others not so soon; the American doctor's cheery ringing laugh sounding long on the quiet night air, as he and the Commander tell alternately the most astounding yarns, each with a *dénouement* more startling than the last.'

This response to a protocol-free acceptance of them as human beings is so consistent a feature of the long narrative that its reporting can have been based by Dalton only on fact. Whatever else the two boys had been made by Motherdear and their father, they were no snobs. Alexandra had seen to that.

They remember with affection the simple kindliness of the Scots farmer, Young, and his family:

'*May 22nd.* [1881]—After sleeping very soundly went down for a sponge bath in the sea-water in the creek off the rocks, and found it very cold. On returning we did full justice to our breakfast. Round each of our two plates Mrs Young had laid a small wreath of rosebuds, "for Sunday morning, and in memory of England." When the things were cleared away we had a short service in the kitchen, at which the whole family attended and joined. This patriarchal and simple praise and prayer ended, we mounted our horses, and having thanked Mr and Mrs Young for their kindness, and the hospitable introduction which they had given us to a settler's life in the Australian bush, we started for Albany soon after noon. Eddy had ridden up on a black horse called "Leo" after the present Pope, and he had a long swinging trot so rare in Australian horses; but he returned to-day on a chestnut called "Hengist," who had a delightful canter.'

There is a little of Dalton's sub-editing here, of course, but the fresh personalities of the princes break through the 'polish'. They liked the Australians and Australia very much, contrasting its sparkling cleanliness with the slums of Great Britain, to which, in condemnation, they return again and again.

They approve of Australian independence, and tell with evident pleasure how the transportation of convicts was stopped by the Australian refusal to accept that shipload which turned out to be the last. They wandered, incognito, amongst the crowds, talking to all; and when, not recognizing one of the princes, a naval officer complained about their having to be taken on to Melbourne, the Prince in question—was it Eddy or George?—enjoys his ability to agree with the unsuspecting officer.

They are normally and healthily free to accept the evidence of their senses, and to believe what others believe:

'*July 11th.* [1881]—At 4 a.m. the *Flying Dutchman* crossed our bows. A strange red light as of a phantom ship all aglow, in the midst of which light the masts, spars and sails of a brig 200 yards distant stood out in strong relief as she came up on the port bow. The look-out man on the forecastle reported her as close on the port bow, where also the officer of the watch from the bridge clearly saw her, as did also the quarterdeck midshipman, who was sent forward at once to the forecastle; but on arriving there no vestige or any sign whatever of any material ship was to be seen either near or right away to the horizon, the night being clear and the sea calm. Thirteen persons altogether saw her, but whether it was *Van Diemen* or the *Flying Dutchman* or who else must remain unknown ... The *Tourmaline* and *Cleopatra*, who were sailing on our starboard bow, flashed to ask whether we had seen the strange red light. At 6.15 a.m. observed land (Mount Diana) to the north-east. At 10.45 a.m. the ordinary seaman who had this morning reported the *Flying Dutchman* fell from the foretopmast crosstrees on to the topgallant forecastle and was smashed to atoms. At 4.15 p.m. after quarters we hove to with the headyards aback, and he was buried in the sea. He was a smart royal yardman, and one of the most promising young hands in the ship, and every one feels quite* sad at his loss. (At the next port we came to the Admiral also was smitten down.) The midshipmen's half-yearly examination began to-day with the Algebra paper.'

This entry seems entirely credible, for only to the very young would it occur to add the reference to the exam paper to a description of a frightful and mysterious death. It is evident, from the allusion to the Admiral's illness later, that the journal was not a day-to-day affair; and it is also evident, from the superstitious linking of the young sailor's death with the fact that he had been the first to see the *Flying Dutchman*, that the princes had listened with all ears to what the Americans call the 'scuttle-butt' of the lower deck. Dalton, too, must have retained his natural belief in wonders, or else he would never have permitted this entry to remain in the finished work.

* In 1881, the word 'quite' had not lost its original force of 'completely' or 'entirely'. The passage is by no means as unfeeling as it might sound to modern ears.

The princes' other activities were of a more normal kind. They played cricket, at which most British of all games the Australians had already shewn their marked superiority; they hunted; they shot game—including kangaroo; they went down mines; they climbed mountains; they listened to speeches, and, if we may believe the journal, Eddy, as the senior of the two Royal visitors, made the answering speeches with fluency and aplomb. We are entitled to accept the record without too much reservation, and believe that when Eddy thanked the Mayor of Adelaide for his citizens' hospitality he actually read and spoke the words attributed to him, in circumstances which did no discredit to his manner or intelligence, because of the attitude taken by the newspapers. For despite the friendly and heart-warmingly down-to-earth reception that the princes enjoyed in Australia, and which caused them to record in the journal that 'After England, Australia will always occupy the warmest corner in our hearts,' there was a strong and widespread feeling of hostility against, if not the Mother Country and her Queen, then certainly against that Queen's government. The mis-management of the Irish question had not made British governments any the more loved amongst the many Australian settlers of Irish origin or descent, and the almost totally defence-less condition of Australia was a constant reproach to Great Britain. The journal mentions the undefended condition of King George's Sound. 'In time of war it would be a matter of vital necessity to Great Britain to secure it against an enemy. It is agreed on all hands that this ought to be done, and done at once, and yet nothing has been done . . . An English man-of-war but seldom condescends to visit it, but the anchorage is very familiar to other maritime powers; it was not long since it was the station for some time of a Russian squadron.' There was plenty of critical comment—but none at the expense of the Princes.

It is obvious that, now seventeen, Eddy was coming out of that mind-numbing state—*petit mal* or whatever it was—which had so retarded him. Its passing was not to make him any brighter a scholar, for he had neither the energy nor the interest to make up for the years in which he had hardly been able to learn at all. But his brilliance as a polo-player on the Uruguayan pampas had impressed even the tough gauchos; the eight hundred guests at an Adelaide ball did not daunt him (he danced with many of the ladies); he did not falter in reviewing a picked detachment of Volunteers; and the crowded time-table, in which entertainment featured far less than the official duties of opening the Adelaide National Gallery, visiting a colony of Cornish miners, dining at Parliament House with all the members, attending divine service at the Cathedral, visiting a Home for Incurables, and so on.

If Eddy really was the half-wit of the traditional portrait, he could not have survived one thousandth part of this exacting itinerary without drawing comment upon his mental deficiency. However much Eddy's would-be educators still complain of his persistent 'backwardness', it seems evident that, so far as worldly experience went, the Prince was growing up fast.

While the *Bacchante*'s broken rudder was being repaired—no easy task in the non-industrialized Australia of the day—the princes transferred to *Inconstant*, rejoining *Bacchante* just before they were due to leave Australia on 20th August, 1881.

By the end of the year, they were at Hong Kong, having visited the Fiji Islands, Japan and the Chinese Treaty Ports of Wusung, Chusan and Amoy.

Yokohama was reached on the 21st October, the anniversary of Trafalgar, though the journal does not record the fact. 'The first Japanese thing we saw this morning was the long black hull of a screw steamer, such as you see them on the Thames, steaming out of Yedo Bay, with the Japanese flag, a red ball on a white ground.'

Whether spontaneously impressed by Japanese progress, or only after having had their attention called to it by Mr Dalton's percipient watchfulness, the lads are unstinting in their praise for Japan.

'Although it is only twenty years ago since the country was opened to foreigners, yet already the lighthouses all round the coast are most excellent, far better than those in some of the southern countries in Europe.' The Princes were impressed similarly by the postal system.

The mystery of Eddy's 'backwardness' appears again in the conversation that the two princes had with the Mikado, 'through Mr Nagasaki as interpreter'.

'[The Mikado] welcomed us to Japan and hoped that the Queen and the Prince and Princess of Wales were well. Eddy assured him they were and thanked him and said, he was glad to come to this most interesting country. He said he had been commissioned by the Queen to announce to the Mikado that Her Majesty had ordered her portrait to be painted in oils and forwarded in token of friendship, and that it would shortly arrive ... George said "the Queen was always glad to see members of other reigning families in England, and that he and his brother hoped that their visit to Japan, and his to England would serve to draw closer the ties of friendly feeling that already united the two countries". A very large party was the witness of this Imperial reception, including several persons not of British nationality and from not one has come any indication that Eddy behaved in other than a normal manner.'

On 27th October, a Japanese artist tattooed their arms: 'a large dragon in blue and red writhing down (our) arms.' The arrival in Yedo Bay of the U.S.S. *Swatara* brought them once again into contact with Americans; and neither of the princes begrudged the American crew its win in the regatta, the boat coxed by Prince George coming in third. Then followed, for the two fortunate boys, a cruise of the Inland Sea, and a visit to Kobe. Christmas Day, 1881, was spent at Hong Kong, before *Bacchante* sailed for China on 31st December.

Save for the weather, they liked Singapore, and in Ceylon almost everything was perfect: 'they liked the hearty young planters of the island, they enjoyed greatly a sambur hunt with Mr Lutyens's pack, and they had one real treat in watching the driving of a herd of elephants into a kraal.' One of the princes notes that 'the cricket here is very good'.

On 6th February, after having attended a ball given by the Governor in Colombo, the princes left for Suez, where the

'Motherdear'–H.R.H. The Princess of Wales.

Sandringham House, Norfolk, country home of the Prince and Princess of Wales, whose portraits are shewn (as King and Queen) above. *Below, left*, Queen Victoria (with Prince Edward of York, the present Duke of Windsor, K.G.). Victoria it was who struggled with Alix over the control of Eddy. *Below, right*, Eddy, aged 13, with his sister Maud, afterwards Queen of Norway.

H.M.S. *Bacchante* under both sail and steam as she leaves Cowes for her first voyage with the two princes in 1879. *Below*, Eddy (right) and his brother Georgy learn the nautical art of splicing from one of *Bacchante*'s petty officers on their first voyage as cadets.

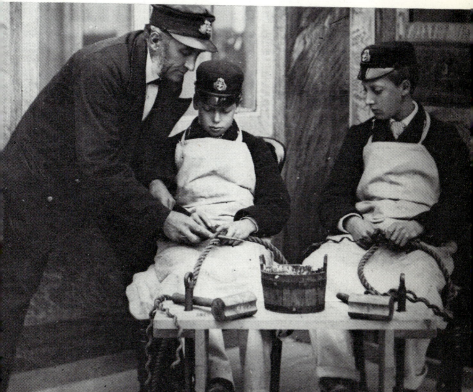

Eddy as Lieutenant-colonel of the 10th Hussars, at South Cavalry Barracks, Aldershot, in 1890. Despite Eddy's reported boredom with a military career, it is quite obvious from this and similar photographs that he thoroughly enjoyed much of military life.

Amongst its obviously appreciated benefits was the opportunity to wear a flattering uniform (subtly differentiated by Eddy's tailor—note the longer tunic with the rounded corners) and be photographed in the company of personable young men.

Below, Eddy as a freshman at Trinity College, Cambridge, in 1883. Though the self-confidence evident in later pictures is not yet fully developed, this photograph makes it clear that he had grown out of the diffidence which marked his childhood. *Opposite*, the two brothers in 1887, the year of Queen Victoria's Golden Jubilee, during the celebrations of which Eddy was one of the Queen's aides-de-camp. Georgy, now a Knight of the Garter, had just been promoted full Lieutenant, Royal Navy. Compare Eddy's established self-confidence with the lack of assurance observable in earlier portraits. Clearly an expanding social life was greatly to his taste. Georgy, it will be observed, had still to acquire a similar maturity.

Father and son—*above*, the Prince of Wales, later Edward VII, and, *below*, the Duke of York, who became the Prince's heir on the death of the Duke of Clarence: a providential happening, avers Sir Philip Magnus in his life of King Edward.

great De Lesseps had kept the Canal clear for the arrival of *Bacchante*.

Egypt, whose lavish and still completely oriental hospitality their parents had already enjoyed, offered it afresh to the two princes, whose visit Fate had timed well. Within a few weeks, Alexandria was to crumble beneath the bombardment of British guns.

But this was in the unknown future when the Khedive welcomed Eddy and George:

'The Khedive was not only courteous and attentive to the Princes, but he roused in them a friendly and personal interest. They pitied his two sons, immersed in an unending round of study, expressing their pity in a sturdy manner instinct with the spirit of the British schoolboy.'

Evidently both Eddy and George had the aristocratic British contempt for the 'swot'. George was persuaded to overcome his prejudice, but Eddy was never to be persuaded to do so.

They went up the Nile, as far as the First Cataract, on the Khedivial yacht, the *Ferouze*, whose costly appointments excited their wonder, and saw the Pyramids and the Sphinx. They left Alexandria on 28th March for Joppa and the Holy Land, and after visiting every place of interest, travelled on to Athens, where a grand reception had been arranged by their uncle, the King of Greece.

The imminence of war with Arabi Pasha being, apparently, unsuspected, it was in the calm enjoyment of a peace-time outing that the princes witnessed and took part in a naval regatta in Suda Bay, Crete.

'The Princes, too,' says Vincent, 'were no amateur seamen. Prince George has proved himself, in later years, a master of his profession; and throughout his life, even up to the premature end of the chapter, Prince Albert Victor took a keen and professional interest in all matters connected with the sea. Thus, when some years afterwards, he was inspecting the great Bute Docks at Cardiff, under the guidance of their master-spirits,

Sir William Thomas Lewis and Captain Pomeroy, those close observers of men were much impressed by the pointed nature of the questions which he asked, and by his evident appreciation of the full significance of the answers.' Once again we have an account that vouches for Eddy's normality.

From Crete *Bacchante* steamed on to Sicily, Sardinia and Gibraltar, where, once again, the princes were welcomed by Lord and Lady Napier. Bad weather caused a stop at the Spanish naval base of Ferrol for coal, but on 5th August, off Swanage, *Bacchante* came up with *Osborne*, on which the Prince and Princess of Wales, with their three young daughters, were awaiting Eddy and George, so that they might conduct the returning princes to pay their respects to Grandmama at Osborne House.

They had gone as boys; now they were returning, if not as men, then as boys on the verge of manhood. Eddy was eighteen, George only a year younger. Motherdear had hated to part with them, but, as she had written to the Queen: 'It is a great wrench—but must be got through—I trust to God that all may go well with them—and that their first step in the world by themselves won't be a too difficult or hard one—poor little boys, they cried so bitterly.'

Dalton had kept both the Prince of Wales and the Princess informed as to their sons' progress, but he may well have concealed from them a development which was not apparent until the publication of *The Cruise of the "Bacchante"* in 1886. Before the princes had set out on their world-tour, Alexandra had asked Dalton to be particularly careful that 'politics of any kind, home or foreign, should be as much as possible kept from them'. She goes on to explain that, though her boys were too young to have any reasoned opinion on the subject, any opinion expressed 'later on and in their position will stick to them for life'. She urges Dalton to see to it that 'our boys should not be influenced by party spirit either in politics or religion'.

In the light of these prohibitions it is curious that Dalton should have managed to compile in his book not only one of the most argumentatively political works of its day, but should have done so by attributing all the most violently combative views to the two adolescent boys in whose name the book purports to be written. Thus Dalton makes them espouse the cause of Home Rule, even though this cause had provoked indiscriminate bombing and carefully directed assassination. At that point in the journal where *Bacchante* is passing through the East Indies, Dalton inserts a scathing attack on French Colonial administration, at the very time that the Prince of Wales was doing his best to maintain his friendly associations with a France whose government had suddenly turned anti-royalist, anti-Church and anti-British. In writing about the West Indies, Dalton does not hesitate to compare the non-productive character of Jamaica with the prosperity of Barbados, attributing the former to the laziness of the native Jamaican and the neglect and maladministration of successive Colonial ministers. He wholeheartedly supports the dangerously explosive policy of importing coolie labour into 'unproductive' colonies, a policy which stiffened the anti-British sentiment of the average Boer. And was it altogether tactful to record, under date of 18th April, 1881, that 'we are reading Sir Charles Dilke's *Greater Britain*', the work of a radical who had made a scandalous exit from political life? Even so, Dalton was made Chaplain-in-Ordinary and Deputy Clerk of the Closet to H.M. the Queen, an appointment which was renewed when the Prince of Wales became King Edward VII. And five years after the publication of *The Cruise*, Dalton was appointed Honorary Chaplain to Prince George, then Duke of York, another appointment which was renewed, when George became Prince of Wales.

Either the Prince of Wales, his wife and mother were prepared to 'overlook' Dalton's intransigence in the matter of keeping politics and the Princes entirely separate, or by 1886 a fundamental change of policy had taken place.

However opinions may differ concerning Eddy's claims to be able to charm Australian mayors, there can be no doubt of his mastery of the Horse and the Gun, and to the majority of 'normal' people in the 1880s, he had thus fully justified his claim to their respectful affection. It is this majority attitude which accounts for the purely quantitative preponderance of the 'evidence' for Eddy's complete normality, compared with the academic's depressed and depressing testimony to Eddy's almost total illiteracy. Even the sneers of Eddy's most inveterate enemy, the old-Etonian, Cantab 'radical', Henry Labouchere, fix him clearly as one whose prejudices belong with the majority opinion. For instance, when the gossip-column of his weekly, *Truth*, comments sarcastically on the news that 'the Prince of Wales drove into Ballochburie Forest with Prince Albert Victor and Lord Cadogan, and there shot six stags, H.R.H. taking three', Labby isn't complaining of what the Prince and his son are doing, but, *from the highest aristocratic point of view*, is objecting to the way in which they do it. The three men had not gone stag hunting, as had been claimed, but had falsely and basely claimed to have done so, simply having been driven comfortably to nothing more than the sort of *battue* in which degenerate foreigners such as the Prince of Monaco took pleasure.

Sometimes Labby notices Eddy in paragraphs which cannot possibly have a double meaning, and into which it is impossible to read hostile criticism:

'Prince Albert Victor is staying at Bicester this week on a visit to Lord and Lady Chesham, and he is to have two days hunting with the Bicester and one day with the Heythrop.' (*Truth*, 528, XXI, Thursday, 10th February, 1887.)

If Labouchere found nothing to criticize in hunting, shooting and fishing, what of the millions of less analytical minds who followed, day by day in the *Court and Society* columns of magazines and newspapers, the unexceptionable activities of Prince Eddy? *They* had no hostile criticism to make.

In his *King Edward the Seventh*, Sir Philip Magnus mentions, without irony, the 'unclouded and humble religious faith' which remained always with Bertie, and which was 'an immense source of strength'. But others have found the undeniable fact of his unremitting search for sexual gratification incompatible with the assertion that Bertie was deeply religious.

King Edward VII was a lecher, without a doubt; but he was not a hypocrite in being, at the same time, deeply religious and unduly sensitive in the matter of his children's sexual morality.

Even as late as 1909, after a good forty years of assiduous and mostly successful woman-chasing, we find him writing, as King, to rebuke Herbert Gladstone, the Home Secretary, for having nominated two women, Lady Frances Balfour and Mrs H. J. Tennant,* to serve on a Royal Commission on Divorce.

The King's reasons may sound curious, but they are characteristic, and their expression is sincere. He warned that divorce was a subject 'which cannot be discussed openly and in all its aspects with any delicacy or even decency before ladies'. Although he had to give his consent, the King did so reluctantly, and told the Prime Minister, Asquith, on 15th September, that he could not but regard the appointments as 'the thin edge of suffragetism, and [the King] feels sure that its adherents and supporters will get stronger and more persistent in their demands when they see the principle, on which they base their claims, partly recognized'.

When Queen Victoria reminded her eldest son once again of the need for protecting both the Princes from contamination by the society in which, as Magnus says, their parents delighted, Bertie, in agreeing with his Mama, went far beyond what the ever-practical Victoria had in mind. He promptly wrote to the Queen (22nd May, 1880) that 'our greatest wish is to keep them simple, pure and childlike for as long as possible'. In a letter dated 11th July of the same year, Bertie reiterated his hopeful belief that the two boys were in no danger of the contamination that the Queen feared—in no danger at all, 'as I have had reason to say before'. He summed up his fatuous complacency thus: 'We both hope and think that they are so simple and innocent, and that those they have come in contact with have such tact with them, that they are not likely to do them any harm'.

In this context, 'innocent' means only 'sexually innocent',

* Asquith had married a Tennant. The appointment of Mrs H. J. Tennant was a 'family' affair.

and sexual innocence here, in so far as its menace could trouble the Prince of Wales, means either personal sexual experience or the knowledge that such experience exists.

As to the first, it may well be that the watchful eye of Dr Dalton prevented any premature tasting of the Fruit of the Tree of Knowledge of Good and Evil. As to the second, it is impossible that, mixing with the ship's petty officers and able seamen, something of the 'facts of life' in their more ribald and grosser aspects should not have come to the wondering ears of the princes. Alexandra herself had urged Dalton to curb the boys' inquisitiveness which, she said, was making them a nuisance to others: 'they always break into everybody's conversation, and it becomes impossible to speak to anyone before them.'

In the same way, it was impossible that they should have remained long in ignorance of their father's affairs of what we may prudently call 'the heart'. The journal makes it clear that letters and newspapers from England followed *Bacchante* throughout her voyage, and there are constant references to the pleasure that the Princes got from receiving news:

'Admiral Willes had sent H.M.S. *Zephyr* with the mail to meet us outside Yedo Bay, but unfortunately she missed us. H.M.S. *Pegasus* was therefore sent to look out for and bring her in, which she did, and brought us our mails at 6 p.m. We were very glad to get eight mail bags of letters and newspapers on board.' (21st October, 1881.)

Perhaps Dalton censored the princes' newspapers, but even if he did, he could hardly have censored those of all the others, from the Captain to the stokers. And in those outspoken days, with *The Times* foremost in reporting royal indiscretions, at least one titbit of High Society gossip would have reached the princes by way of the newspapers, the Rosenberg libel action of October, 1879, in which not only several of Papa's valued friends were mentioned—Mrs Lillie Langtry, Mrs Mary Cornwallis West, Lord Londesborough and Lord Lonsdale—but even Papa himself.

Since this case has been recorded in detail in my *Painful Details*,* and referred to at lesser length in my *Fanfare of Strumpets*,† it is only necessary here to say that Adolphus Rosenberg, owner and editor of a scandal-sheet, *Town Talk*, was charged at the Central Criminal Court with having libelled Mrs Cornwallis West, Mrs Langtry, Lord Londesborough and Lord Lonsdale. There were two libels: that against Mrs West claimed that she sold her 'pin-up' photographs; that against Lillie Langtry claimed that her husband had been prevented from divorcing Lillie, and citing Bertie, and his two friends, Lord Londesborough and Lord Lonsdale as co-respondents, only by his having been bought off by a lush diplomatic appointment. Rosenberg got a year's imprisonment with hard labour, while the plaintiffs, having won their case, left court 'without a stain on their character'. *The Times* reported the case in full, as did most of the other newspapers.

About the same time London was buzzing with the news of Bertie's latest infatuation, Sarah Bernhardt, who had come to England with the Comédie Française company. Lady Frederick Cavendish described her as 'a woman of notorious, shameless character', who 'not content with being run after on the stage, is asked to respectable people's houses to act, and even to luncheon and dinner; and all the world goes'.

A piece of news which, though not of a scandalous nature, yet scandalized many people in January, 1881, was the report, carried by all the newspapers, that the Prince of Wales had attended the synagogue wedding of Leopold de Rothschild and Marie Perugia, the sister of that Mrs Arthur Sassoon to whose beauty, said the scandal-mongers, the Prince of Wales had not been insensible. The report said, correctly, that the Prince had even signed the marriage register.

It was not that this broad-mindedness offended the religious or social prejudices of the less tolerant, as that it was made the basis of an absurd but widespread and widely believed rumour: that the Prince had gone to a synagogue because of a promise

---

* *Painful Details: Twelve Victorian Scandals.* London: Max Parrish, 1962.
† *Fanfare of Strumpets.* London: W. H. Allen & Co. Ltd, 1971.

that he had made to Sarah Bernhardt, who was of Jewish origin.

But that 'innocence' on which the Prince of Wales continuously harps relates also to the fact that, as a boy, he was protected from those crude initiatory rites to which his sons, educated in the traditional manner denied to him, were exposed.

All initiatory rites, no matter into which society or sub-group within that society, have a sexual element, more or less important within the totality of the ritual.

Most brutal, and brutally obscene, of all initiation rites in the last century were those traditional in the Royal Navy, and it is foolish to think that the two princes were spared the ritual customary in 'introducing' cadets to a naval career.

These consisted in two parts: a short, sharp initiation involving the stripping of the initiate, a 'belaying' on the bare buttocks with a leather dirk-scabbard, and as the climax of the initiation the filling of the luckless cadet's rectum with tallow (later changed to Lifebuoy soap). That the ritual buggery was practised long after it had been officially forbidden under the reforms of 1863 is certain.

The second part of the initiation rites was a long-drawn-out affair, which consisted, as in the majority of public schools, in formalized bullying.

Any offence by a cadet—smelly feet or nose-picking were considered exceptionally grave offences against good order and naval discipline—was punished by a gun-room sub-lieutenant or a senior midshipman, under the general supervision of the gunnery lieutenant. More serious breaches of discipline were dealt with by a committee consisting of the senior gunnery lieutenant, the midshipmen, and at least one 'Captain's clerk' (paymaster-midshipman). These disciplinary meetings were always held in the gun-room on the orlop deck, and by tradition were autonomous in that the ship's senior officers rarely ventured to enquire into the conduct or the verdicts of these self-constituted bodies.

At sixteen and fifteen respectively, Eddy and George can

have had no more of that 'innocence and simplicity' that their papa hoped to preserve than any other public-schoolboys of their ages. Even on a warship commissioned to take two Royal Princes on a tour around the world, life at sea was tough in 1879, and the men who went to sea in those days were no milksops.

. . . .

4. Preparing for the World

Before *Bacchante* 'like any other ship at the end of her usual three years' commission', was paid off on Thursday, 31st August, 1882, she had been visited by the Queen, the Prince and Princess of Wales, the Duke of Cambridge (Commander-in-Chief) and several lesser notables. But before this a most important event in the princes' life had taken place, their confirmation.

The royal yacht *Alberta* had been despatched, on 7th August, to fetch the Archbishop of Canterbury, Dr Tait, and Miss Tait, to Osborne House, where they were to stay as guests of the Queen. At 10.30 a.m. on the following day, the Prince and Princess of Wales took their sons to Osborne House, where they were examined before the Archbishop. On the same afternoon Eddy and George were confirmed, in the presence of the Queen, at Whippingham Church, where, from 1869 to 1871, the Reverend Mr Dalton had served as curate.

'After the laying-on of hands, the Archbishop pointed out that Confirmation is the admission to Holy Communion, and urged upon us to be henceforward regular Communicants.' On the following day, after the Queen had crossed over to Southampton to inspect transports leaving for Egypt, where, a few weeks before the princes had been so royally entertained by the Khedive, they went up to Whippingham Church to make their first communion. 'In the absence abroad of the

65

Rev. Canon Prothero through ill-health, the Rev. G. Connor, vicar of Newport, assisted by the acting chaplain of the *Bacchante*,* administered the Holy Sacrament.'

Although all boys brought up in the Anglican branch of the Catholic Church go through the two moving ceremonies of confirmation and first communion, not so many become what Archbishop Tait urged the princes that they should become, regular Communicants.

Yet this, in fact, was what they did. As the Archbishop said in his long address to the princes, 'From this time forward, your course of life, which has been hitherto unusually alike, must, in many respects, diverge. You will have different training for an expected difference of position.'

More of what he had said must have impressed the boys than the Archbishop had humanly the right to hope. He must have been an unusually impressive father in Christ, or the princes were in an unusually impressionable mood. For eight years later, when Eddy is twenty-six, and, even on his Papa's sad admission, innocent no more, we find him writing to his brother, George: 'I wonder if Motherdear has thought of the Communion for us on Sunday for that is the only thing that could bring me back before Tuesday.'

Apparent in this letter is both the touching love for their mother and the desire to do what will give her pleasure, and that resolute intention, no matter what the pull of worldly temptation, to stick to the faith of childhood and boyhood, that faith to which, with all their faults, both Motherdear and Dear Papa have paid far more than mere lip-service.

Georgina Battiscombe, in her excellent biography of Queen Alexandra, makes the important point that, consciously or otherwise, Alexandra sought to retard her children's development, to keep them childlike for as long as possible. Mrs Battiscombe points out that her daughter, Princess Louise, celebrated her nineteenth birthday with a children's party! 'Her mother, in fact, never properly realized that everyone of necessity grew up. Years later she caused some embarrassment

* The Rev. J. N. Dalton's modest way of referring to himself.

to one of her nieces, a girl in her twenties, by sending her presents suitable for a child of ten. On one occasion this elegant young woman, who was nearly six foot tall, received a parcel with a verbal message delivered by a footman, 'To darling little Patsy from her silly old Aunt Alix." ' One wonders how the footman delivering Alexandra's present kept a straight face.

Quoting a letter from Alexandra to her children in which she says that she is 'a bad old Motherdear not to write', Mrs Battiscombe remarks that 'even in her letters to her children, Queen Victoria never forgets that she is Queen of England; the reader of these letters to Prince George is seldom, if ever, aware that their writer is the Princess of Wales'. One letter quoted was written by Alexandra when her son, George was 'a full-blown naval officer commanding a first-class gunboat'. The letter ends 'with a great big kiss for your lovely little face'. Mrs Battiscombe was never more percipient than when she remarks that 'although written as early as the seventies and eighties these letters are Edwardian rather than Victorian in tone; to read them is not to be reminded of Victorian mammas in fact or in fiction but of Barrie's Mrs Darling. Here is more than a little of *Peter Pan*, the embarrassing whimsy, the un-doubted charm, the understanding of children, the curious horror of growing up. This time, however, it is not the boy who refuses to grow up, but the mother who will not allow him to do so.'

Whoever did the refusing, it is clear that both Eddy and George retained their adolescent immaturity until long after they ought to have been fully adult males. 'All love is sweet, given or returned,' but the love of Motherdear for her children was of the most damaging kind. That there were elements in his manly career to protect him from the vampirish love of Motherdear was something for which, it is evident, George came to be consciously grateful. It is he who, still with un-diminished affection, pronounced Motherdear to be the most selfish woman of his acquaintance.

But Eddy was lost. He was Alix's first-born, the son over whose birth there had hung a mystery, who had crept into the world, as it were, when no-one was expecting him, in a house devoid of the usual reception-committee. Besides, Eddy was so *beautiful*, as beautiful a man as Motherdear was a beautiful woman. He did not live to see what Motherdear's 'love' could do to a daughter, but the face of Princess Victoria, denied marriage so that she could stay with the Motherdear who 'could not spare her', is sufficient testimony to the destructive power of selfishness which may persuade itself that it is love at its most generous.

On a more practical level, Motherdear's interest in her sons' educational progress caused her to take little satisfaction in what Eddy had learned or rather had *not* learned.

Already, when only half-way through his terms in *Britannia*, Eddy's 'backwardness' had caused Alexandra to write to Dalton as a result of the suggestion that Eddy should be removed altogether from *Britannia*, 'his standard of intelligence being too low to make it possible for him to compete with the average naval cadet'.*

'I must write you one line to say how *dreadfully* distressed I am with all the different reports about poor Eddy's progress; it is indeed to be regretted and deeply deplored that he should have got on so little this term—and in fact according to Lord Ramsay's account the Britannia has been a complete failure as far as he is concerned! and he as good as advised us to remove him from there!

'Now I am sure this would be a great mistake and I am sure you will agree with me that nothing could be worse for him in every way than to be *educated at home alone* this time without even his brother! But whatever is done must be most carefully weighed before anything definite is settled.'

In this important respect, the Princess of Wales had her own way, and, if the evidence of *The Cruise* is to be believed, Eddy's backwardness was sufficiently overcome that he could pass out of *Britannia* into *Bacchante* and impress a couple of dozen

* *Queen Alexandra*: G. Battiscombe.

Australian municipal councils with his fluent command of the traditional phrases of sub-diplomatic intercourse.

But although the two princes might claim a fair mastery of their mother tongue, their only other language was their mother's Danish. Outside Denmark the talent was little regarded since, throughout Europe and Asia, French was the *lingua franca* of the educated classes, and German the family language of European royalty. Despite their 'backward' father's extraordinary fluency in these, Eddy and George spoke neither. To rouse their interest in French, Dalton had got the boys some of Dumas's novels, an enterprising move which gained him rather reproof than commendation from the Princess of Wales:

'Though I have no doubt that Dumas' novels are very interesting still I cannot help thinking that *Novels* are not useful reading and do the boys no good. In French literature there are so many useful and most entertaining books in the shape of memoirs and historical works which would be far better for them. Lamartine's *Girondins* for instance is most interesting.'

Some have found this objection of Alexandra's to novels narrow-minded, in sharp contradiction to her known and widely reported broad-mindedness. But it must be recalled that Dumas permitted himself a freedom in treating of certain subjects which, in those days, was not permitted to the average British novelist, over whose choice both of subject and expression the library-monopolists, Mudie and Smith, exercised autocratic control.

In any case, exciting or not, Dumas's novels didn't improve the princes' French, and the Princess of Wales began to be seriously disturbed about a failing which had to be rectified if the boys were to take their due place in European society. At the end of the summer of 1882, Eddy and George, still in the care of Dalton as 'tutor'—he was yet to be promoted to the rank of 'governor'—were sent to Lausanne, to learn German and French as it were 'on the spot'. The boys liked Lausanne and the new freedom that even Dalton's relative strictness could not impair. But their progress in the languages that they had been sent abroad to learn failed sadly to come up to their parents' expectations. On 11th March, 1883, after Eddy and George had spent six months in Lausanne, Alexandra is writing despairingly to Dalton about Eddy:

'Although you kindly beg me not to distress myself about the contents of your last letter I cannot, I confess, help being very much grieved by the unsatisfactory account you are unfortunately obliged to give me of Eddy! It is indeed a bitter disappointment that instead of steadily improving as we hoped he had begun to do during the first half of his stay at Lausanne he should have relapsed into his old habits of indolence and inattention. It does indeed seem strange that at his age he does not yet see the great importance of exerting himself to the utmost, and lets his precious time slip by which can never be recalled.'

In a later letter to Dalton Alexandra acknowledged sadly, in talking of Eddy, that 'we are neither of us blind to his faults'.

It was in this March, 1883, that Queen Victoria lost that oddest of all royal servants, John Brown, whose eccentricities would have been better understood in an age in which the royal jester was still a recognized appanage of kings and queens. Sympathizing deeply with the bereaved Queen, even though that sympathy stopped short of an approval of Brown, Alix strove to give what comfort she could, so that the Queen wrote: 'Dear Alix has been here for two nights and nothing could exceed her tender sympathy and complete understanding of all I feel and suffer.' And because Alix could find and give sympathy in circumstances that others might have found absurd, irritating or even contemptible, she found sympathy, too, in her own troubles. The Queen both loved and pitied Eddy—a sympathy all the more remarkable when we consider how accomplished Victoria was, being an expert linguist, a very competent artist, and an excellent pianist. Her love for her odd grandson excused his faults (even, later, those most serious faults which were to threaten a throne-rocking scandal), in taking pleasure in what, to her, were excellent qualities which amply compensated for Eddy's obvious failings. Lord Napier, then Governor and Commander-in-Chief of Gibraltar, met Eddy twice and wrote of him that 'he does the right things as a young gentleman in a quiet way'. This praise might be dismissed as mere good policy on Napier's part if the judgment, expressed in varying ways, had not been held by many others. Even Sir Henry Ponsonby, no consistent flatterer of royalty, praises in very much the same way when he remarks that Eddy 'is pleasing, talks well, and will be popular when he gets more at his ease'. The main difficulty, Ponsonby thought, in fitting Eddy for his exalted position as King of Great Britain and Ireland and Emperor of India was the fact that Eddy could not 'apply himself for a length of time'. Ponsonby also noticed the hereditary deafness.

Alexandra possibly did not wish to put forward deafness as a possible cause of Eddy's backwardness in learning as she was understandably sensitive on the subject of imperfect hearing. That Eddy, in her own words, was 'a little slow and dawdly' Alexandra always attributed to her son's having grown so fast.

In other respects, too, Alexandra's reluctance to face any unpleasant facts or surmises connected with her sons is shewn in a letter that she wrote to the Queen after Eddy had gone up to Balmoral, in the summer of 1883, to be invested with the Garter. After thanking the Queen for the good advice that she has given Eddy, Alexandra rather ambiguously adds that she is glad that the Queen did not allude to any of the other subjects that she had intended speaking about, 'such as races, clubs, etc. as he really has no inclination that way and it might only have put them into his head beside placing his father in rather an awkward position'.

Eddy was to become, within a very short time, a member of many clubs, not only the Marlborough, the club that his father founded, but of some far more raffish establishments of a type that his pleasure-loving father had long since given up as being beneath his dignity.

With letters and diaries of this time full of references to Eddy's charm and fluency of speech—though perhaps it is the manner, rather than the fluency, which is meant by that constantly repeated phrase, 'he speaks well'—and with about the same number of letters and diaries bemoaning Eddy's backwardness, it may seem a little difficult to determine exactly how 'dawdly' he was. What, I think, has been forgotten is the fact that teaching in those days laid great—we have come to think of it since as excessive—stress on the catechistic, *viva voce*, method of imparting knowledge; the very method, indeed, least suited to an 'abstracted' child and youth whose hearing was already impaired. In learning which involved no questions or answers Eddy was as bright as the brightest, being able not only to play an excellent hand of whist, but to hold his own against such noted Cantab whist-players as H. H. Turner, H. L. Stephen and his 'governor', J. N. Dalton. If change has brought improvement in few things since 1883, surgical and psychological skill today might well have broken through the neurotic armour in which this deaf, troubled lad had encased himself.

That even his parents had conceded the fact of *some* improvement in Eddy's general level of intelligence seems to be obvious in their consent to part him from his brother. Until Eddy's nineteenth year, it had been an article of faith with the decision-making members of the Royal Family—the Queen, Princess Frederick of Prussia and the Prince and Princess of Wales—that, *on no account*, ought Eddy to be separated from his younger, brighter brother. It was the suggestion, made by the First Lord of the Admiralty, W. H. Smith, and tacitly endorsed at first by the Prime Minister, Benjamin Disraeli, that the princes should be sent around the world on separate warships, which angered the Prince of Wales to unbridled language.

But now—on whose advice was it?—it was decided to reverse this policy and separate the princes, George being commissioned as a sub-lieutenant to H.M.S. *Canada*, and Eddy entered as an undergraduate of Trinity College, Cambridge.

No-one, rightly, was at all anxious about Prince George. Although somewhat slow, he was sure, and his parents were confident that he would prove a credit to them and to that Service in which he had chosen to make his career.

As for Eddy, it was felt that if his 'prop', George, were to be taken away, another must be supplied in the shape of some brilliant, eminently 'suitable' young man who would act, partly as crammer, partly as 'companion', under the general supervision of Dr Dalton, who was to continue as Eddy's 'governor'. The young man selected was James Kenneth—'Jim'—Stephen, nephew of that Sir James Stephen, Professor of Modern History at Cambridge, who had recommended his ward, Gibbs, to the Prince Consort as the most suitable tutor for Bertie. It was Gibbs who had recommended Dalton as tutor for his former pupil's two sons, and now Dalton's sense of obligation to the Stephen family caused him to speak up for Sir James's nephew. J. K. Stephen was brought to Sandringham, inspected, and pronounced a fit and proper person to be appointed to the task of steering Eddy into and through the University. The young tutor's background was excellent, coming from a family with long and successful connections with the law. J. K. Stephen, like his father, Sir James Fitzjames Stephen, was an Etonian, and like Dalton, a member of Trinity College, Cambridge, to which Eddy was going for the academic year, 1883–4. It certainly never occurred to anyone investigating young Mr Stephen's background to notice the recurrent breakdowns, usually referred to as 'severe illness, caused by overwork', which ran through the history of the Stephens, and which was to attack Sir James himself in 1885. Even the notice in the *Dictionary of National Biography*, written by Sir James's nephew, Leslie (afterwards Sir Leslie) Stephen,* cannot conceal the gravity of the mental disturbance which terminated one of the most successful legal careers of the century:

'A disease which had been slowly developing began to affect his mental powers. Upon hearing that public notice had been taken of supposed failure, he consulted his physician, and by

---

* Whose daughter, the brilliant Virginia Woolf, did not escape 'the curse of the Stephens'. She committed suicide.

his advice at once resigned in April, 1891. . . . From this period
he gradually declined, though he was still able to collect some
of his old *Saturday Review* articles for publication.'

Since the illness of both Sir James Fitzjames Stephen and his
father, Sir James Stephen, will be mentioned again in the course
of this history, the reader's attention is called to the following
significant dates.

In 1885, Sir James Fitzjames Stephen was elected an
honorary Fellow of Trinity College, Cambridge.

In 1885, Sir James had what his son describes as a 'serious
illness'.

In 1886, despite this 'serious illness', Sir James was appointed
chairman of a Committee assembled to enquire into the management of the Ordnance Department.

In 1888, Sir James was the judge at the trial of Mrs Maybrick, accused of having poisoned her husband with arsenic.
The accused was found guilty and condemned to death, but
later reprieved, and sentenced to life imprisonment. Sir James's
conduct of the trial so aroused public resentment that he had to
be given police protection.

In 1891, because of what his nephew describes as 'a disease
. . . [affecting] his mental powers', Sir James resigned his high
judicial office. He died in Ipswich, in 1894.

It must be borne in mind that the 'disease . . . [affecting] his
mental powers' which drove Sir James to premature retirement
from the Bench was, as Leslie Stephen says, a disease which had
been slowly developing. It had, in other words, laid its fatal
hand upon his mind not only as early as the year of his 'serious
illness', 1885, but, one must assume, a good deal earlier—as
early, perhaps, as the year in which the Prince and Princess of
Wales were arranging to appoint his son, J. K. Stephen, tutor
to a future King of England.

The Stephen family will be discussed in more detail later, but here we must consider the character and personality of the young man who was to prove one of the most important influences in Eddy's life, James Kenneth Stephen.

It is hard to accept the value of contemporary estimates of a personality which has vanished without ever having impressed itself upon posterity by means of books, paintings, a brilliant political or military career or (as in the case of Dr Johnson) by inspiring a dedicated disciple to record the ephemeral *persona* for later generations.

Clearly, 'Jim' Stephen fascinated not only the men of his own age but also those of an older generation with his rare physical beauty and his quite unusual intellectual brilliance. It is evident that Vincent, like all those who came into contact with Stephen (Vincent met him at Cambridge), was impressed by his personality, but in his case one senses the reluctance to admit the power, to yield to the charm.

'Mr Stephen was . . . a man of striking personality. He was the son of one of Her Majesty's judges, who owed his seat upon the Bench to exceptional circumstances and exceptional powers. Some men are promoted to the Bench because they have served faithfully this political party or that; some owe their position to the skill and learning which they have displayed as advocates. Sir James Fitzjames Stephen rose to his high office without having argued many cases, without having been prominent in politics—by force of the sheer intellectual power, the profundity and the precision of thought which he had shewn in dealing with Indian law, and in books upon English law treating of subjects which, since his books appeared, no wise man has so much as attempted to handle. Mr J. K. Stephen, an Etonian and Cambridge man to the finger-tips, added to his father's powers and force of intellect a cultivated taste in the delicacies of scholarship. He was no mere bookworm, but a man with a natural bent towards dainty and exquisite language in prose and verse. "He was (writes his friend, Mr H. F. Wilson . . .) by general consent the ablest of the younger generation . . . No better choice could have been made [i.e. than in selecting him to be Eddy's tutor], for Mr Stephen, to an extraordinarily brilliant and subtle intellect, united a geniality of disposition that made him, to those who knew him well, one of the most lovable of men." A hearty man was this, and a vigorous, warm-hearted, large in mind, versatile in taste, intensely human.

'Such was the man under whose immediate personal influence Prince Albert Victor was brought, *and for whom, until death parted them, taking first the pupil and then the tutor, Prince Albert Victor had ever an affectionate regard.*' [My italics.]

Such would have been the opinion expressed by all who knew Jim Stephen. He was one of those handsome, 'brainy', yet universally popular men who even in school-stories seem a little too good to be true. It seems inevitable that, after he had appeared as 'Ajax' in a Greek play at Eton, a contemporary should not hesitate to approve the choice of Stephen for 'a part for which he was filled by a massive frame and striking face'.

The longest-surviving portrait of J. K. Stephen prefaces *Lapsus Calami*, one of the two small volumes of verse that he published in 1891, and which proved an immediate success. This portrait, engraved from a photograph and idealized in the manner of the well-known Brooke portrait, shews Stephen as his friends wished him to look. The idealization apart, there is no doubt that he was a good-looking man whom his contemporaries thought 'classically' beautiful.

Yet there is no doubt that of all those whom the Prince and Princess of Wales could have chosen as their elder son's tutor, Jim Stephen was the worst possible choice.

Book II *Youth*

5. College days

The Stephens were social climbers, and it was possibly the constant worry of deciding whether or not the next step was to be the right one which brought on those 'nervous breakdowns' which punctuate the otherwise successful progress of this ambitious clan. They were, in their dedicated climbing, one of the typical successful families of the nineteenth century, a century whose ruling classes were, on the whole, ready to help the climber and welcome him to the higher levels as soon as he had attained them.

The founding father was James Stephen (1758–1832), whose connection with the law began in the somewhat dubious employment of 'evidence collector' for the still-existing firm of Freshfields, solicitors. He is known to have collected evidence against Queen Caroline and for Sir Fowell Buxton's enquiry into the slave trade. He rose to the rank of Master in Chancery and became an M.P., a violent anti-slavery agitator and close associate of Wilberforce. His second son was Henry John Stephen (1787–1864), serjeant-at-law, and author of *A Treatise on the Principles of Pleading in Civil Actions*. His younger son, George Stephen (1794–1879), is described as 'a miscellaneous author'. Called to the bar of Gray's Inn in 1849, he settled in Liverpool, built up a fair practice in bankruptcy cases, and in 1855, after his practice had declined, emigrated to Australia. His officious 'honorary' activities in the Anti-Slavery campaign

79

earned him a knighthood. James's third son was Sir James Stephen (1789–1859), Colonial Under-Secretary in 1822, a famous contributor to *The Edinburgh Review* (an epilogue to his collected 'Review' essays earning him a charge of heresy) who was known in the Colonial Office as 'King Stephen' or 'Over-Secretary Stephen'. He suffered 'a severe illness caused by over-work', and in 1849 was appointed Professor of Modern History at Cambridge, where, as has been noted, he was in a position to recommend Gibbs as tutor to the young Prince of Wales. Sir James Stephen's son was Sir James Fitzjames Stephen, Bart., KCSI, the father of J. K. Stephen. Sir James Fitzjames was not only a distinguished lawyer—as codifier of the Indian legal system, he earned his KCSI—but a well-known journalist, contributing to those socially conscious journals, *The Saturday Review* and *The Pall-Mall Gazette* for the better part of his adult life. It should be noted that as the Stephens advanced, they exchanged radical for more orthodox beliefs.

In far less than a century, the Stephens had come from a sort of attorney's odd-job-men to established senior civil servant, serjeant-at-law, chief justice, Cambridge don, master in Chancery, judge of the Queen's Bench. One of the most consistently exacted and least-recognized penalties of success is that haunting sense of having betrayed something; of having 'sold out'. Reproached by the slavery-abolishing, anti-royalist, anti-Anglican self-helpers of only a generation or two back, the rapidly rising Stephens must have known tensions indeed to create fundamental neurotic conditions over at least three generations of these brilliantly successful *arrivistes*.

The family background of J. K. Stephen illustrates clearly the nature of the clan's two principal links with the Establishment, the university and the law. Of these, the law was by far the more important, and it was through his close connection with the law that Jim Stephen planned to gain a control over his royal pupil far more total and complete than any imagined by Eddy's parents.

The introduction of Jim Stephen to the Prince and Princess of Wales and their elder son took place in the summer of 1883, between the Prince of Wales's visit to Berlin in February, for the silver wedding celebrations of his sister, the Crown Princess of Germany, and a stay at Homburg in August, where his gambling and generally sportive behaviour caused much head-shaking and mouth-pursing amongst the British wowsers. On Michaelmas Day, 1883, the Prince of Wales joined Alexandra at an important house-party at Fredensborg, one of the Danish King's palaces, and on 17th October Bertie returned to Marlborough House, so as to be able to take Eddy to Trinity College, Cambridge, on the following day.

In the meanwhile, Eddy had been receiving three months of the special Stephen system of tutoring.

It is amusing to read the patronizing words in which Stephen seeks to hide his own pride and sense of self-importance on having been appointed tutor to his future King. After his first meeting with Eddy he wrote, 'He is a good-natured, unaffected youth, and disposed to exert himself to learn some history.'

To indoctrinate Eddy into university ways—for there were to be no University examinations—it was arranged that a select and carefully screened party of actual or prospective undergraduates should be invited to Sandringham to spend the Long Vacation as the guests, not so much of Prince Albert Victor as of an experimental tutorial system from which, it was hoped, the guests would derive no less benefit than their royal host.

It is clear from Stephen's letters that the ideas behind the 'experiment' were his, and not Dalton's. Stephen was lucky in that on one of the Prince of Wales's flying visits to Sandringham, he had been seated next to the Prince at dinner, and that afterwards 'they discussed the future career of the young Prince at length and in such a manner that Mr Stephen was deeply impressed with the Prince's interest in his son's welfare'. However careful Vincent is in allocating responsibility, crediting Stephen with more, and the others with less, initiative, it is clear from his account of the arrangements for Eddy's tutoring that Dalton had already dropped out of the directing body, and that the Prince and Princess of Wales, impressed by the way in which Stephen had 'sold' his ideas, had turned over the management of the affair to him:

'Mr Stephen also took a decided step towards what may be called the social preparation of the Prince for the University. With the sanction of Mr Dalton, and, of course, of the Prince of Wales also, he contrived a preliminary introduction between the Prince [Eddy] and some of those who were to be associated with him at Cambridge later. Thus we find Mr Stephen writing to Mr H. F. Wilson, of Rugby School and Trinity College, Cambridge, to ask him to come to Sandringham, and saying, "If you came on Saturday (the letter is dated August 7th*) you might meet Goodhart." '

Though Wilson is described by Vincent as 'a very elegant scholar, given to epigrams and verses in English, Latin and Greek, fond of exercise in the open air, a genial and merry companion', the real reason for his having been selected *by Stephen* to join the tutorial party at Sandringham was that he, too, like Stephen, was reading law.

At first the party was a mere half-dozen, and to accommodate them, the Prince of Wales had made over to Dalton the 'Bachelors' Cottage' in Sandringham Park.

As Stephen wrote home:

'We are six in this little house, a sort of adjunct to the big one in whose grounds it stands, and we lead a quiet and happy reading-party sort of life with all the ordinary rustic pursuits. I have a fat and speedy nag all to myself, and I give him plenty to do.'

The other members were Dalton, whom Stephen found too prone to 'depreciate himself and others', but in whom he recognized 'a keen interest about the welfare of Prince Albert Victor and all that concerns him', a 'lively little Frenchman', 'a young aristocrat, whose father is the Earl of Strathmore [*the*

* 1883.

Hon. Patrick Bowes Lyon], and a naval lieutenant kept on shore by a bad knee, [*Sub-lieutenant F. B. Henderson, RN*] both of whom are very pleasant and have more brains than they take credit for'.

As it is in this same letter that Stephen describes his discussion with the Prince of Wales after dinner, it is clear that he has already planned to round out the 'reading-party sort of life' with some additional guests of his own careful choice. Behind the studious façade of young Mr Stephen, there hid a man-manager of no ordinary skill.

The Cambridge of 1883 was a very different place, both as town and University, from what it is today. One hears now and then of the Christ Church riots at the sister University, when a number of rioting undergraduates broke into the staff rooms, and destroyed a number of valuable manuscripts and books. The story is offered as an excuse for similar behaviour today when a number of Cambridge undergraduates invaded the dining-room of an hotel, destroying property and attacking guests and servants. But the key-difference is that, with all his high-spirits, the undergraduate of 1883 did not question the right of Authority to punish him.

Of course, these undergraduates included the sons of the well-to-do middle classes, and even boys who had made the grade through scholarship and exhibition, or who had been given their chance of a university education by the grant of some philanthropic association or by the benevolence of their fathers' employers or territorial landlords.

It had been the Prince Consort's wish to see the 'under-privileged' have access to all the good things which, up to his time, had been mostly the prerogative of a small class of over-privileged and underworked grabbers. He was not the first Prince to develop a non-political socialistic desire to see the Meek inherit the Earth, but he was certainly the first—and still perhaps the only—man of his position to have attempted to realize his social beliefs in a practical way.

What he left behind, as a tradition in that royal family to which he brought stability and respect, was a recognition of the fact that a monarch is ruler of all his subjects, irrespective of their racial, social or religious origins. After his death, his son had the good fortune to marry the most unsnobbish princess in the world, and whatever the Prince and Princess of Wales had in mind when, with Dalton's open, and Stephen's subtly concealed, planning, they sent Eddy up to Cambridge, it was certainly with no intention of making him a snob.

Significantly only one of his 'chosen' companions came from an aristocratic background, the Honourable Patrick Bowes Lyon, who had served with Eddy on *Bacchante*, and since he was the third son, was very unlikely to succeed to the family title.

Much more representative of the 'entourage' was the brilliant Harry Wilson who, as Sir Henry Wilson, KCMG, KBE, CMG, was to progress, through a first appointment as a barrister in the Colonial Office's legal department, to a world-reputation as one of Imperial Britain's greatest colonial administrators.

Yet Wilson, Foundation Scholar and Fellow of Trinity College, Cambridge, First Class in Classical Tripos, 1882, Bell's University Scholar, and Chancellor's Medallist for English Verse, was the son of a Norfolk rector, with no 'connections' and precious little money beyond his modest stipend.

The hand-picked companions of Prince Eddy were all brilliant young scholars and they all played games extremely well. If any person of royal blood had a chance of becoming 'human', these young men gave Eddy that rare opportunity. They were the cream of that generation of Cambridge men: hard-working without being 'swots', brilliant without being rapt in learning, hard-playing without being bone-headed hearties. But what neither Dalton nor Stephen could control in their selection were the choices which had already been made. They had to accept existing University appointees and the influence of some of these on Eddy has been seriously under-estimated.

Vincent reports that 'Prince Albert Victor's inner life was passed at first among the friends whom he had made at Sandringham, and later within a gradually widening circle of which those friends were the nucleus and centre. In the selection of these friends some care was exercised. With what seems an excessive complacence Vincent mentions 'an interesting photograph' of the majority of these carefully selected friends of Eddy's:

'In the centre sits Prince Albert Victor, as broad and square in the shoulders as any of the constituent units of the group; on his left hand is Mr H. L. Stephen [later Sir Herbert Stephen, Bart., Jim Stephen's elder brother], on his right is Mr H. F. Wilson. Immediately behind the Prince stands Mr J. K. Stephen, smothered in a soft white hat, not to be divorced from his indispensable pipe, with a cheery smile upon his face. Mounted high above Mr Stephen, apparently sitting on his shoulders, is Mr J. N. Langley. Reclining on the ground in front are Mr Dalton [he was not yet a Canon of Windsor], Mr J. W. Clark, and Mr Goodhart;* the remaining members of the group are Professor Stanford, Mr A. H. Clough, Mr F. B. Winthrop, Mr J. D. Duff, Mr A. H. Smith and Mr H. B. Smith. By universal consent this fellowship of kindred spirits was one of the most delightful ever known; and those who have met many of the fellowship since will not hesitate to say that it was an assembly of brilliant wits no less than of pleasant men.'

As we have seen, Wilson became a barrister, as did H. L. Stephen, J. K. Stephen, Joseph Tanner (he practised as a conveyancer and equity draughtsman) and James W. Clark (another conveyancer and equity draughtsman, who was also resident legal adviser to the Board of Agriculture).

'It was with the younger of these men and a few more', Vincent continues, 'that Prince Albert Victor was most closely associated.' There were, however, older men whose influence, for all that they were perhaps not amongst those with whom 'Prince Albert Victor was most closely associated', exercised an

---

* Harry Chester Goodhart, afterwards Professor of Latin at Edinburgh University. Died 1895, aged 37.

undeniably profound and arguably corrupting influence on him. Of these peripheral influences the most important was undoubtedly the sinister Oscar Browning, already the principal figure in a school scandal given far too wide publicity when the headmaster of Eton, Dr Hornby, had sacked him from his lucrative housemastership for what another Eton housemaster, Woolley-Dodd, had termed Browning's 'undue friendliness' with one of Dodd's boarders, the then good-looking future Viceroy of India, George Nathaniel Curzon. Browning, having refused to accept the implications of Hornby's complaints, had taken the quarrel to the newspapers before eventually he was forced to go.

Browning held a Fellowship at Cambridge, and, on leaving Eton, took up his residence at King's College. There he stayed for thirty years, becoming more and more mistrusted, and failing to get any of the appointments or titles for which he continued to apply.

Browning's homosexuality was of the exhibitionistic kind, though he did not wish to pay the penalty of his exhibitionism. He enters Eddy's story in what Dr Hornby would have agreed was a typically sinister way. Browning thought that J. K. Stephen had secured the plum appointment as tutor to Eddy only because, as Rupert Croft-Cooke says in his excellent *Feasting with Panthers*,* 'the official arranging the matter had failed to find him in his rooms'. The mixture of ambition and revengeful jealousy is not infrequently found in homosexuals of Browning's type. But that he should have thought that a mere malignant trick of fate had deprived him of a lucrative and influential position and given it to Stephen must have filled him with a consuming desire for revenge. The most obvious way would have been to usurp Stephen's by no means completely established dominance over the Prince by inducting Eddy into that 'Greek'† secret fellowship of which Browning was an acknowledged initiate.

* *Feasting with Panthers: A New Consideration of Some Late Victorian Writers.* London: W. H. Allen, 1967.
† Victorian academic homosexuals' cant word for 'queer'.

In *Feasting with Panthers*, Rupert Croft-Cooke makes Oscar Browning's interest in youth quite unambiguous:

'His friendships were never intense or soulful but cheerful affairs chiefly with young roughs, sailors and the like, to whom he was kind and hospitable. If the age in which he lived was narrow it was also ignorant—at least until Havelock Ellis and Symonds informed it—about sexual phenomena and no one seemed to think it strange that the O.B. should fill his rooms with blue-jackets shouting nautical songs and drinking, or with rescued stable-boys, or "several boys who are protégés of mine, a young blacksmith, a young printer and a young instrument-maker," or that he should always have a well-chosen man-servant to sleep in his rooms at night "in case he were seized by sudden illness," or that he might (as on one recorded occasion) have two youths in his rooms, one drying him after his bath, the other playing the violin, or that he sometimes employed three young secretaries and two young language teachers at the same time. Perhaps his friendships with Simeon Solomon and Oscar Wilde or Robbie Ross may have raised eyebrows when their public scandals came, but his addiction to boys of the working class was put down to his kind heart or to his general oddity of character. Even his mother, a shrewd old lady, explained as enthusiasm in his profession the fact that he never came to stay with her without a young man in tow.'

There is one fact in Browning's life which has not yet been commented on. After being sacked from Eton and coming to Cambridge as a Fellow of King's, his income dropped from £3,000 to £300. It is true that one could live far better on £300 a year at Cambridge than on the same sum in a villa at Beckenham, but it does not seem that Browning had any other source of income, even though he still enjoyed the rare editions of books and wine and expensive foreign tours during Long Vacation (always with a personable lad or two in tow). Where did he get the extra money to enable him to live as well at Cambridge on £300 a year as he had lived at Eton on ten times that annual income? One is forced to the conclusion that he earned money either by pimping or blackmailing.

Evidence for this surmise may be found in Browning's statement that he first met the young Jewish homosexual painter, Simeon Solomon at Fryston Hall, Ferrybridge, Yorkshire, one of the four country seats of the immensely rich and notably perverted Richard Monckton Milnes, 1st Baron Houghton. For Fryston, nicknamed 'Aphrodisiopolis', housed the greatest collection of erotica ever put together by one man, sex-struck to the point of obsessive lunacy. It was a house to which only oddities came, the house of an aesthete who was also a pervert. The fact that Browning was a guest at Fryston shews only too clearly what manner of man he was, even without the evidence of his dismissal from Eton and his open, propagandist friendship with Simeon Solomon.

And this was the person who was to thrust himself into that 'carefully selected' group of men who were to guide Eddy through the pitfalls of adolescence and bring him safely to the firm ground of adult responsibility.

There was another homosexual don at Cambridge when Eddy went up in the autumn of 1883, but of a very different type. Where Browning was noisily extrovert, Edmund Gosse made every effort to conceal his sexual aberration, not least from himself.

But to those who understood the mentality of the homosexual, Gosse's fundamentally homosexual character was as apparent as was that of Browning. In a manner only too frequently encountered in the history of his kind, he played both the attacker and the attacked. In spite of an inferior scholastic background, Gosse had obtained the plum appointment of the Clark Lectureship in English Literature, and wrote *From Shakespeare to Pope*, a book for which his learning, although not at all contemptible, did not qualify him. The work was harshly criticized in *The Quarterly Review* by a friend of Gosse, John Churton Collins. As Croft-Cooke explains: 'It was a reasoned and documented attack which no writer who depended on his scholarship could survive, and as such Gosse did not survive it

. . . he never swam in such deep waters again, and to the end of his life was touchy and opinionated with an over-bearing self-assurance which revealed his inner insecurity.'

In the Cambridge of the 1870s and 1880s there lay behind the façade of an academic order, of a communion of souls in which all met in an atmosphere of High Anglican sexlessness, this tightly meshed fellowship of homosexuality. That this was ever exposed was due to the fact that it had powerful enemies, though generally it was neither suspected nor revealed, and trusting mamas and papas trustingly confided their sons to summer holidays spent abroad in the company of those whose very appearance, in our more sophisticated world, would have put us, as parents, instantly upon our guard.

Nor can it be said that this secret society of 'Greeks' was intellectually, asthenically aesthete. On the contrary, their philosophy, though necessarily to be imparted in secret and only to the chosen few, was an active, aggressive, proselytizing affair.

So we have Pater and Browning, Gosse and William Johnson ('Cory'), Dr Vaughan (another public school casualty—Harrow, this time), Arthur Sidgwick and Henry Dakyns, masters at Clifton and Rugby respectively. All of them, and very many others, entrusted with the care and education of the young.

The Prince of Wales, following the carefully devised plan of his father, had had the unusual experience of attending three universities, Cambridge, Oxford and Edinburgh, though in the common meaning of the word, he was never an undergraduate. Living at Madingley Hall, some three miles from Cambridge, Bertie was rather *near* the University than *of* it. That he resented the arrangement is clear from his decision that Eddy should be as far as possible an ordinary undergraduate, sharing the daily life and studies of his fellow students.

'In those days,' says Vincent, 'there was nothing except the old-fashioned silk gown of the fellow-commoner—the Prince never wore the gold tassel*—and the privilege of escaping University examinations, a privilege properly accorded to his high

* Though others say that he did.

rank, to distinguish Prince Albert Victor from his fellow undergraduates.'

His college tutor was Joseph Prior, a Senior Fellow. J. K. Stephen 'continued to give him general advice as to his course of reading; and besides this private tuition, he attended Professor Seeley's historical classes, and occasionally the excellent "Clark" lectures of Mr Edmund Gosse on English literature, in both of which he is known to have taken real pleasure.'

As Vincent notes, Eddy 'had . . . always shewn a natural predilection for history and for genealogies, which some men find dull'. In other words, Eddy, not being able to hear well, preferred to read.

However, outside the self-congratulation by which all those entrusted with Eddy's education were persuading themselves and others that they were making a good job of it, there was one discordant voice—that of George, Duke of Cambridge, the Queen's bluff old cousin. With no great pretensions to intellectual superiority, the Duke of Cambridge had what Johnson would have approved a 'sound bottom of sense'. He was immensely popular with the masses—perhaps the most popular member of the Royal Family in all its long history.

Despite Stephen's and Vincent's testimony to Eddy's partiality for history, the Duke of Cambridge, who saw much of Eddy and his brother George at Sandringham, was shocked by Eddy's ignorance of what the Duke considered to be things that anyone should have known. He thought Eddy 'charming . . . as nice a youth as could be', but he did not conceal his opinion that Eddy's 'unaffected simplicity . . . and lamentable ignorance' were likely to prove serious drawbacks to his worldly progress. One night at Sandringham, when Eddy sat next to the Duke at table, the talk turned on the Crimean War: '*He knew nothing about it!!!!* Knew *nothing* of the Battle of the Alma*!!! It is past all conceiving! One other sad failing he has from the Prince [*of Wales*], he is an inveterate and incurable dawdler, never ready, never there.' One would have more justly

* At which the Duke of Cambridge commanded the Brigade of Guards.

Prince Eddy dining in Hall as an undergraduate at Trinity College.

attributed this dawdling to Eddy's mother, who was even late for her coronation.

Unlike Alix, and, to a lesser extent, Bertie, both of whom were inclined to put the whole blame for Eddy's faults on to Eddy himself, the Duke espoused the evidently unpopular view that an indifferent pupil usually means an incompetent teacher.

'We talked of how right alas! our judgement of stupid Dalton was, who taught Prince Eddie *absolutely nothing*!! Major Miles the instructor he has been under at Aldershot is quite *astounded* at his utter ignorance . . . It is clearly Dalton's fault, for it is not that he is unteachable, as Major Miles, having found him thus ignorant, is equally astonished how much he has got on with him and thinks, under the cirumstances his papers are infinitely better than he dared to expect. He has his father's dislike for a book and never looks into one, but learns all orally, and retains what he has learnt.'*

This open attack on Dalton is revealing, and one would like to have had the Duke's views on Dalton's protégé, J. K. Stephen. Certainly, had the Duke ever found himself at one of Mr Oscar Browning's 'Sunday evenings', that would have been the end of Cambridge, Browning, Stephen, and all the other more-or-less epicene *literati* who had been 'carefully selected' to effect 'the social preparation of the Prince for the University'.

Eddy's two years at Cambridge were spent in two sets of rooms—what are known at Cambridge as 'attics'—on the top floor of the last staircase as one faces the library of Nevile's Court. The ground-floor set was at first occupied by F. B. Henderson, who had been a sub-lieutenant on *Bacchante*, and later by another ex-*Bacchante* sub, Patrick Bowes Lyon, both of whom had been members of the pre-University party at Sandringham. Halfway up the staircase, Professor Stuart, one of Eddy's special tutors, had his rooms.

* Lady Geraldine Somerset's *Diary* quoted in *The Royal George*. This should be compared with Vincent's remark, quoted earlier, page 90.

Vincent records that 'the Princes's rooms, though comfortably furnished, were not noticeably different from those of the ordinary undergraduate. Indeed, it is said that of the two sets of rooms those of Mr Dalton were the brighter and more interesting, ornamented as they were with many mementoes of the cruise of the *Bacchante*.'

Leaving aside the odd appearance of the average modern undergraduate, little of the outward form has changed at Cambridge since this was written by Harry Wilson nearly a century ago:

'Nevile's Court, in spite of the tasteless reparations of Essex, has a look of old-world dignity about it, with the great façade of Wren's noble library at one end and the College Hall, from which two flights of shallow steps with balustrades descend to the level of the grass ploy, at the other. It is the chosen abode of dons and scholars, and seldom re-echoes the sound of undergraduate revelry, presenting in this respect a strong contrast to the adjacent New Court, where pianofortes are numerous and noisy, and a pleasant stir and bustle prevails both by day and by night.'

Vincent remarks that 'it was undoubtedly agreeable to Prince Albert Victor to be the occupant of rooms in a court in which the spirit of quietness prevailed'. Be that as it may, Eddy, who, according to the panegyrists, 'did his daily work regularly and conscientiously, as he did everything, and shewed a constant desire to make use of the advantages which the University offered to him', took part wholeheartedly in the social life of the University.

It is hard to explain why he did not join the two best-known and most 'select' of Cambridge's many clubs, the Pitt and the Athenaeum. However, he was a member of the Amateur Dramatic Society, to which his by now intimate friend, Jim Stephen, belonged. As Jim had been President of the Union in 1882, the year before Eddy went up to Cambridge, Eddy, as

Vincent rather oddly expresses it, 'was fond of attending as a silent member at the Cambridge Union whenever his friends were speaking'. Vincent's following remark that Eddy 'was a most constant listener at all University concerts, whether of chamber or orchestral music' is far more comprehensible, since a love of music has been a consistent characteristic of the British Royal Family for generations.

Although no musician himself, a Bluethner concert grand pianoforte was installed in his room, and Stephen saw to it that Cambridge's most skilful performers, led by Professor Stanford, gave small concerts of the highest quality in the Nevile's Court 'attic', to which, says Vincent, Eddy 'listened with delight'.

A photograph taken in October 1883, shortly after Eddy had joined his college, shews him in the very elegant uniform of the Cambridge University Rifle Volunteers. Evidently his advisers felt that he could not begin too early to familiarize himself with the military life, and so fit himself for that career of army officer which has traditionally been considered the proper vocation of an heir to the Throne.

There were two reasons why Eddy enjoyed the friendship of a small circle of intimate acquaintances: his natural reserve ('shyness', though a word frequently used in connection with him, is inexact) which meant that friendships were initiated by the approach of others, never by his own act, and, secondly, the jealousy of Jim Stephen, who was not prepared to let his control of the future King be threatened by Eddy's finding friends not of Stephen's selection.

Stephen had been particularly acute in seeing how this domination might be acquired, by keeping at bay the boredom from which Eddy congenitally suffered. Stephen, the ambitious member of an ambitious family, who had written in half-affectionate contempt that Eddy 'is a good-natured, unaffected youth, and disposed to exert himself to learn some history', had soon discovered what interested Eddy.

Eddy shared with his father a liking for, and skill in playing, cards. He was a first-class whist-player—a fact which somewhat contradicts the frequent complaints of both Dalton and Stephen that Eddy couldn't fix his attention on anything for more than a few minutes at a time. A skilful whist-player needs to concentrate on the game all the time.

Stephen's choices of partners for Eddy, for we must assume that it was Stephen who controlled the whist, as he controlled everything else, shews the bent of Stephen's ambitious mind. Generally the fours were made up of Eddy, Dalton, H. H. Turner and Jim Stephen's elder brother, Herbert (afterwards Sir Herbert Stephen, Bart.).

A dinner given by Eddy to his friends on 2nd November, 1883, in his 'attics', reveals the same pattern, with all the guests belonging to the closed circle. Wilson's diary records: '*Nov. 2.*— dine with hrh, jekstudd, hcgoodhart, ronald, etc., to cust's later.' 'Jekstudd' was Kynaston Studd, who married the great Russian prima ballerina, Lydia Kyasht; 'ronald' was the sinister Lord Ronald Sutherland-Gower, son of the 2nd Duke of Sutherland, and uncle of that 4th Duke who was so close a companion of Eddy's father. Lord Ronald, some twenty years older than Eddy, must have seemed to the naïf Dalton to be an admirable companion for Eddy on account of his Trusteeship of the National Portrait Gallery and his faked reputation as painter and sculptor. One wonders whether Stephen suspected his total homosexuality—there is no doubt that Oscar Browning recognized in Lord Ronald a fellow-uranian as esurient and exhibitionistic as himself.

Not all the parties that Eddy attended—'into society, in a quiet way, the Prince went with some freedom'—were of the crypto-queer type which seemed to be the developing pattern of Eddy's more intimate social gatherings. On 11th December, 1883, just as Trinity was about to break up for the Christmas vacation, Dr Munro, 'the great Latinist' who enjoyed a contemporary European reputation for his masterly edition of Lucretius, gave a dinner-party for Eddy. One hopes that Dr Munro did not touch on *De Rerum Naturâ* during dinner. But, seeing that he was the host and that his commentary on that great poem of despair was a life work of which he had cause to be justly proud, perhaps he did. This may explain the entry in Harry Wilson's diary:

'It was delightful to witness the unaffected courtesy and deference which the Prince displayed to older men, and especially to the distinguished scholar who was entertaining him. I can recall many other pleasant evenings of a similar kind, but this particular evening will always hold a definite place in my memory. Alas, that of the merry party no less than three should have passed away!—the host himself, his princely guest, and that kindliest and most genial of men, the Vice-master, Mr Edward Blore.'

'One of the charms of life at Cambridge', says Vincent, 'and an advantage which is less easily to be obtained at Oxford, is to be found in the modest dinner-parties which bring men, whether Princes or commoners, into closer intimacy. It was by means of them, principally, that Prince Albert Victor's circle of acquaintance was enlarged.' The quiet way into which, as Vincent says, the Prince went with some freedom, was not always provident of that raffish enjoyment that 'the occasional "Sunday evenings" at Mr Oscar Browning's' could be counted on to afford. Whether or not he wore the gold tassel, there were tuft-hunters in plenty tracking down Eddy—it is not in every academic year that the undergraduates include a Knight of the Garter. In March, 1884, Professor Newton gave a highly formal party for the Prince in Magdalene College, and on 9th June in that same year Eddy's college tutor, Joseph Prior, 'gave a ball in honour of the Prince, many hundreds of people being present'.

The more strenuous sports did not appeal to Eddy, though like every other freshman he went down to the Cam during the first few weeks of his University career to learn the art of 'tubbing'. Although no expert himself, to the end of his life he always took a keen interest in the performance of the Light Blues on their annual appearance between Putney and Mortlake.

He was a regular attender at Mrs Jebb's lawn-tennis parties, a sport which had achieved a sudden snobbish popularity when the Prince of Wales had added that game to his fencing as a means of reducing weight. Mrs Jebb who had forcibly placed herself in the very van of Cambridge academic smartness, had her lawns levelled, drained and rolled, and to her lawn-tennis parties came the cream of university society, of which the lion was, naturally enough, Prince Eddy. May, of course, is the month of light-hearted pleasure-taking at Cambridge, and it was in May that Mrs Jebb's tea-and-lawn-tennis parties were given. A contemporary diary notes that 'hrh plays better than he did'. A similar garden-party was given at King's College later in the same month, where Eddy played even better.

Eddy did not play cricket and football, but in hockey, a game which, in those days, had not yet been taken over by the heartier of our public-school females, he took great pleasure. He played it often and well, and those who have a tendency to attach importance to coincidences may recall that it was in order to see her husband play ice-hockey on frozen Virginia Water that Alix had herself driven over from Frogmore, on the day on which Eddy was prematurely born.

A year after Eddy came down from Cambridge, Harry Wilson wrote to ask his still close friend if he would accept the Presidency of the newly formed Hockey Association of Great Britain:

> Marlborough House,
> Pall Mall, S.W.,
> Feb. 10th, 1886.

'MY DEAR HARRY,—I must apologize for having kept you waiting for an answer to your letter respecting the Hockey Association but I was unable at the time you wrote to give you a definite answer, which I am now able to do. You must let the Association know that I was extremely flattered by their wishing to make me President of the Association, which I am now able to accept. I always did, as you know, take a great interest in the game of hockey, and think it an excellent idea to start an Association, which is likely to make the game more popular. It seems a long time since I saw you last, and I am glad to hear that you have settled down to your reading at the bar, and before long I have no doubt we shall see you a prominent attorney. But I daresay you must find it a bit dull working in harness. I am going down to Cambridge soon to be present at the opening of the New Union Building, which I have no doubt will be an interesting ceremony. I daresay you regret leaving Cambridge, in some ways, as much as I do, as I think, taking it all round, we had a very delightful time there, and the two years spent there went by like lightning. I hope old Jim Stephen is very flourishing, and I have no doubt he is doing well, as a better man never existed. Well, my dear Harry, I am afraid I must close now, but will write to you again from Aldershot and tell you how I am getting on.

Believe me, ever

Yours sincerely,

EDWARD

Several newspapers of the time published statements that Eddy found life at Cambridge irksome, and wished to leave the University. This letter surely makes it plain that the very opposite was the case, and that he could number his university days amongst the happiest of his life. 'Of a character naturally simple and docile,' says Vincent, 'he had been trained in habits of strict discipline on the *Bacchante*; it was hardly likely that he should find the almost imperceptible discipline of Trinity College troublesome. On the contrary, all the evidence goes to shew that the Prince was, during his Cambridge career, a quiet and moderately industrious young man, who gave to his various teachers, amongst whom in the second year Mr H. C. Good-hart* and Mr J. R. Tanner† of St John's were included, as little trouble as possible.'

A picture which appeared in *The Illustrated London News* of late 1883 shews Eddy dining in Hall with six elderly dons,

---

* Afterwards Professor of Humanity at Edinburgh University.

† Afterwards a barrister, specializing in conveyancing and equity draughtmanship. Editor of *The Historical Register of the University of Cambridge to 1910*.

though it must be confessed that he is not looking at his happiest. He played lacrosse and his favourite hockey; 'for the rest he rode often in a quiet way, and often gave his friends a mount; and like many another man who has grown weary of rowing as a systematic and laborious pursuit, would frequently spend a pleasant summer evening with a friend upon the water among the beautiful surroundings of the "Backs".'

The first great tragedy of Eddy's life occurred on 28th March, 1884, in his second year at Cambridge. This was the sudden death, whilst dancing, of his uncle, the haemophiliac Prince Leopold, Duke of Albany, fellow-rival of his brother, Bertie, in the chase after Lillie Langtry's widely accessible charms. As his Mother's confidential private secretary, Leopold had exerted immense influence over Queen Victoria, who granted him keys to the cabinet despatch boxes which were denied to the Prince of Wales.

Eddy, of course, saw only the charm, and Vincent is probably right when he says that Leopold's death 'produced an abiding feeling of sorrow in that nephew's mind'.

In the 1870s and 1880s, Cambridge was the more fertile source of the smut which emanated from both the universities. It is smut of a specialized kind, full of allusions obviously not intended to be appreciated by the outsider. The following is, of course, Oxonian:

Three Students went slumming out into the High,
  Out into the High, as Big Tom went down,
Determined to slum till their taps ran dry,
  And the bull-dogs stood watching 'em
Right through the town.
For men must slum, and women will try
To gain a small pittance by walking the High,
  While Peter stiff is standing.

What is common to both Oxford and Cambridge smut is, first, a distinctly anti-clerical (rather than anti-religious)

99

bias—*The Reverend Pimlico Poole* is a typical example of the clergyman-lampooning 'poem'—and, second, a preoccupation with two subjects that are now seen as neither amusing nor sexually exciting, menstruation and venereal disease. The mildly anti-religious tendency gave rise to the parodies, all pornographic, of many of the favourites from *Hymns A. & M.*

Beside that of Oxford, Cambridge pornography is—if the word doesn't sound too fatuous in this context—a little less irreverent, less self-conscious and a great deal more vulgar. Dim little rugger clubs in unfashionable south-east London suburbs have paid Cambridge's manliness and vulgarity the tribute of honouring it to this day.

Of particular significance for what follows is the long narrative poem, *Kaphoozelum*. Later this bawdy ballad must be examined in detail, but here it is necessary only to point out, not merely that it was familiar to Jim Stephen (and so, presumably to his royal pupil and the other members of the Stephen clique), but that Stephen assumed that it was equally familiar to anyone likely to read his volume of verses, *Lapsus Calami*, in which it is quoted. Stephen's publishers, Bowes and Macmillan of Cambridge, obviously did not object to the inclusion of the reference to *Kaphoozelum*. The reader should bear this in mind, for it brings us to another most important aspect of upper-class Victorian behaviour: the addiction to lower-class slang.

What with 'sports' like ratting and making a book on the first type of hat to be on the head of the first man entering some frowsty East End pub, it is no wonder that men added to their Latin (rarely Greek) and French, the waywardness of small-trading and smaller criminal secret talk. A familiarity with Cockney rhyming slang was a fashion amongst the products of Oxford and Cambridge, and this skill was by no means confined to those circles whose common centre was Romano's and the dipsomaniac, classically educated staff of the Pink 'Un. In this language a dollar is an 'oxford', a pocket is a 'sky', a woman is a 'bramah', and so on. They were also habitual users of the slang of the Turf and the (especially illegal) card-room. They called ten shillings A 'half a bar', a pound a 'thick 'un', a 'jimmy o' goblin', five pounds a 'flimsy',* twenty-five pounds a 'pony,' five hundred pounds a 'monkey', and so forth.

To explain this addiction we must accept what is rarely considered in discussing and analysing the Victorian social scene, the fact that 'poverty did not make a member of the upper-class *déclassé*. The law of primogeniture, whereby the heir inherited everything, and the younger sons, nothing, created a class of well-bred parasites whose morals had been so corrupted by their completely accepted poverty that there was *literally* no shabby expedient for 'raising the wind', as it was then called, to which these well-bred paupers would not resort. If they succeeded—and generations of dealing with their 'inferiors' had given them a moral dominance which generally enabled them to get their own way—their success was the talk and the toast of the town. If they failed—and even if a hasty trip to Paris or a term of imprisonment were the penalty for failure— no-one *in their class* thought any the worse of them. In Paris, where the expatriates no longer welcome in the Home Country gathered, the Prince of Wales was always glad to see the cheque-bouncers, the race-riggers, the con-men. The true difficulty in understanding the Victorians is that we have based our opinion of them on the pictures of Victorian life painted by such people as E. P. Roe, Mrs Southworth and on the more mawkish parts of Dickens, Thackeray and Albert Smith. Many of the stories that Osgood Field recounts in his *Uncensored Recollections* are far nearer the reality.

A representative member of this world was Alfred, Duke of Edinburgh, Eddy's uncle, reputed to be the meanest, as well as the most foul-mouthed, member of contemporary royalty. He cadged from relatives and friends alike, and acquired wealth by many devious means. Born in 1844, he entered the Royal Navy in 1858 to pursue a successful career, in the course of which he held the command of the Channel Squadron (1883-4) and of the Mediterranean Fleet (1886-9). Created Duke of Edinburgh, Earl of Ulster and Earl of Kent, in the peerage of

* Hence the modern Cockney 'flim.'

the United Kingdom, in 1866, Parliament granted him, in that same year, an annuity of £15,000, to which an additional £10,000 was granted, in 1874, on his marrying the Grand Duchess Marie Alexandrovna of Russia. He supplemented this income and his naval pay by the fees he earned as professional introducer of snobbish parvenus to members of European royalty. Thus while beating up the town with brother Bertie, he cannot have enjoyed less than about £30,000 a year.

The presence of such exemplars as the Duke of Edinburgh and 'The Yellow Earl', Hugh Lowther, 5th Earl of Lonsdale, made it possible for Eddy's inherited pleasure-seeking to become established in the least desirable of patterns. Of the 'respectable' element in Eddy's education, the Dalton–Stephen–Prior committee, far too much has been written and made. The Duke of Cambridge had been brusquely correct when he called the royal tutor 'that *stupid* Dalton', and right when he claimed that Dalton had 'taught Prince Eddy *absolutely nothing!!*'

Stephen, before the great change which will provide the most dramatic chapters of this book, was a worthy enough young man, though, as his reference to *Kaphoozelum* indicated, he was probably no more cleanly spoken than Eddy's uncle, the Duke of Edinburgh—'But the Duke of Edinburgh (most charming when he liked) could be, and I grieve to narrate, not unfrequently was, as rude and rough as an angry navvy.'*

But Stephen belonged to a family in which ambition had become traditional, and he could not have resisted the temptation to profit, not only for himself but for his clan, by his fortunate propinquity to a future king. Of all those 'good fellows' who linked arms to keep out the interlopers from the charmed circle about Eddy, only Harry Wilson, the future colonial administrator, seems to have escaped that appeal to ambition that daily intimacy makes inevitable with so many royal companions.

No-one will ever understand the actions of the Victorians until they take the trouble to study their prejudices; and they

* *Uncensored Recollections.* Anon (i.e. Julian Osgood Field) London: Eveleigh Nash and Grayson Ltd, 1924.

will never understand those prejudices until they understand that the least trustworthy guides to Victorian thinking amongst the people who 'mattered' are the novelists, with one or two notable exceptions, of whom Miss Braddon, daughter and wife of a solicitor, is perhaps the most outstanding.

The novelists of yesterday and the historians of today talk of the 'complicated stratification' of Victorian Society, and of 'the endless ramifications of its caste-system'. That these stratifications existed, and that millions of people were concerned with them is true enough. But those who were concerned with them were the Middle Classes. And with them, and their preoccupations with 'etiquette' and 'precedence', the Nobs were not concerned at all. It would not be untrue to say that the Britain of Victorian times had only three social classes: the Aristocracy, the Middle Class and what perhaps might be called the Classless. What irritated the Middle Classes most was the obvious fact that when the Aristocracy went outside its own class for pleasure, profit or the enjoyment of common interests, they usually went, not to the Middle Class, but to the Classless.

'Strahan was a mystery . . . Everyone knew and liked him; he was a member of the Jockey Club and a great personal friend of the late Duke of Beaufort (the very beau ideal of a grand seigneur) and of the Prince of Wales and went everywhere (among men) smoking his big meerschaum . . . The Prince of Wales was particularly fond of him, and so also was the Duke of Edinburgh . . . Strahan was always full of amusing gossip that the Prince liked, and sometimes Strahan would be the whole day long in Paris with him.'*

There is no mystery about Strahan's origins. He was the son of one of the three partners of a London bank, which had defaulted for over £1,000,000. The three partners were sentenced alike to fourteen years transportation.

The Middle Class would have 'cut' Strahan.

The pages of *A Pink 'Un and a Pelican* or *Pitcher in Paradise*, besides being crammed with references to money-lenders, dud

* *Uncensored Recollections*, op. cit.

cheques, unmet promissory notes, turf swindles, and unpaid 'debts of honour,' are also full of the sort of anecdote which in illustrating the close friendship between the Nobs and the hangers-on, gives the true explanation of Victorian Britain's caste-system. Here is a typical anecdote. It concerns the Duke of Teck and a wealthy biscuit-manufacturer, who, on being presented to the Duke, found that he had no visiting-card on him. He asked the barmaid for a penny Abernethy biscuit.

' "There, that's my name, yer royal highness—the second one. If yer mind accepting this in lieu of a card—"

'And determined that it should be so, he grabbed the left front of the Duke's frock coat, and pulling it open, stuffed the biscuit forcibly into the Duke's breast-pocket!

'Ducal is as ducal does, and Teck accepted the stodge with princely obsequiousness; but supposing he had been run down by a fly as he strolled down Richmond Hill, what a story the society gossips might have spun round a Royal Duke found dead with a penny abernethy in his pocket.'

They all frequented the same raffish clubs and bars: the Argyll Rooms, the Pelican Club in Gerrard-street, Evans's, the Empire, the Holborn Music-hall, and the buffets of the big railway-stations, for they were always travelling to and from race meetings.

Eddy's first long vacation was mostly spent at Heidelberg, where Professor Ihre, only too Teutonically conscious of the exalted rank of his pupil and the heavy responsibility laid upon him by the Prince's parents, joined the large body of those who had set out to teach Eddy something, in this case German. Heidelberg has always had a reputation as a place where students have always demanded their own way, and, though it was vacation time in Germany as well as in England, Eddy soon made friends with some of the more adventurous and aristocratic members of that famous university. He did not, of course, learn to speak German, but he did manage to enjoy himself. That 'innocence' which must have begun to lose its primal bloom in the coarse initiation ceremonies in *Britannia* and

Bacchante, and had become distinctly corroded at Cambridge, can have barely survived when he returned from Heidelberg.

It was a pity that Professor Ihre failed to teach Eddy the tongue of Schiller and Goethe, for in the following year, when Eddy accompanied his father to Berlin to attend the 88th birthday celebrations of William I, the German Emperor, a knowledge of German on his son's part would have helped the Prince of Wales in his efforts to woo German opinion.

Distance made no difference to those friendships that J. K. Stephen carefully cultivated both before and after Eddy had gone up to Cambridge. But of the letters written to Eddy at Heidelberg, only those of Harry Wilson have survived the general destruction of the Prince's papers. His friends were all versifiers, at a time when verse-writing was a fashionable occupation for the educated young of both sexes. In a letter to Eddy, Harry Wilson, the Chancellor's Medallist for English Verse, displayed his expertise in rhyming:

> Upon my soul there lies a load
> Of song, not sin—the promised ode.
> By day these unproductive brains
> Are cudgelled for befitting strains;
> And when at eve I seek my bed,
> Slumber deserts my weary head,
> What time I turn and toss about,
> And try to 'beat' my 'music out'.
> So now, Prince Edward, deign to take
> These verses, fashioned for your sake.
> To wish you health and happiness,
> A shadow never growing less,
> Fine larks by day, sweet sleep at night,
> And undiminished appetite.
> I often wonder what you do
> Beneath those skies of 'Prussian blue';
> What joys and sorrows serve to chequer
> Your life beside the silvery Neckar.
> I seem to hear you reading Heine

(No poet sure can be diviner),
And catch the approving *'Das ist besser'*
Of the benignant Herr Professor.
I see you at the students' duel,
Thinking the business tame and cruel;
Now bathing there, now riding here,
And now imbibing *lager-bier*.
Whate'er your occupation be
In sunny lands beyond the sea,
We trust there reaches you at times
The echo of St Mary's chimes,
That through the dark Teutonic trees
You spy the roofs of 'King's' and 'Caius',
That western breezes oft recall
The fragrant subtleties of Hall,
While a thought-pilgrimage is made
To Nevilles cool and cloistered shade.

Now that I'm master of my Muse,
You'd like, perhaps, to hear the news:
It's dull enough, but then the 'long'
Is not provocative of song.
We rise—a few of us—at six
(A different hour *I'm* wont to fix);
Breakfast at seven, or sometimes eight,
Though that's considered rather late.
A pipe discussed, the books come down,
We fall into a study brown,
And doze and wake and yawn, then munch
(At one p.m.) a frugal lunch,
Until the lengthening shadows grow
Beneath the trees, when out we go
To take or lose a shaky wicket
At very unpretentious cricket;
Or scull a boat along the 'Backs';
Or slowly jog on hireling hacks
(Of action anything but free)

To Trumpington and Madingley;
Or bathe in Byron's storied pool
Like little boys let loose from school;
Or stretched beneath the evening star,
Inhale the fleeting, fair cigar.
Our company is most select,
But that, of course, you would expect;
Goodhart was here for half a day,
Then found it slow and rushed away;
Inches of unregarded dust
Lie on the chairs of Harry Cust.
We don't know what's become of Clough;
Benson's at Lambeth; only Duff,
And I, and half a dozen more,
Remain to vote our life a bore.

Excuse a postscript, to confess
A crime that I've committed—yes,
To-day pray grant your pardon for
This raid upon your royal door—
I made burglarious entry vile and
Took from the shelves the "Treasure Island".
My brother wanted it to read,
So please forgive the desperate deed.

Your kitten broadens to a cat,
And wonders what her master's at;
Is she to wait your Highness' will,
And stay with Mrs Jiggins still?
Or shall we pack her in a box,
And send her off from London Docks?
Meanwhile she slays the casual mouse,
And dreams at night of Marlborough House.

And finally a word we send
To our Philosopher and Friend;
They say he's coming in July—

We hope 'tis true, for, verily,
We miss our mine of curious knowledge,
And when we get him back in College,
We mean to drop a pinch of salt on
The tail of Mr J. N. Dalton.

But '*Halt! Genug!*' I hear you say,
I've done, and wish my Prince good-day.

The poem tells us two things which make Eddy seem very 'human' indeed, that he liked cats and Robert Louis Stevenson's *Treasure Island*, a novel to which even novel-disapproving Motherdear could hardly have taken exception. But the poem cannot be quite as domestically innocent as it seems to be. It is obviously a communication intended to convey a certain impression to the outside reader, and quite a different meaning to its recipient. Is 'our Philosopher and Friend', who is returning (from Heidelberg?) to Cambridge in July, really J. K. Stephen, and whether he is or not, what is that 'curious knowledge' of which he is 'a mine'? The allusion to J. N. Dalton, too, is puzzling. The meaning of the old phrase 'put a bit of salt on his tail' is to catch an elusive animal. Where had Dalton been secreting himself for so long that his tail needed salting? Had he at last decided to neglect duties that all his diligence had proved would never achieve their end? That Eddy could read and enjoy *Treasure Island* must have seemed to Dalton no mean achievement on the tutor's part.

The 1880s saw the apogee of travel, in luxury, in punctuality and in the ability to go literally anywhere in the civilized world. What made travel the luxury that it was until 1914 was the co-ordination of the means of travel, the railway and the steamboat, with an international hotel system the like of which the world will never see again. Money was international—and exchange-rates stable. The telegraph system was, in most cases, superior to that of today, and already the telephone had begun to link up the main centres of Europe and the Near East. There was, indeed, nothing to prevent Bertie's less reputable friends from 'dropping in' on his young son to 'cheer him up', and to teach him those facts of life not included in the curriculum of even so broad-minded a university as Heidelberg, of which so many of the Prince of Wales's friends were former students.

A more respectable member of the Prince of Wales's entourage who visited Eddy was Lord Suffield, who had been a Lord of the Bedchamber to the Prince since 1872. But there also appeared the shifty race-rigger, 'Duppy', Lord Dupplin, and some others even less desirable.

'Heidelberg', reports Vincent, 'had made no alteration in his warm affection for the friends whom he had made during the first year. We find him playing whist as before, playing hockey, going to see "Princess Ida" at the Theatre Royal, inviting Prince George to meet his special friends at dinner at Trinity, and one of these friends writing "Prince George is all that fancy painted him, a good-hearted lively sailor".'

On 8th January, 1885, Eddy came of age, an event which was celebrated by the usual Victorian large-scale feasting, to which came all available members of the Royal Family, though not the Queen, and to which some of Eddy's 'special' Trinity friends were invited. These select guests, who included the Stephen brothers, were 'delighted', says Vincent, 'to find him as quiet, as kindly, and as simple as if he had been in their rooms at Trinity'.

However, history was to repeat itself very soon after. Just as the Prince Consort had visited Cambridge to enquire into a scandalous rumour concerning Bertie's sexual activities, so now Bertie himself, disturbed by rumours that Eddy had become what Sir Philip Magnus calls 'dissipated and unstable', decided to go to Cambridge and remonstrate with Eddy.

Vincent, in his usual commissioned public-relations style, writes that 'the notable event of the term was a visit of his Royal Highness the Prince of Wales to Cambridge and to his son's rooms. There the Prince of Wales met some of his son's friends, one of whom* records in his private diary the pleasure and the honour which he had of a short conversation with the Heir to

* Harry Wilson, almost certainly.

the Throne, who, on that occasion, had brought in his dog "by special permission".'

But though it is true to say that the reason for this 'notable event' was Bertie's desire to see some of his son's friends as it were 'on their home ground', it was in no very amiable mood that the heir to the Throne visited the 'attic' in Nevile's Court, and caused Eddy to summon his friends to meet Papa. Bertie, with his insatiable sexual urge, still had his mother's middle-class morality to make him worry continuously about his boy's 'threatened innocence'.

The destruction of Eddy's correspondence, and the discreet silence maintained about his private activities, have made the task of assessing his character no easy one for this historian. However, there can be no doubt that he was a panerotic.

Eddy liked sex in most of its available forms simply because he remained, psychically, at that immature stage of human development in which the sexual urge manifests itself rather as curiosity than as what we usually call 'sexuality'.

Had he developed into a complete homosexual, with the possibility of coming to terms with his 'difference' and a world which demanded from the homosexual concealment in return for acceptance, most, if not all, of the tragedy of Eddy's life might well have been avoided. There have been homosexual kings of England who have caused great scandal, but neither Edward II nor James I was a bad *king*; and as for that other homosexual, William III, though he started the world off on a chain-reaction of fighting which hasn't stopped yet, he caused no open scandal by his preference for men over women.

Two women at least loved Eddy, and one of them at least he loved to distraction, as they say. And one at least of these two claimed that her beautiful, but otherwise worthless, son had Eddy for a father—it was not Prince Henry de Ligne, said Sarah Bernhardt, who was the father of her handsome, illegitimate Maurice, but Prince Albert Victor of Wales. One needn't believe her, of course, but if Eddy had been the 'obvious' into which ill-informed history has typed him he would hardly have been a suitable candidate for this rôle. Granted his rather effeminate beauty, it clearly did not condemn him in the eyes of his contemporaries—especially the females—to the ranks of the queer.

Whatever had come to trouble Bertie's peace of mind in regard to his son, it must be accepted that the two Stephens, Harry Wilson, Cust, Tanner, Clark and Bowes Lyon had managed to persuade him that *their* influence was no bad thing. In the previous year J. K. Stephen had been called to the Bar, Cust had taken his B.A., and joined the *Pall Mall Gazette* of which he was soon to be editor; Patrick Bowes Lyon had also graduated and was now reading for the Bar, as was Harry Wilson. Bertie must have been half-reassured that rumour was taking too many liberties with his elder son's good name, since he let Eddy enter—in a highly formal way, of course—the profession that his friends were preparing to enter. On 21st January, 1885, less than a fortnight after his twenty-first birthday and only a day or two after Bertie's investigatory visit to Nevile's Court, Eddy became a Bencher of the Middle Temple, and thus Stephen's nominal superior.

This was to be Eddy's last year at Cambridge, and already preparations were being made to equip him for entry into that larger world in which his position as his father's son would make him outstandingly conspicuous.

Already he had had some experience of military duties as a member of the Cambridge University Rifle Volunteers, even if he turned up later at Aldershot without any idea of the most elementary drill. On his twenty-first birthday, in preparation for a career as a regular army officer, Eddy was gazetted lieutenant in the 2nd Brigade, Eastern Division, Royal Artillery. It was a curious choice on his parents', or on their advisers', part, since though Eddy could both shoot and ride, he knew little mathematics. But this was purely a formal appointment and entry into a regiment far better suited to Eddy's limited military capacity was awaiting him at the close of his Cambridge days.

However, 1885 was to be a far more memorable year for the

young Prince on account of a terrifying experience that he was to undergo.

He was coming out into the world. The old King and Emperor, William I, was celebrating his eighty-eighth birthday, and Bertie took Eddy to Berlin to join in the celebrations. Once there, Bertie made a lifelong enemy of his twenty-six-year-old nephew, Prince William of Prussia (afterwards the Kaiser Wilhelm II), by encouraging a romance between the nineteen-year-old Princess Victoria of Prussia, Bertie's niece, and the thirty-year-old 'Sandro', Crown Prince of Bulgaria. The marriage was against German policy, and although in the end it did not take place, Prince William never forgave his uncle—'that old peacock!'—for having interfered in German affairs.

But worse was to come. On 8th April, 1885, exactly one month after the Emperor's birthday, the Prince and Princess of Wales, accompanied by Eddy, crossed over to Ireland, on one of the regular state visits that political ineptitude considered would compensate the Irish for Britain's refusal to let them manage their own affairs.

The Dubliners let the Royal party carry out its elaborate formal programme, the highlight of which was the Princess of Wales's visit to Trinity College to receive her honorary degree of Doctor of Music. Writing to Prince George of the ceremony, she remarked, 'I don't think any Irishman here would do us any harm; they are all very nice and friendly.' But at Mallow, half-an-hour before the Royal train was due, the military had to be called out to quell what Mrs Battiscombe calls a 'near riot'.

From Dublin, on 13th April, the Royal visitors had gone south to stay with Lord and Lady Listowel at Convamore, near Cork, and on the following day, the Marquess of Waterford (brother of Bertie's present great friend, and future great enemy, Lord Charles Beresford) invited sixty of the county's most presentable guests to meet the Prince and Princess of Wales and their elder son at Curraghmore, a splendid house set in 7,000 acres of park and 100,000 acres of property. But on

14th April, 1885, nothing within the noble mansion suggested the horror that was to erupt on the following day, from whose deep emotional impact it would take all years to recover.

The Lord Lieutenant of Ireland, Lord Spencer, had written reassuringly to his Sovereign that all would go well on the visit, but those with a sharper eye for realities were full of apprehension, especially with regard to that ancient centre of disaffection, Cork.

As Bertie wrote to his son, George, 'the loyalists received us with the greatest enthusiasm, but the nationalists, who are virtually separatists, as badly as possible.'

Such a comment hides the truth of an experience as ugly as the Prince of Wales was ever to endure. Much clearer was Arthur Ellis when he told Queen Victoria that 'the truth (and Your Majesty will wish to know the truth beyond every other thing) is that the lower class, the *lazzaroni* of Cork, which exists in overpowering numbers, were rabid rebels. No other word can convey their hostility and behaviour ... and no one who went through this day will ever forget it ... It was like a bad dream. The Prince of Wales shewed the greatest calmness and courage.'

But so, too, did Alix and Eddy. As the few loyalists nervously raised their hats, clapped and shouted the traditional loyal slogans, the quay across Cork's narrow harbour was a dense crowd of screaming enemies, waving black flags and black handkerchiefs, and shouting every imaginable obscenity. 'Never', wrote Arthur Ellis, 'were there so many dirty, ill-looking countenances gathered together ... streets filled with sullen faces, hideous, dirty, cruel countenances, hissing and grimacing into one's very face, waving *black* flags and *black* kerchiefs—a nightmare!' Despite this, and the rotten vegetables pelted at the Royal carriage, the Prince of Wales determined that his visit to Cork would go as planned.

That night, at Lord Waterford's table, sparkling with the glass and silver of fruit-and-flower laden epergnes, and waited on by liveried servants, it was possible to face the still remaining twelve days of the Irish visit with a little more equanimity. The

Prince of Wales refused ever after to discuss the terrifying reception of the Cork *lazzaroni*, and from that time forward the pleasant little city became 'out of bounds' to the Royal Family. It says much for Eddy's courage that, two years later, he should have agreed to return to Dublin to receive his honorary degree of LL.D. from Trinity College and to be installed as a Bencher of the King's Inns, Dublin.

On the day following the disastrous Cork visit, all applied themselves to the fashionable Victorian exercise of letter-writing. The Prince of Wales wrote to Georgie, as did his wife; Arthur Ellis wrote to the Queen; and the newspaper correspondents got their wires off to their respective editors. 'It says volumes', comments Mrs Battiscombe, 'for the determinedly ostrich-like attitude adopted by the loyalist element, both English and Irish, that next day the headline in the *Daily Telegraph* ran "Royal Visit to Cork, Enthusiastic Reception in the City".'

And Eddy wrote to Harry Wilson and, particularly, Jim Stephen, on whom Eddy's rather simple description of the vilely insulting crowd, especially of the women amongst them, made a far deeper impression than at the time Stephen realized.

At this point reference must be made to an unresolved problem of dating: when did J. K. Stephen become involved in some sexual difficulties which, known or not to the highly tolerant authorities of those happy times, although apparently not harming his position as Fellow and barrister, made him the subject of one of the most cryptic of 'rugger songs' ever to have come from Cambridge. In the collection, *Why Was He Born So Beautiful and Other Rugby Songs,** the song about Stephen, like so many other songs in the book, has been modernized, and the last two stanzas are inaccurate additions. This is the actual song:

> There was a maid of the mountain glen,
> Seduced herself with a fountain pen;
> The pen it broke and the ink ran wild,
> And she gave birth to a blue-black child.

---

* Selected by Harry Morgan, Preface by Michael Green: Sphere Books (paperback), London, 1967.

Chorus: They called the bastard Stephen,
They called the bastard Stephen,
They called the bastard Stephen,
For that was the name of the ink.

Stephen was a bonny child,
Pride and joy of his mother mild,
And all that worried her was this:
His steady stream of blue-black piss.

Chorus: They called the bastard Stephen,
They called the bastard Stephen,
They called the bastard Stephen,
For that was the name of the ink.

At first glance, this is too cryptic for any possible attempt at explanation. The well-known manufacturers of their patent 'blue-black' ink, Messrs Stephen, were amongst the dozen really big advertisers of the latter part of the last century, and their advertisement is a masterpiece of expertise, even judged by modern standards: just a vast, careless 'splodge' of blue-black ink on a white ground, with simply the one word 'Stephens' on the 'splodge' of ink. Of course, any boy with Stephen or Stephens as his name might be liable to pick up a nickname with 'ink' in it—there was a master at Harrow, Kesteven, who was always called 'Inky Stephen'. But there are reasons for thinking that the 'Stephen' of the dismal doggerel above quoted was one of the famous Stephen family, and, in all probability, Jim Stephen himself.

Leaving aside, for the moment, the question of the 'maid's' identity, 'the mountain glen' could be Avondale, a little-known royal property in Scotland, which attracted attention because Eddy, in being created Duke of Clarence and Avondale, 'shocked' many by the 'unlucky' associations of the first place name, and puzzled them by the obscurity of the second. Now, to any schoolboy the name 'Avon' inevitably recalls that phrase in the histories of English Literature, 'The Swan of Avon'. And if 'Avon' inevitably would suggest to the least educated mind 'The Swan of Avon', then 'Swan' would inevitably recall the trade-name of the then most popular (because most widely advertised) fountain-pen, 'The Swan'.

Thus it may be suggested that the verses contain some obscure reference to a scandal, or a *supposed* scandal, in which Eddy and J. K. Stephen were linked. The 'poem' cannot be earlier than May, 1890, in which month Eddy was created Duke of Clarence and Avondale; but by that time his ill-omened friendship with Jim Stephen had involved him in both scandal and tragedy.

It must have been a sadly subdued Eddy who returned from Ireland to Cambridge, to finish the last few weeks of his final year at the University. May Week, in the Cambridge of those days, was a brilliant social occasion not at all confined to University circles, and an anonymous fellow student, probably H. L. Stephen, has recalled a moment at which his life must have been at its most perfect.

'Another occasion of which I have a very distinct remembrance was in June, 1885, just at the end of the Prince's second and last year at Cambridge. There had been a ball in St John's Lodge —one of the most successful functions of a brilliant May Week— and we had all danced until the sun was high in the sky and we could dance no more. Prince Albert Victor walked back to Trinity with my brother and myself and two or three other men, and when we reached the Great Court, the charm of the fresh summer morning made the thought of bed impossible. It struck some one that it would be a good idea to turn into the Bowling Green (there were Fellows of the party) and have a final cigar before we separated. In a day or two we should all be going down, some of us for the last time, and it seemed a pity not to see the thing out to the end. How clearly I recall the very sounds and scents of that delicious June day—the gay squealing of the swifts as they circled round the old towers, and the moist odours of the shaven turf at our feet. It was as though the quintessence of our happy life at Cambridge had been distilled into a golden cup and offered as a final draught to our regretful lips.'

Eddy's days of 'learning' were ended, and, on 17th June, 1885, *The London Gazette* carried the news that Lieutenant H.R.H. Prince Albert Victor of Wales, K.G., had been commissioned a lieutenant in the 10th Hussars, the cavalry regiment of which his father was Colonel.

It is the custom that every subaltern joining his regiment has a month's leave, but for Eddy, now beginning to learn the full tedium of royal life, his month's leave could hardly have been called a holiday.

On 24th June, Midsummer's Day of a particularly hot summer, he performed his first public function when he accepted, from the Prime Warden and Livery of the Fishmongers' Company, the honorary freedom of their ancient guild. Two days later he attended a similar, but even grander ceremony, when he was made a Freeman of the City of London by the Lord Mayor, the parchment enrolling Eddy being presented in the usual elaborate silver casket so beloved of Victorian functions of this type.

The Illustrated London News, *The Graphic* and other picture-journals carry drawings of the occasions. To the journalists, especially the one who attended the ceremony at the Mansion House, Eddy shewed a marked elegance of phrase in thanking 'My Lord Mayor' and the City Corporation for the proposal— 'carried unanimously, with great enthusiasm', says the reporter —that a medal be struck to commemorate the Prince's first visit to the seat of the City's government.

On the following day, 25th June, accompanied by Lord Suffield, an intimate of the Prince of Wales, and by Eddy's equerry, Captain the Honourable Alwyn Greville, brother in law of Lady Brooke, Papa's 'darling Daisy', the Prince went down to Sheffield to open the Cutlers' Exhibition. The three men must have been glad to get out of smoky Sheffield for the lush Victorian comfort of Brocklesby Park, Lincolnshire, the country seat of Lord Yarborough, who had come down from

Trinity only the year before. The official reason for the visit to Yarborough was that Eddy should inspect the new sea defence works and public gardens at Grimsby. In reality, the few days' visit, beginning 1st July, 1885, was an opportunity for three young men to have a little quiet fun before Eddy joined his regiment five days later.

In the whole history of the British Army, there has never been a regiment which has acquired for itself quite the distinction attaching to the 10th Hussars, even if other regiments have gained more, and more glorious, battle honours.

Raised in 1715, by authority of a warrant from George I, the 10th Dragoons, as they were then called, had a most distinguished service throughout the century, fighting Jacobites and French with equal vigour and success. In 1783, the title of the regiment was changed to 'The 10th or Prince of Wales's Own Regiment of Light Dragoons'; ten years later, at his own request, the Prince of Wales was appointed Colonel-Commandant, in time to welcome in his old friend and favourite, Beau Brummell. In 1806, the regiment was equipped with Prinny-and-Brummell designed uniforms, and changed its name to the 10th Hussars. The regiment fought throughout the Peninsular War, at Waterloo, in India, in the Crimean War, in the Afghan and Egyptian campaigns. There is no doubt that the memory of Eddy inherited by the present officers of his old regiment is one of a man in whom they find no more than the most venial of human faults. Indeed, according to Major Robert Archer-Shee, 'There's no doubt that the members of the mess tended to grow noticeably more aristocratic after Prince Albert Victor arrived'—a fact that the noble names signing the mess-register makes unquestionably apparent. The 'scrap book' of the Tenth, in which drawings and photographs cut from magazines have been pasted with care, exhibit, over the latter half of the 1880s and the first two years of the 1890s, what seems to be an undue proportion of illustrations having Prince Eddy as subject. This must denote the Prince's popularity.

Yet what sort of a soldier did Eddy really make of himself during those seven years in which he rose from lieutenant to major? From the point of view of his day, with the then small emphasis placed on mechanized warfare, Eddy did not do at all badly. He was taken in hand by Captain Peary, the Riding-master, who kept him hard at it for six months. Every morning, the new subaltern was on parade at the riding-school at 6.30. Only after a month did Peary even permit his pupil to attend the regiment's normal turn-out. Eddy notes in his diary for 14th August, 'Attended drill under C.O. in the Long Valley— first time on parade.'

Evidently he had to fight hard, to keep his mind on things, even under the soldierly tyranny of Peary, for there is a note that Prince Albert Victor was fined a half-dozen of champagne for appearing on duty without a belt. The six months in the riding-school, however, may be partly explained by the fact that Eddy had to neglect his strict regimental duties for activi-ties which varied between the 'official' and the domestic.

For instance, only a few days after he joined his regiment, he was taken from his duties to listen to a deputation of City notables informing him that the Lord Mayor and Corporation had ordered a medal to be struck to commemorate his having received the freedom of the City on 29th June; and, on 22nd July, he went down to Cowes to attend the wedding of Princess Beatrice, his aunt, to H.R.H. Prince Maurice of Battenberg, P.C., K.G., which took place on the following day.

Four days after his first parade, Eddy returned to Aldershot, with his father, the Regiment's Colonel, his brother George, and Colonel Wehrner, who came to inspect the Wellington Monument, which had recently been transferred from Hyde Park Corner to Aldershot. That evening the Prince of Wales dined with the regiment. On the following day the Prince of Wales inspected the regiment in the Long Valley—in the absence of his son who, with his commanding officer, was paying 'a flying visit to the Queen at Osborne'. One gathers that the Queen, having heard from the Duke of Cambridge what Colonel Wood thought of his Royal subaltern's progress, decided to interview them together, and to stiffen both Colonel and subaltern.

At any rate, after this Eddy stayed at Aldershot, whilst others visited him. Not until the end of November did Eddy request four days leave of absence, during which he visited the Empress Eugénie at Farnborough, dined with his uncle, the Duke of Connaught, at Bagshot, spent two nights (but not two days!) at Marlborough House, and passed his last day at Cambridge, mostly with Stephen, who had written to say how worried he had been by his father's illness. It was the hereditary 'breakdown' of the Stephens, so little a secret that even Sir Leslie Stephen, himself a victim, was to have to discuss it in the case of no fewer than four members of his family when he came to write their entries in the *Dictionary of National Biography*.

What the two friends could not know was that in the following year the 'Stephen disease' would hit a great deal nearer home and with results far more terrible.

At Cambridge, J. K. Stephen had proved himself a brilliant scholar, winning his Fellowship with a masterly dissertation on 'International Law'. But with the breaking up of his Cambridge court, much of J.K.'s influence, which obviously depended on his personal presence, waned, and when he was called to the Bar in 1884, he had found himself faced with competition against which all his oratory, beauty, authority and charm counted for little indeed. His future developed in a very different way from what had been foreseen: 'his high reputation as a speaker led his friends to anticipate for him a career of particular success, and his singular sweetness and frankness gained him innumerable friends.'

Not that his old friends neglected him. In the club-like atmosphere of the various Inns of Court, he still met Patrick Bowes Lyon, Harry Wilson and the rest, and he met them again at Marlborough House and in those many fox- or stag-hunting activities to which both Eddy and his father were devoted, and to which they invited all their 'special' friends. But the members of the Stephen court at Cambridge were growing up, and though they retained, it is clear, their liking for J.K. as an old companion, they had renounced their allegiance to him as a former leader. Besides, it began to look to these young men that far from being the outstanding success that had seemed inevitable when they were all under his command, he was being left behind in the race for distinction.

For all his supposed laziness, Eddy exchanged letters regularly with his friends, and though the majority of these letters of Eddy's no longer exist, sufficient have survived to let us see how Eddy shaped as a correspondent. His letters to Harry Wilson give the impression of a simple, frank and, above all, normal personality.

At the beginning of 1886, Harry Wilson had written to Eddy to suggest that he might care to see a performance of *Twelfth Night*, given by the Oxford University Dramatic Club. Eddy replied:

> South Cavalry Barracks
> (Aldershot)
> *February 18th, 1886*

MY DEAR HARRY,—Many thanks for your letter, which I was very glad to get. I should have liked very much to go down to Oxford and see the 'Twelfth Night' as you suggest, but I am afraid it is impossible just now, as I have so much to do, and am not able to get away much except on special occasions. Will you let the committee, or whoever they are, know how pleased I should have been to have come down and seen their new theatre, and thank them very much for their kind invitation. I suppose you will not be able to go down to Cambridge for the opening of the new Union Buildings, but I trust I shall see you again some time. If you would care about it you might come down here some time during the spring or summer and see what sort of a life I lead here, as I could easily put you up. You have no idea what a lot we have to do, and I am sure it would interest you to see Aldershot. Excuse this short scrawl, but I am rather hurried to-day, being on duty.

> Ever yours, very sincerely,
> EDWARD

The excuse for the curtness was justified, for Eddy *was* busy, both with regimental and official duties.

After finishing at the riding-school on 10th December, 1885, he was able to join fully in the life of the regiment. 'He had, it is said,' Vincent records, 'a certain shrinking from the robust horseplay which has been known to exist among subalterns, although the 10th was about the last regiment in the world in which it was likely to be carried to excess. Still, the holiday of a month or more which followed these months of drill must have been passing pleasant.'

There was the usual 'family' visit to Sandringham, where Eddy planted an oak tree in front of the house, then shooting for three days and dancing for three nights at Burghley House, near Stamford, seat of the Marquess of Exeter, and then, after two nights at Sandringham, a trip to London to attend Lord Airlie's last bachelor dinner at the Hotel Métropole before his marriage on the following day to Lady Mabell Gore, daughter of the 5th Earl of Arran.

After the Airlie marriage, the Prince of Wales, with Eddy and George, went up to Eaton Hall, seat of the Duke of Westminster, whose granddaughter, Lady Constance Grosvenor, would marry another of Eddy's brother-officers, Lord Shaftesbury. On 1st February, 1886, Eddy returned to South Cavalry Barracks, full regimental duties being varied, of course, by duties inseparable from his rank.

On 24th February Eddy went to Cambridge to open the new Union buildings. He managed to get up to London once or twice, and not always for reasons as 'official' as a visit to the Shire Horse Show at Islington. He had a run with Mr Garth's hounds, and on 30th March he again went up to London 'officially', this time to receive the freedom and livery of the Goldsmiths' Company, a traditional ceremony which was followed, in traditional City fashion, by Eddy's taking up the freedom of the Mercers' Company.

Eddy, one feels, can have been the last to complain that his Colonel overworked him—on 10th March, 1886, Eddy and Colonel Wood both took the day off to ride with the Bicester—

'fruitlessly', as Vincent puts it, 'because frost put an end to the hunting'. It may have been a kindhearted gesture on Eddy's part to invite the Colonel to hunt with this most famous of all packs, since Wood was shortly to be replaced.

The newspapers and 'society' journals of the day make it clear that Eddy was being, in the modern phrase, 'groomed for stardom'. His presence in the London Season was more marked than it had been before, and 'there was much duty done of the princely kind, in attendance at State functions; at dinners, such as that of the Elder Brethren of Trinity House, in distributing prizes and in like matters'.

What was not so agreeable was that that rich, *déclassé*, spiteful Liberal, Labouchere, began to turn his malignant attention on Eddy, and a taste of what was to come was apparent in the tone of the references to Eddy and his father in the gossip-column which was the feature which really accounted for *Truth's* circulation and baneful influence.

By the middle of 1886, Eddy, under the gruelling discipline of Captain Peary, had become not only a presentable but a reasonably efficient officer. At least, he could take his place on parade without the Colonel's having to implore the Duke of Cambridge not to ask Eddy to perform even the simplest military drill. Peary had succeeded where Dalton had failed, perhaps because he had taken his duties a great deal more seriously than had the tutor-cleric.

As July ended, and August took the toffs off to the grouse-moors and the soldiers back to their headquarters, Eddy managed with credit some exacting field days under the Duke of Cambridge, a period on duty as orderly officer, attendance at a 'feast' of the Tenth's N.C.O.'s, and at the presentation of colours to the Buffs.

Though he had not yet been created Duke of Clarence and Avondale, and was thus not yet a peer, Eddy obviously held various political opinions. He could never forget the reception that he and his parents had endured at the hands of the Cork mob, and so the matter of Home Rule was one which engaged his feelings. Harry Wilson, determined to maintain the friendship begun at Sandringham, and hearing that Eddy was to dine at Downing-street with Gladstone, then Prime Minister, sent Eddy some verses on the Home Rule question.

South Cavalry Barracks,
May 25th, 86.

MY DEAR HARRY,—Many thanks for your letter, received this day week. I ought to have answered it before, but thought I would wait and see whether I could ask you down here this week, which I am afraid I cannot do now, as I am going off to town tomorrow, for the Darby (*sic*) and shall be away nearly all the week. But, if possible, next week may do, and I will let you know what day. I must appear very unwilling to have you down here; but you must not think so, as my plans are so unsettled just at present that I cannot find a day that will suit. But I will do my best about next week, so I hope you will not be disappointed. I have signed the photograph for your brother, which you asked me to do. I thought the poems you sent me very good, and they certainly do you great credit as they are only too true ... So hoping to see you again before very long.

Yours
EDWARD.

The excised portion was presumably cut out by reason of its political bias.

Clearly the separation from his friends troubled his conscience.

South Cavalry Barracks,
December 29th, 86

MY DEAR HARRY,—I was very glad to hear from you again, as it is a very long time since we met. I am afraid it is the natural result of leaving college, as one sees so little of one's old friends. It has just struck me that, as I am going up to town to-morrow afternoon on some business—would you care to

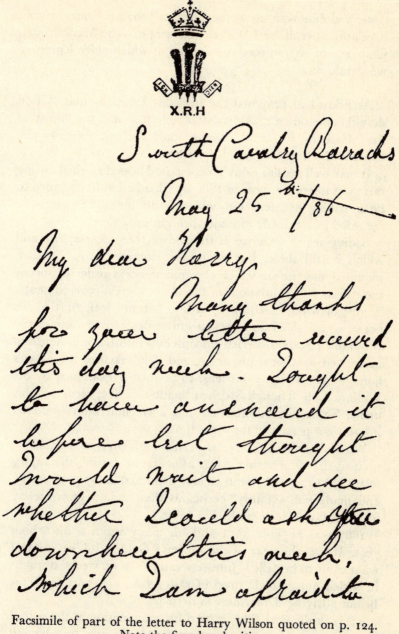

X.R.H

S. with Cavalry Barracks
May 25th/86

My dear Harry,

Many thanks
for your letter received
this day week. Ought
to have answered it
before but thought
I would wait and see
whether I could ask you
down here this week,
which I am afraid to

Facsimile of part of the letter to Harry Wilson quoted on p. 124.
Note the firm handwriting.

come and dine with me at the Club, as I shall not be returning here until after dinner? Will you telegraph to the Marlborough Club as soon as you receive this, and at which place I propose we should dine.

As Eddy had proposed the previous February that Wilson should come down to Aldershot, the letter—and the dinner at the Marlborough—must have soothed the conscience of the one and the hurt feelings of the other.

It may well be that Eddy's feelings had been disturbed during this most important year of 1886 by what had at first seemed to be a trifling accident but which, with hindsight, must be regarded as a tragedy of major proportions.

Riding near Felixstowe at the end of 1886, near a windmill which is still there, but no longer working, J. K. Stephen mounted the rise on which the mill stood in order to survey the still lovely undulations of the smooth, grass-covered chalk. A gust of wind, catching up a late autumn leaf, startled his horse, which shied and backed into a descending vane of the windmill. J.K. was carried unconscious into the mill-house to be treated by a local physician, and then taken to his father's home at 32, De Vere Gardens, to be further examined by Sir William Gull. Though Stephen 'made a perfect recovery', his uncle, Sir Leslie, admits that this accidental blow 'inflicted injuries not perceived for some time'.

Whether or not Eddy, with his half-feminine sympathy, divined that 'the accident was affecting his brain', this injury to his old tutor and friend clearly depressed Eddy profoundly, and made him (guiltily) conscious that he had grown away from his Cambridge circle.

1887 was an important and, in many ways, a disturbing year. It was the year of the Queen's Golden Jubilee, and of what came to be called 'Jubilee weather'—a six weeks' drought in which not a single drop of rain fell in any part of Great Britain, driving the farmers to despair.

Early in the year Eddy passed his examination at the end of his garrison course of instruction; in March, the 10th having moved to Hounslow, he was attached to the 3rd Battalion of the 60th Rifles, at South Barracks. On the day of the Queen's Jubilee, Eddy was promoted captain in the 10th, and appointed an additional aide-de-camp to the Queen. It was in this capacity that he attended many of the State functions connected with the Jubilee, and rode with Her Majesty on that 'solemn procession of thanksgiving' to St Paul's. The main celebrations over, Eddy was moved to York, where, says Vincent, 'he entered heart and soul into his regimental life'.

The measure of Eddy's strengthened confidence in himself may be gauged by his willingness to return to Ireland in mid-1887, to become a Bencher of the King's Inn, Dublin. This time there were no hostile demonstrations: his extreme personal beauty, allied with an elegance which seemed to belong to an earlier generation, enchanted the crowds, and his simple dignity captured the hearts of all who came into personal contact with him.

The records of the 10th shew that Eddy did not neglect his duties. His name is constantly amongst those who sign as having been present in mess for dinner; although as 1888 draws near, the absences are frequent. An accident in the hunting field may account for this.

As Eddy explained to Harry Wilson:

MARLBOROUGH HOUSE,
November 1st, 1887.

DEAR HARRY,—I was very glad to hear from you again, as it is a very long time since we last met. Yes, I have been rather unfortunate to get laid up like this and at this time of year. I did not exactly sprain my foot, but struck it going through a gate while out hunting last week down in Northamptonshire. It did not hurt much at the time, but began to swell a day or two after, and I was obliged to go on the sick list, and have been so for over a week, as I am not able to put my foot to the ground; but I hope to be about again in a few days, as it is well on the road to mending.

So you have taken a house for your people in the Isle of Wight for the winter. I hope Ventnor is a sheltered spot in winter, as you know parts of the island are very exposed at this time of year. I was at Cowes for a short time this summer, and had a delightful time of it, sometimes yachting, which I think very enjoyable on a fine warm day.

I suppose you are aware Dalton is now the proud possessor of a son? I had the honour of being godfather, but was unable to be present, being abroad at the time. Directly I am able to get about again I am going up to York for the winter. I have not stayed there before, and I hope to get some shooting and hunting in the neighbourhood. Hoping we may meet again some time,

Believe me,
Yours very sincerely,
EDWARD

Wilson's invitations continued to be turned down by Eddy. On 28th February, 1888, Eddy replied from Settrington House, near York, to another Wilson letter:

DEAR HARRY,—I was very glad to hear from you again, and it is very good of you to think of asking me to come to your place to see the boat race from. I should be delighted to do so, for it would be very nice to meet some of our old Cambridge friends again whom I have not seen for a long time.

But the question is whether I shall be in town then or not at the end of March, for if I am not I fear I shall be detained at York then by my duties with my regiment. But I had better let you know again for certain a little later on, if that would be the same to you.

We are having it very cold here still, and there has been more snow the last few days. I am staying here, where one feels the effect of the east winds pretty freely, as it is on the Wolds, which are a certain height up, and the highest hills in Yorkshire.

In spite of the weather, I had several good days' hunting last week. Hoping I shall be able to come,

> Ever yours,
> Very sincerely,
> EDWARD

The following letter cannot have been a surprise to the patient and ever-hopeful Harry Wilson:

> CAVALRY BARRACKS [*York*]
> *March 26th (1888)*

MY DEAR HARRY,—I put off writing to you before in the hope of still being able to give you a favourable answer. But I now find, very much to my regret, that I shall not be able to get away for next Saturday, which is very tiresome, for I should have much enjoyed paying you a visit at Chiswick and seeing some of my old friends again. If it had only been last Saturday I might have managed it, for I was in town for five days; that is the chief reason why I am unable to get away again just for the present, and have a certain amount of work to do here. I hope, at any rate, you will have a pleasant day for it, and I shall think of you all when the time comes. I met the C——s the other day, and think him a very lucky man to have secured so charming a lady for his third wife. I think you will agree with me when you see her. I hope you will come and dine with me some evening when I am in town again, and go to the play, and we shall be able to talk over old times, as we have not met for so long.

> Ever yours,
> Very sincerely,
> EDWARD

The apparently innocent nature of this friendship is clear from part of an undated letter of Eddy's belonging to this period.

Another example of Eddy's handwriting.

The songs you sent me I am sure were good although I have not heard them played yet for Villiers Stamford always writes such pretty music. By the way have you heard Sullivans new opera yet, for I have not, and believe it is very fine? Thanks for enquiring after my injuries I am luckily quite sound again; but it took some time, for I had strained the muscles in my shoulder rather badly by a fall out hunting. However I have been more fortunate lately. I am sorry you say Cambridge has not a good crew this year, but perhaps they may pull round in time and give Oxford a hammering which I sincerely hope they may.

Ever your very sincerely,
EDWARD.

But though Eddy, with new responsibilities as well as new companions, appears to have kept his older friends at a distance, he did not break with them completely. On 8th June, 1888, he went down to Cambridge, in company with a number of the nation's most distinguished subjects, to receive the degree of LL.D., *honoris causâ*. The brilliance of the company competed successfully with the Australians who were playing a Cambridge XI in what was ideal cricketing weather, for crowds gathered about the Senate House in such density that the distinguished visitors had some difficulty in entering themselves. In addition to 'the star attraction', Prince Albert Victor, there were also present the Marquess of Salisbury, the Earl of Selborne, an ex-Lord Chancellor, the Earl of Rosebery, and that 'political star of eccentric orbit', Lord Randolph Churchill. Afterwards, Eddy dined with these notables in the Hall of his old College, and later attended the reception in the drawing-room of the Master's Lodge.

Harry Wilson was not present, even as a spectator, but he dutifully sent Eddy one of his poems:

TO H.R.H. PRINCE EDWARD OF WALES
ON HIS TAKING HIS LL.D., JUNE 8TH, 1888

Five years ago! and yet to me
It seems as if 'twere yesterday,

And I am now a staid M.A.,
And you, Sir, are an LL.D.

Five years ago—we rode, we read,
    Boated, played hockey, whist, La Crosse,
    Listened to *Seeley*, laughed with *Gosse*,
And went at shocking hours to bed.

O days of gold! O sunny prime,
    Wherewith no season may compare!
    What words can paint a scene so fair?
How may I render into rhyme

The subtle charm of lawns and trees,
    Of lichened walls and chapels dim,
    Of pictured saint and soaring hymn,
Of that high carnival of ease,

And health, and loyal friendship free,
    When *England*'s best and brightest meet
    For blameless mirth and converse sweet
Within the courts of *Trinity*?

'Tis gone! the friends are scattered far,
    And one is scorched with *Indian* suns,
    And one is blest with dogs and guns,
And one is slaving at the Bar.

But you, the Prince of this dear Isle,
    The loftiest destiny awaits,
    To see yon realm's unnumbered States
Conjoined in one. May Heaven smile

Upon that great, that glorious aim!
    And like her *Edwards* Third and First,
    May you, for England's weal athirst,
Add lustre to a royal name.

Required by the scansion, the omission of the second Edward
need not be of great significance.

Major Miles and Captain Peary had realized some of the hopes that the Duke of Cambridge had rather hopelessly uttered. Outwardly, at least, their respectful yet iron discipline had turned Eddy into a soldier. In the previous year, Eddy had taken his place in the Royal Review at Aldershot; now, in 1888, he was a captain commanding 'B' Troop of the 10th Hussars. A picture of him leading his troop shews a smart young officer as competent as any of the other members of his mess. The fact is that he liked York, perhaps because it was the first posting in which he realized, with what astonished pleasure one may well guess, that he had overcome his nervousness, had mastered the military evolutions, that his men accepted him as one of themselves. He was out of his military apprenticeship.

His new confidence was apparent at several of the functions which, as he grew older, became more and more frequent. On 18th July, 1888, he acquitted himself with composure and dignity throughout the long ceremony by which he was admitted a Knight of Justice of the Order of St John of Jerusalem, and nominated Sub-Prior of that Order in England. Ten days later, he drove, with a full escort of his own Tenth through the crowded streets of the ancient Roman city of York, to the Mansion House, to receive the freedom of the city.

But, as in the plot of some Gothic melodrama, horror of the most unimaginable kind was waiting to displace the seeming invulnerability of this young hero. The horror was to come so near as to involve him in its terror. Nearly a century later, people are still asking questions: to what extent was Eddy caught up in that nightmare of beastliness? how much did he know? how much did he conceal? how intimately was he concerned in its concealment?

Book III   *Manhood*

6. The Lurker in the Shadows

In November, 1970, the extraordinary rumour swept through the world that the Whitechapel mass-murderer, notorious in criminal history as 'Jack the Ripper', was none other than Prince Albert Victor, Duke of Clarence and Avondale. The spark which fired this train of blazing scandal was an article by the late Dr T. E. A. Stowell, C.B.E., M.D., which appeared that month in *The Criminologist*.

The 'Ripper' article was 'picked up' by a *Sunday Times* staff feature-writer, Mr Magnus Linklater, who, naturally, set out to interview Dr Stowell and to pin him down, if possible, to a more detailed statement of the murderer's identity than had appeared in *The Criminologist*. Subsequently interviewed on television, it was inevitable that Dr Stowell, whilst refusing to state positively that his 'suspect' *was* the Duke of Clarence and Avondale, seemed equally reluctant to state positively that Eddy was *not* the Ripper.

Under a picture of Eddy, *Time* asked the question: *Was this the Ripper?* Many other journals were even less sensitive in their approach to the identification of a sadistic and maniac murderer with one who had been in the direct line of succession to the Crown of Great Britain.

If the editors and feature writers had read Stowell's article they would have realized that the author had set out to convey the impression, though without actually committing himself to a positive statement, that he not only believed, but actually knew, that Eddy and the Ripper were the same.

Stowell had, it is clear, convinced himself that a man of whom he had got some particulars *at third hand* was Eddy. It is true that certain dates in the lives of both the real Ripper and of Eddy do tally, but Stowell preferred to believe that he was hearing about Eddy, rather than about someone of lower social rank. It made a better story.

Before considering Dr Stowell's claims in detail, it is necessary briefly to look at the dreadful crimes whose commission has given Jack the Ripper a dubious immortality as the sadistical murderer *par excellence*.

It is not generally agreed that there were only five murders, and some criminologists include in the series a murder as early as 1887 and another as late as 1892. But *all* agree that five murders were the work of a single killer, the self-styled 'Jack the Ripper', since the *modus operandi*, varying only in savagery, but never in type, recurs as the characteristic 'signature'.

These dominant features may be summarized as follows:

1. Although sexually motivated, the murders are not sexual assaults in the ordinary meaning of the phrase. The murderer in no case attempted sexual intercourse, either normally or abnormally, with the victim, and the pudenda were not attacked in any way.

2. The five women were silenced, almost certainly by the clapping of a hand over their mouths, and were killed by having their throats slit with a knife.

3. Once dead, the woman was eviscerated. The extent of this depended upon the amount of time available to the murderer.

4. The murderer not only eviscerated his victim, but also took away with him, in most cases, the organs he had removed. His principal interest, according to the evidence of what was missing from the corpses, seems to have been the uterus, although other organs—ovaries, kidneys, bladder—were sometimes cut out.

But the focus of the murderer's obsession would appear to have been the uterus.

There is no need to go into the ghastly details of the crimes, for these are readily available in recent books by Colin Wilson, Tom Cullen and Donald McCormick. My tracking down of the murderer has depended not on what he did, but *how he managed to do it*, an awkward question that all the commentators on the Ripper crimes have understandably declined to tackle. The fact that the evisceration of a woman differs only in the minutest detail from the gralloching of a stag has, of course, been noticed. Indeed, it is one of the arguments used by Dr Stowell for fastening the crime on Eddy. But to accuse a man simply because he knows how to gralloch a stag is as absurd as it is unjust—Stowell might as well have accused almost any land-owner of the day or his many guests.

The seriousness with which the Home Office took, not so much the crimes, as the terror inspired by them, is sufficiently in-dicated by the fact that General Sir Charles Warren, Chief Commissioner of Metropolitan Police, summoned back the Chief of the Criminal Investigation Department from holiday in Switzerland. The latter promptly assigned seven senior C.I.D. officers to assist the six hundred police already serving with H Division and those men of the City Police who had been brought into the case when the last-but-one victim died just within the City limits.

The efforts of all these men were hampered, as they always are in similar circumstances, by lack of any eye-witness evidence and by an overplus of surmise. This latter is hardly surprising in the light of the extensive newspaper coverage of the crimes. Even Queen Victoria was interested in the Ripper—and not, as one writer suggests, because she feared that he might be her beloved grandson, Eddy! The tone of the letters that the Queen wrote, both to the Chief Commissioner of Police and to the Editor of *The Times*, are clearly not those of a woman fearful that her own family was mixed up in these awful crimes.

When modern commentators are spinning their theories

about the identity of the Ripper, they make great play with the fact that a man—or men—seen talking to the women victims was—or were—'softly spoken'. Dr Stowell, for example, asks, 'What do we know of the murderer? Witnesses stated that he was under medium height—5 ft 6 in. to 5 ft 7 in. He spoke "softly", this probably meant that he spoke like a gentleman.'

Surmise apart, there is no reason why the 'softly spoken' man seen talking to Mary Jane Kelly, most diabolically-mutilated of all the victims, should have been her murderer.

Even assuming that 'softly spoken' means 'well-spoken', it is not true, as so many assume, that the well-spoken man was a rarity in the East End of the 1880s. Almost as many professional men worked there as in the West End—bank-managers, civil engineers, doctors in both private and hospital practice, senior officials of the Port of London Authority, Trinity House, H.M. Customs.

But—and the significance of this fact appears to have missed most of the investigators—there was also another type of 'toff' with which the East End had become familiar in the twenty years or so before Jack the Ripper initiated 'the Autumn of Terror'. For a non-Socialist, non-political, interest in the 'underprivileged' had swept through the upper strata of society, and 'social work' became fashionable, not only in the universities, but even with such shallow thinkers as the Prince of Wales.

In February, 1884, during Eddy's first year at Trinity, the Prince of Wales had accepted nomination to membership of a Royal Commission on the Housing of the Working Classes. The membership of the Commission reflects the 'pioneering' character of its intentions, and consisted of Lord Brownlow, whose heir, Lionel Cust, was a friend of Eddy's, Lord Carrington, Jesse Collings, G. J. Goschen, Lord Salisbury and Cardinal Manning, under the chairmanship of Sir Charles Dilke, soon to fall from grace and political power through the notorious Crawford case. As well as attending the regular meetings of the Commission, the Prince, in disguise and accompanied by Lord Carrington, explored some of the Clerkenwell slums.

POLICE NOTICE.

TO THE OCCUPIER.

On the mornings of Friday, 31st August, Saturday 8th, and Sunday, 30th September, 1888, Women were murdered in or near Whitechapel, supposed by some one residing in the immediate neighbourhood. Should you know of any person to whom suspicion is attached, you are earnestly requested to communicate at once with the nearest Police Station.

Metropolitan Police Office,
30th September, 1888.

Further, to shew his sincerity, the Prince invited a working-class Liberal-Radical M.P., Henry Broadhurst, to spend a December week-end at Sandringham. While there Broadhurst enjoyed many frank discussions with his host and hostess, as well as with Prince Eddy and Prince George, and he noted happily that he 'left Sandringham with a feeling of one who had spent a week-end with an old chum of his own rank of society.' Today, one would hardly expect 'an old chum' to serve one's meals in one's room, away from all the other guests; but *tempora mutantur, nos et mutamur in illis* . . .

What is important here is that, on the Prince's returning from his visit to the slums of Holborn and Clerkenwell 'in time for luncheon', Eddy was at Marlborough House; whilst Henry Broadhurst, in his 'many frank discussions . . . with Prince Eddy and Prince George', must have filled in the picture of London's slums.

As I said before, 'social work' was one of the many fashions with which the all-too-idle rich of the 1880s sought to beguile their leisure.

This interest in the poor was not confined to mere sentimental sighing. Being Victorians, albeit rich and class-conscious, they did something to shew their sincerity in a practical way. They put the hat around, and, with the money raised, they built those 'settlements' in the East End which exist to this day, while universities and public schools set up 'missions'. Perhaps the most famous of these is Toynbee Hall, the original of which dates from 1867, and adjoins St Jude's Church in Commercial Street. On the other side of St Jude's Church was yet one more of these Samaritan institutions, the East End Universities Settlement, another establishment where the presence of a 'toff' would not only not be noticeable, but, on the contrary, be both expected and accepted. Like Toynbee Hall, its back doors also provided easy access to any of the dark yards of Whitechapel.

One thing, however, remains clear, that Eddy was not the Ripper. Such evidence of witnesses as exists, and this was never more than that a victim was seen talking to a man, is so contradictory that it is of no use at all. As all the murdered women were prostitutes, the very nature of their calling would have made them accost men, so that the sight of their talking to a man assumed sinister significance only because of what happened to them later.

One such witness was an ex-night-watchman named Hutchinson, 'who saw the Ripper talking to Mary Kelly'. This is Colin Wilson's account from his excellent *A Casebook of Murder*:

'After she left [Hutchinson], he saw her picked up by a swarthy-looking man in Commercial Street. He thought the man looked too well-dressed to be hanging around the East End at such an hour, but he had no suspicion that it was the Ripper. He had a gold watch chain and a heavy moustache that curled up at the ends'.

Now Eddy had a moustache which curled up at the ends, but the fact that *Pomade Hongroise* was a best-seller at chemists' and barbers' shops makes it clear that so did most of the moustaches in the 1880s. In any case, Eddy's little moustache could in no way be described as 'heavy'. Neither was Eddy swarthy nor, going back to earlier 'evidence', was he 'below the medium height', being, in fact, a little under six feet tall.

Even if the Court Circular did not provide an alibi for Eddy for every one of those nights on which an 'unfortunate' was horribly done to death, the evidence of contradictory witnesses shews that no-one resembling Eddy was ever seen talking to any of the women.

But the Court Circular does provide the necessary alibi. If the murders were all the work of a single murderer, then an alibi for only one would prove innocence of all the crimes. For instance, when the woman, Alice McKenzie, was murdered on the night of 16/17th July, 1889, Eddy was accompanying the Shah of Persia on a wearisome tour of the principal centres of commerce and manufacture in England and Scotland. The Shah arrived at Gravesend on 1st July and took his leave of the

Queen at Osborne on 29th July. In all that time Eddy was in constant attendance on the Shah.

Of course Eddy visited the University Settlements, as did his father and his Cambridge friends; and, though they were never founded as a sort of harem for homosexuals, the very fact that they were packed nightly with the youth of the East End inevitably made them attractive to that type of homosexual who is attracted to youth, especially of a lower social stratum.

Since I know, and shall, at the proper time, reveal this unfortunate madman's identity, it is clear that no-one did see him, for otherwise the police and the Whitechapel *vigilantes* would not have been searching for men of so widely different physical type that the huge Polish-Jewish barber, 'Chapman'; the shy, neurotic English barrister, Druitt; and 'the mad Russian doctor', Michael Ostrog, could all rank as suspects.

Following the publication of Dr Stowell's article in *The Criminologist* and the subsequent publicity, a letter, signed 'Loyalist', was printed in *The Times*. Though anonymous, this letter was authoritative, and merely stated what was true: that the innocent movements and activities of the Duke on all the relative dates were on public record and could be checked by anyone interested.

On the following day, 9th November, 1970—by coincidence, the anniversary of Mary Jane Kelly's horrible murder in 1888— a letter appeared, signed by Dr Stowell. In it he said that he too was a loyalist, and that he had never said nor even thought that the Duke of Clarence had been the Ripper.

And then came one of those occurrences which are so unacceptable in fiction, but with which life is so full. In *The Times* of 10th November, 1970, a small paragraph reported the death, *on 9th November*, of Dr Stowell. Interviewed by several reporters, Dr Stowell's son said that 'the papers' on which his late father had based his sensational story, had been destroyed, unread, immediately after Dr Stowell's death.

Dr Stowell's article, '*Jack the Ripper*'—*A Solution?* takes up twelve full pages in *The Criminologist*. The article begins by listing *his* five victims, and their dates of death. He describes the ghastly details of the mutilations, ending with the most horrible of all, the butchering of Mary Kelly in the night of 8th/9th November, 1888.

The article then goes on to describe the feelings of terror inspired by the murders, the efforts of the police to find the murderer, the false clues, the half-lynched 'suspects', and the various 'descriptions' of what Dr Stowell himself calls, without any justification whatever, 'the murderer'.

Dr Stowell rightly defends General Sir Charles Warren against the charge of ineptitude:

'It seems obvious that all the efforts of Sir Charles Warren and the police were primarily directed towards preventing further murders and secondly to avoid the embarrassment that would be caused by the bringing to trial for these murders, the heir of a noble and prominent family. Clearly he was a lunatic, and was not responsible for his actions. Such however was the indignation of the public that it would have been satisfied with nothing less than a capital sentence.

'His activities were probably known to his family after the second murder, perhaps even after the first. After the murder of Annie Chapman [8th September, 1888] he disappeared and nothing was heard of him until letters first posted from Liverpool were received from him one or two days before the murder of Stride and Eddowes [both on 20th September, 1888] and in these he announced his intention.

'I believe that within an hour or two of the murder of Eddowes on 30th September [1888], he was apprehended and certified to be insane and was placed under restraint in a private mental home in the Home Counties. But the police were busy with preparations for the Lord Mayor's Show. The murderer escaped from his custodians and got to his Whitechapel haunt, where he murdered Mary Jane Kelly and left the scene an hour and a half before sunrise on 9 November [1888].'

So far, this is acceptable. The Ripper was a lunatic, he was taken into private custody, he must have escaped from restraint in order to murder Kelly—though not necessarily from the restraint of a lunatic asylum. Although not the heir, the murderer was a younger son, but his family was 'noble and prominent', and there were excellent reasons why the scandal (a word preferable to Stowell's milder 'embarrassment') should have been covered up. The criminal lunatic could have brought many a reputation crashing down with his own.

Now for Dr Stowell's argument, in his article, that so many people were willing to accept as convincing 'proof' that Eddy was the Ripper. Remembering that, but a few hours before he died, Dr Stowell denied that he had ever thought or suggested that Eddy and the Ripper were one and the same, his assertion seems to me to be one of the most maliciously ambiguous ever made.

All the same, though Dr Stowell became exceedingly cautious when challenged to state definitely that Eddy *was* the Ripper, Colin Wilson, in an article written for *The Leicester Chronicle* some ten weeks after Dr Stowell's death, says unequivocally that Stowell did name Eddy as the maniac Whitechapel killer.

Colin Wilson had been commissioned to write some articles for *The Evening Standard*, a series under the title of *My Search for Jack the Ripper*. Many people wrote to Wilson, among them Dr Stowell.

'He explained,' wrote Wilson in *The Leicester Chronicle*, 'that he was a brain surgeon and that he had always been interested in the Ripper problem. From my articles, he said, he was pretty sure I knew the identity of Jack the Ripper. Would I like to meet him for lunch and talk about it?

'I wrote and told him that I hadn't the faintest idea of the identity of the Ripper, but I would be pleased to meet him for lunch.

'I met him at the Athenaeum . . . He was in his early seventies; a friendly, likeable man. He told me he was still practising surgery—although, noting the way his hand shook as he cut his steak, I wondered how much longer that could go on . . .

'He came to the point fairly quickly. He was convinced, he

told me, that Jack the Ripper was the Duke of Clarence, grandson of Queen Victoria, son of Edward the Seventh, heir to the throne of England. If he had not died in 1892, he would have become king of England in 1910 . . . an interesting thought.

'And how had he come by all this knowledge? He had seen the papers of the late Sir William Gull, Physician in Ordinary to Queen Victoria . . . What the papers revealed, he said, was that the Duke of Clarence had *not* died in the flu epidemic of 1892—as the history books state—but in a mental home near Sandringham, of "softening of the brain" due to syphilis.'

So much for Dr Stowell's positive statements in 1960, when, at his own invitation, he met Colin Wilson in the Athenaeum. Now let us see what Stowell had to say ten years later, after the article in *The Criminologist* had found a far wider audience than that unsensational, specialist journal usually reaches.

This is Dr Stowell's case, as set out in the *Criminologist:*

'Now for my suspect.

'I prefer not to name him but to call him "S".

'He was the heir to power and wealth. His family, for fifty years, had earned the love and admiration of large numbers of people by its devotion to public service to all classes, particularly the poor, but as well to industry and the workers. His grandmother, who outlived him, was very much the stern Victorian matriarch, widely and deeply respected. His father, to whose title he was heir, was a gay cosmopolitan and did much to improve the status of England internationally. His mother was an unusually beautiful woman with a gracious personal charm and was greatly beloved by all who knew her.

'After the education traditional for an English aristocrat, at the age of a little over 16 years, "S" went for a cruise round the world with a number of high-spirited boys of approximately his age group.

'He was, perhaps, too popular and gregarious for his own safety. It is recorded that he went to many gay parties ashore.

147

'It seems to me that for a young man of his age and personality and his great prospects of wealth and rank in the years to come, the temptations which inevitably lay in his path were not given proper consideration by those responsible for his safety and welfare; and I believe that at one of the many shore parties which he enjoyed in the West Indies on his world journey, he became infected with syphilis.

'Some six weeks later he had an important public appointment in what was then one of our Colonies. At the last moment he cancelled that appointment on account of "a trifling ailment". The abandonment of an important engagement on account of a trifling ailment is unusual unless it is causing severe pain or obvious disfigurement, e.g. toothache or the development of a visible rash.

'This "trifling ailment" may well have been the appearance of the skin rash of secondary syphilis appearing six weeks after the primary infection acquired in the West Indies.

'As to whether this was recognized and adequately treated, I have some misgivings in the light of later events.

'He arrived back in England before his 19th birthday. At the age of 21 he was gazetted to a commission in the Army where he was successful, popular and happy.

'He resigned his commission at about the age of 24. This was shortly after the raiding of some premises in Cleveland Street, off Tottenham Court Road, kept by a man named Hammond, which were frequented by various aristocrats and well-to-do homosexuals [see *Their Good Names*, H. M. Hyde, London, 1970, p. 95].

'I have seen a photograph of my suspect which suggests paranoia by the extravagance of his dress, for which I am told he became a butt.

'In this photograph he is seen by the riverside holding a fishing rod, wearing a tweed knickerbocker suit of perfect cut, not a fold misplaced and without a crease. On his head is a tweed cap set far too precisely, and he has a small moustache. He is wearing a 4in. to 4½in. stiff starched collar, and is shewing two inches of shirt cuff at each wrist (I was told by my elders that he was given the nickname of "Collar and Cuffs"). This photograph of him is more suitable for a tailor's showcase than for the river bank, but it must be remembered that this was the period of extravagance of the "aesthetes," and also that the photographic plates of those days were slow, and subjects had to be "posed." I have already said that I believe that the Ripper was apprehended after the murder of Eddowes in September, 1888, and placed under medical care, whence he escaped and murdered Kelly on 9 November and after which he was again apprehended. He was, throughout, under the care of the great physician, Sir William Gull, who treated him with such success that in 1889 he was able to take a five months cruise during which he enjoyed some big game hunting in which he was a remarkably fine shot.

'His father and mother accompanied him part way out from England, but little is recorded of his return. Before his return, he probably suffered a relapse and was brought home quietly for further intensive treatment. In the summer of 1890 he took the leading part on three great public occasions.

'On each of these occasions, important though they were, he made speeches, but each speech contained little more than 100 words. This indicates that he had lost much of his former ebullience and that he was on the downward path from the manic stage of syphilis to the depression and dementia which in time must inevitably overtake him.

'We hear little more of him before his death a year or two later. As is usual in general paralysis of the insane, he was kept alive so long only by means of medical skill and unremitting careful nursing—in his father's country house.'

So much for Dr Stowell's statement of his suspicion and his description of his suspect. At first reading it does, indeed, look like a positive identification of Eddy, Duke of Clarence and Avondale, especially with that remark 'I was told by my elders that he was given the nickname of "Collar and Cuffs" '—this was Labouchere's taunting name for Eddy in the pages of *Truth*.

But if one examines the text of this malicious double-talk

carefully, one finds that Stowell never committed himself to an actual statement that his suspect *was* Eddy.

Without examining every 'fact' in the statement, let me point out a few of Stowell's 'facts' which *cannot* apply to Eddy (my remarks follow each statement of Stowell's).

'At the age of a little over 16 years, "S" went on a cruise round the world with a number of high-spirited boys of approximately his age group.'

[Eddy went as a cadet on H.M.S. *Bacchante*, on a cruise to the Mediterranean and the West Indies. *He* was 15.]

'In the West Indies on his world journey he became infected with syphilis.'

[Under the care of the Rev. Dr Dalton, it seems highly unlikely that Eddy would have had the chance of contracting syphilis. Nor is there the slightest evidence that he did.]

'Some six weeks later he had an important public appointment in what was then one of our Colonies.'

[The West Indies were left on 13th April, 1880, for Spithead, which was reached on 2nd May. Six weeks after the last possible day at Bermuda, Eddy was on leave with his family, mostly at Sandringham and Marlborough House.]

'At the last moment he cancelled that appointment on account of a "trifling ailment." This "trifling ailment" may well have been the skin rash of secondary syphilis appearing six weeks after primary infection acquired in the West Indies.'

[The 'trifling ailment' of which Stowell speaks occurred *in June, 1881, in Western Australia*, over a year after Eddy had left the West Indies, and the 'important public appointment' was a private kangaroo hunt up country. Incidentally, Eddy was fully recovered on the next day.]

'He resigned his commission at about the age of 24.'

[Eddy was 24 in 1888, the year in which he was appointed Captain in command of 'B' Troop, at York. In 1889, he achieved field rank as Major. He never resigned from any of his military appointments.]

'Collar and Cuffs'. A posed studio portrait of Eddy, about 1890, showing the high collar and very visible starched cuffs which inspired Labouchere to give Eddy his sarcastic nickname.

Opposite, the north side of Postern Row in George Yard, Whitechapel. Near this dismal street, typical of the district, Martha Turner met her violent end, second of the Ripper's victims. *Above,* James Kenneth Stephen in 1887, from a chalk drawing by F. Miller—the frontispiece to *Lapsus Calami* (1898), the collected edition of Stephen's poems. *Below,* 'the mad judge,' Sir James Fitzjames Stephen, Bt, K.C.S.I., Q.C., (J.K.'s father), whose insanity became apparent during the trial of Mrs Maybrick, so disastrously conducted by Mr Justice Stephen that he was forced to retire from the bench.

One of the Ripper letters considered genuine by the police. It was addressed to Mr Lusk, a prominent and active member of the White-chapel Vigilantes, organised to protect local women from the maniac murderer.

From hell

Mr Lusk

Sor I send you half the Kidne I took from one women prasarved it for you tother piece I fried and ate it was very nise I may send you the bloudy knif that took it out if you only wate a whil longer

Signed Catch me when you can Mishter Lusk

A fine kill by Eddy, in Travancore State, November, 1899: Eddy proudly sits on the bison that he has just killed. At rear: Captain Holford, Eddy's equerry, Mr Bensley and Iyappen Nilghiri, the head-man who acted as tracker.

Photograph by a Mr Haryngton.

Cleveland Street, as it appeared from the front steps of the notorious No. 19. This is the one part of the street which retains its eighteenth-century aspect unaltered. Mrs Hannah Morgan's confectioner's shop at No. 22 is in the extreme left of the picture. All the neighbouring shop-keepers were witnesses of the comings and goings at Hammond's house. *Below, left*, Sir Henry Hawkins, Q.C. A judge whose fairness belied his nickname of 'the hanging judge', his severest trial was to preside over the farce of the Cleveland Street case. *Below, right*, leading for the prosecution, Sir Charles Russell, Q.C., M.P. *Bottom, right*, leading for the defence, the Solicitor-General, Sir Frank Lockwood, Q.C., M.P.

Photograph by Anthony Mann; author's collection.

All; W. & D. Downey.

THE WEST-END SCANDALS.

COMMITTAL OF THE EDITOR OF THE "PRESS" FOR TRIAL

A DEFENCE FUND OPENED.

Lord Euston emphatically denies the libellous statement, and explains the circumstances under which he once visited the house in Cleveland-street.

The editor of this paper has been committed to take his trial at the sessions of the Central Criminal Court, which open on Monday, 16 December. The proceedings were initiated last Saturday morning, when on the application of Mr. Lionel Hart, instructed by Messrs. Lewis & Lewis, Justice Field granted his fiat for the commencement of criminal proceedings against Mr. Ernest Parke, whose solicitor, Mr. Minton Slater, offered no opposition. At Bow-street Police Court the same afternoon, Mr. George Lewis obtained from Mr. Vaughan a warrant for

LORD EUSTON.

Mr. Parke's arrest, the Earl of Euston supporting the application by testifying to the truth of the affidavit he had made denying the libellous statements complained of. Sergeant Partridge was sent with the warrant to the *Star* office, but being by inadvertence informed that Mr. Parke had left, went to his place of residence at Clapham. Meanwhile, however, Mr. Parke heard of the issue of the warrant, and at once went to Bow-street

TO SURRENDER HIMSELF,

accompanied by gentlemen who offered bail to the amount of £1,500. The magistrate had, however, left, the hour being half-past five, and Detective-Inspector Conquest—who was in charge —had no authority to accept bail. The Chief Commissioner Mr. Monro was consulted, but finally at 10.30 Mr. Parke and his friends were informed that the ordinary course could not be departed from and he must be detained in the cells till Monday morning. Everything was done for his comfort that the police regulations permitted, every officer from Mr. Conquest downwards treating him with all the consideration permissible. On Monday morning he was brought up, but to the disappointment of a crowded court the proceedings were

PURELY FORMAL.

Mr. Asquith applied for a remand, which after some opposition on the part of Mr. George Lewis was granted till 3 o'clock the next afternoon. Mr. Lewis asked that Lord Euston should there and then go into the box and deny the libel, but Mr. Vaughan declined to allow that course to be adopted.

Mr. Parke was allowed out on bail in two sureties of £50 each. Strong comments have appeared in several papers upon the fact that the warrant was applied for and issued so late that Mr. Parke's detention without bail from Saturday till Monday was rendered inevitable. It is usual, we believe, to proceed with libel cases by summons instead of by warrant, unless the prosecutor has reason to think that the defendant will attempt to escape. It is the more difficult to understand how Mr. Lewis could have gained this impression, inasmuch as Mr. Parke had received formal notice of the proceedings on the preceding Tuesday, and thus had had ample time to get out of jurisdiction if he had so desired.

regarded as the disgrace and opprobrium of modern civilisation." The paragraph concluded by warning Mr. Matthews, the Home Secretary, that if he did not take action before Parliament met he would have a heavy reckoning to settle. Mr. Lewis continued that the accusation was a very atrocious one, and he should ask that the defendant be committed for trial. The circumstances, so far as Lord Euston was concerned, were these. He had never committed any crime of any sort or kind. That statement was

ABSOLUTELY WITHOUT ANY FOUNDATION

so far as he was concerned. He had never left the country, and there had been no warrant issued so far as he knew for his apprehension. If there was any warrant out, Lord Euston was present that day to be apprehended : but it was perfectly untrue that such a warrant had issued. All that he knew about the case was simply this. One evening at the end of May or the beginning of June Lord Euston was walking in Piccadilly at about 12 o'clock at night when a man put into his hand a card on which were the words "Poses Plas-

HAMMOND.

tiques.—Hammond, 19, Cleveland-street." About a week later

LORD EUSTON WENT TO THE HOUSE,

between 10.30 and 11 at night. A man opened the door to him and asked him for a sovereign, which Lord Euston gave him. Lord Euston asked about the poses plastiques, when the man made an indecent proposal to him, on which Lord Euston called him an infernal scoundrel, and threatened to knock him down if he did not at once allow him to leave the house. The door was then opened and Lord Euston at once left the house. That was all he knew of the matter.

Formal evidence was then given of the publication of the libel and of the connection of Mr. Parke with the paper, but Mr. Lockwood observed that the evidence was hardly necessary as the responsibility of the defendant was not disputed.

The Earl of Euston was then examined by Mr. Lewis. He said—My name is Henry James, Earl of Euston. When in London I reside at

4, GROSVENOR-PLACE.

When not in London, I reside at Euston Lodge, Thetford, or Wakefield Lodge, Stoney Stratford, my father's place.

You have seen the copy of the paper of the 16th of November, *The North London Press* ?—I have. I at once gave instructions for a criminal prosecution for libel in respect of the matter contained in that paper.

Is there any truth Lord Euston, in the statement that you have been guilty of the crime alleged in that newspaper ?—Certainly not.

Is there any truth, so far as you know, that any warrant has been issued for your apprehension ?— No. There is no truth whatever in the statement that in order to abscond from arrest I went to Peru. I have not been out of England since I came from Australia in 1881.

Will you state to the court

WHAT YOU KNOW OF THIS HOUSE ?

All I know is that one night I was walking in Piccadilly. I cannot quite say the date. It was either the end of May or the beginning of June. A card was put into my hand, which, on reading afterwards, I saw was headed, "Poses Plastiques, Hammond, 19, Cleveland-street." I do not remember whether Tottenham Court-road was on the card. About a week afterwards I went there. It was about half-past ten or eleven o'clock at night. The door was opened to me by a man. He asked me to come in, and then asked me for a sovereign. I gave it to him. I then asked him when these poses plastiques were going to take place. He then said, "There's nothing of the sort."

Mr. Lockwood here objected to the conversation being given, and the objection was upheld.

Mr. Lewis—Did he say something to you ?—He did.

Did you express anger ?

You say the statement was first made in the month of October ?—Yes.

Have you made a statement at the Home Office about it ?—No.

Or at the Treasury ?—No.

You made no statement to any official ?—None whatever.

Just wait and hear my question. You made no statement to any official at all either at the Treasury or the Home Office ?—I have had no communication of any sort or kind either with the Treasury or the Home Office.

That you swear ?—That I swear.

You said you first made your statement in October. That I take it meant to some friends ?— Yes, privately.

IS LORD ARTHUR SOMERSET

a friend of yours ?—I know him.

When did you see him last ?—Last summer some time during the season. That is as near as I can remember. I was in London during May June, and July. I saw him in society. I was in the habit of meeting him constantly.

Did you meet him in society ?—Yes.

You have not seen him since ?—No.

Do you know where he is ?—No.

Now just tell me with regard to this occurrence in May or June, you say you afterwards read the card. How long afterwards ?—When I got home I think. I don't remember particularly. I think when I got home and took my coat off. I did not read it in the street. I just shoved it in my pocket and looked at it when I got home.

Just tell me what it was that was on the card ; was it a printed or a lithographed card ?—It was a lithographed card, but the words *poses plastiques* at the top were in writing.

Was the gentleman giving out these cards promiscuously, or ʼ

WERE YOU PARTICULARLY FAVOURED ?

—Witness (laughing) : I cannot tell you. He shoved one into my hand, and I put it in my pocket.

Was he giving them away to other people ? —I really cannot tell you. I was walking along pretty smart home. I do not walk slowly as a rule.

Did you see him give a card to anyone else ?— No. It was near 12 o'clock as I was walking home.

I suggest to you that you had not time to stop and read it ?—Well (laughing), I did not stop to read it under a lamppost.

Mr. Lockwood—I do not know what there is to laugh at.

Mr. Lewis—Well. it was a comical question.

Mr. Lockwood—Well. how long was it between your reading it and your going to see whether the promises in the card would be carried out ?—Oh, at least a week.

Then you kept the card during the whole of that time ?—Yes.

YOU WENT ALONE ?—YES.

Did you bring the card back with you ?—I brought it home.

What did you do with it ?—I destroyed it. I was disgusted at having been found in such a place, and I did not want to have anything more to do with it.

You say you destroyed it. Did you burn it or tear it up ?—Well, I think I tore it up. I should not have a fire in my room at that time of year.

You tore it up in disgust ?—Yes.

In indignation ?—Yes. I was very angry with myself for having been brought there.

Lord Euston, from what passed in that house you had no doubt what the character of the house was ?—Not the smallest.

It is a house, as I understand you to say, of your own knowledge, where crimes such as those alluded to in the libel were probably committed ?— I should think they might be, and probably were, from what was said to me.

Mr. Lockwood—That, sir, is at present all I have.

1891: the affianced couple. Eddy and the Princess Victoria Mary ('May') of Teck, later Queen Mary, wife of George V. This appears to be the only portrait of the pair taken together.

'I have seen a photograph of my suspect which suggests paranoia by the extravagance of his dress . . . he is wearing a 4in to 4½inch stiff starched collar . . .'

[The collar was 3¼ ins, and was not exaggerated by the sartorial standards of the time. In any case, he wore a high-collar to hide the same scar, from the same cause, which disfigured his Mother's neck.]

'. . . in 1889, he was able to take a five months' cruise during which he enjoyed some big game hunting . . . His father and mother accompanied him part way out from England, but little is recorded of his return. Before his return he probably suffered a relapse, and was brought home quietly for further intensive treatment.'

[In 1889 Eddy made a tour of India, as his Father had done in 1875, leaving the Prince and Princess of Wales at Port Said on 31st October, 1889, and reaching Bombay on 9th November. He left India on 20th March, 1890, visiting Cairo and generally sightseeing in Egypt in numerous and distinguished company before returning to London in early May, to be created Duke of Clarence and Avondale. Although he did enjoy considerable big game shooting in India, he also carried out numerous public engagements such as laying foundation stones for docks, leper hospitals, schools, etc. He was always accompanied by a large staff of both British and Indians, and reporters of both races and all nationalities were constantly present.]

'In the summer of 1890 he took the leading part on three great public occasions. On each of these occasions, important though they were, he made speeches, but each speech contained little more than 100 words. This indicates that he had lost much of his former ebullience and that he was on the downward path from the manic stage of syphilis to the depression and dementia which in time must inevitably overtake him.'

[Eddy took the leading part in far more than three 'great public occasions' in 1890, but Stowell here is probably referring to Eddy's taking his seat in the House of Lords as Duke of Clarence and Avondale in June; his installation at Reading as Pro-Grand Master of Berkshire Freemasonry; and his review of the King's Royal Rifle Corps on the occasion of his being appointed to the honorary colonelcy of the Corps. None of these occasions called for more than the shortest and most formal speech, although there were many occasions in 1890 and 1891 when Eddy made some quite long speeches, notably at a hospital dinner at the Hotel Métropole.]

'We hear little more of him before his death a year or two later. As is usual in general paralysis of the insane, he was kept alive so long only by means of medical skill and unremitting careful nursing—in his father's country house.'

[It was not merely those journals—*The Times, The Illustrated London News, The Graphic*, etc.—friendly to Eddy which reported his activities; one might even suppose a pious fraud to keep the sad truth from the nation; but his enemies, including Labouchere. Besides there is the evidence of the photographs; and as Eddy stands in these family groups he is certainly not suffering from G.P.I.]

Clearly, then, Stowell is *not* talking of Eddy, though Stowell wishes us to think that he *is*.

It is now time to examine the sources of Stowell's story. Unfortunately, there is hardly any other *external* evidence than his own, but it can be shewn, from *internal* evidence, how the story came to Stowell, and what deductions Stowell made from his third-hand 'facts'.

As he says in his *Criminologist* article:

'Many false trails were laid. Some, no doubt, were intended to mislead the police, some to mollify the angry press and public, and some, no doubt, to puff the egoism of the neurotic exhibitionist.

'One of these was that the murderer must be a surgeon to have removed the kidneys and pelvic organs. This is nonsense, for in those days, before the advent of antiseptic and aseptic surgery, the abdomen was almost inaccessible to the surgeon.

'To support this fantasy, it was not unnatural for the rumour mongers to pick on a most illustrious member of my profession of the time—Sir William Gull, Bt., M.D., F.R.C.P., F.R.S.

'He was physician to Guy's Hospital, Physician in Ordinary to Her Majesty, Queen Victoria, to H.R.H. the Prince of Wales, and physician to a large number of the aristocracy and the wealthy, including, if I am right in my deductions, the family of Jack the Ripper. It was said that on more than one occasion Sir William Gull was seen in the neighbourhood on the night of a murder. It would not surprise me to know that he was there for the purpose of certifying the murderer to be insane, so that he might be put under restraint as were other lunatics apprehended in connection with murders.'

Stowell is right in saying that it needed no surgical skill to carry out the excisions. The fable that 'only a person skilled in surgery' could have made the eviscerations was due to a Dr Llewellyn, who gave medical evidence at the inquest on the first 'Ripper' victim, Mary Ann ('Polly') Nicholls.

Not even asked for his opinion on the skill involved in disembowelling 'Polly', Dr Llewellyn volunteered to the Coroner's Court that 'the mutilations of the lower part of the abdomen were extensive' and 'deftly and fairly skilfully performed'. Though the tribute to the Ripper's 'surgical' skill was instantly and quite widely disputed throughout the successive inquests, the original opinion of Dr Llewellyn had established virtually that the Ripper 'had surgical skill (and, almost certainly, therefore, surgical training)'. In fact, a butcher could have done the jobs more neatly, an obvious point which set Robin Odell* speculating that the Ripper might have been a *schochet*, or Jewish ritual slaughterman.

What is particularly hard to understand is Stowell's statement that, 'it was not unnatural for the rumour mongers to pick on . . . Sir William Gull'. On the contrary, one would have thought that to pick on one of the most illustrious medical men

* *Jack the Ripper in Fact and Fiction*, George G. Harrap & Sons, London, 1965.

of his day would have been the most unnatural thing in the world. Yet, perhaps, in this remark, we may have a clue, if not to the identity of the killer, to the fact that somehow the news had leaked out that the killer was Gull's patient.

Gull might well have been seen in the vicinity of Whitechapel, but he was so well known to the police that his presence there could not have brought him under suspicion of being involved in the crimes. He could, though, have been thought to know or suspect the identity of the murderer. We have only Stowell's word that Gull was there, but my own theory makes Stowell's statement at least probable, as both Stowell and I state (though in our different ways), that Sir William Gull was the Ripper's physician.

The weakness of Stowell's account is simply explained, in that he was repeating gossip, and not discussing facts whose evidence he could have examined. The source of his information was Caroline, the daughter of Sir William Gull. For Stowell, as a young medical man, had studied medicine at St Thomas's and Brompton Hospitals under Caroline's husband, Theodore Dyke Acland, son of Sir Henry Wentworth Acland, Bart., one of the most internationally famous medical men of his day and Honorary Physician to the Prince of Wales.

In his article, Stowell relates the following story:

'Fred Archer in his book* tells an interesting story that Lees, the medium† was asked by the police to "use his uncanny gifts to help them". Lees led them to "an impressive mansion in the West End". The house was the home of a fashionable and highly reputable physician.

'The chief inspector accompanying Lees asked if he could speak to the doctor's wife who, Archer said, made some amazing disclosures under questioning. These were to the effect that her husband had exhibited sadistic behaviour and that she had

---

Ghost Detectives, W. H. Allen, London, 1970.

† Robert James Lees, scholar, philanthropist and friend of Gladstone and Disraeli, arranged the *séances* at which the Queen endeavoured—perhaps succeeded?—to communicate with the spirit of her dead husband.

noticed that his absences at night had coincided with the East End murders!'

Stowell continues:

'It interests me to speculate whether the "imposing mansion" to which Lees led the police was 74, Brook Street, Grosvenor Square, the home of Sir William Gull, and whether Mr Archer's story is a variation of one told to me by Sir William Gull's daughter, Caroline . . .

'Mrs Acland's story was that, at the time of the Ripper murders, her mother, Lady Gull, was greatly annoyed one night by an unappointed visit from a police officer, accompanied by a man who called himself a "medium", and she was irritated by their impudence in asking her a number of questions which seemed to her impertinent. She answered their questions with non-committal replies such as "I do not know", "I cannot tell you that", "I am afraid I cannot answer that question".'

This sounds much more probable, than that the wife should voluntarily have accused her husband of being a sadistic night-wanderer, with the strong probability that he was the Ripper! The rest of the episode seems far less likely:

'Later Sir William himself came down, and in answer to the questions, said he occasionally suffered from "lapses of memory" since he had had a slight stroke in 1887; he said that he had once discovered blood on his shirt. This is not surprising, if he had medically examined the Ripper after one of the murders.'

What is impossible is that Sir William Gull, physician to the Queen and to the Prince of Wales and half the 'nobs' of Britain, should have volunteered such information to a casually-calling police-inspector. Possibly the truth behind this story is not that the police were led by Lees to Gull's house in Brook-street, but that Lees came to warn Gull that his lunatic patient, who may well have been at Brook-street at the time, had been followed, and that Gull should prepare himself for a call from the police.

Stowell continues:

'Jack the Ripper was obviously Sir William Gull's patient and Mrs Acland told me that she had seen in her father's diary an entry, "informed Blank that his son was dying of syphilis of the brain". The date of the entry was November, 1889, after "S" had returned from his recuperative voyage. Evidently, towards the end of 1889, "S" had another relapse which caused Sir William Gull to make his sad and gloomy but accurate prognosis. The patient did not recover but passed into the inevitable stage in which he was unaware of place and time; he died little more than a year later.'

We have seen that it cannot have been Eddy who was dying 'of syphilis of the brain'. In November, 1889, he was in India, from which he did not return until the March of 1890; and he died, not 'little more than a year' after November, 1889, but more than two years later. Nor, curiously enough, was it the Ripper himself, as I am about to shew. The identity of 'Blank' whose son was dying of syphilis of the brain, we do not know, but 'his' son was *not* the Ripper, as Stowell seems to think and as he tells us that Mrs Acland believed.

In any case, I am doubtful whether Sir William Gull was, in November, 1889, in a position either to make diagnoses or even to keep a diary. For following his first stroke in 1887, he had a further stroke in the autumn of 1889, which resulted in a paralysis so severe that Sir William had to abandon his practice. His third attack, on 29th January, 1890, whilst Eddy was hunting elephant and other big game in India, caused Sir William's death.

James Kenneth Stephen was Jack the Ripper. He first became a patient of Sir William Gull, a specialist in paraplegia, diseases of the spinal cord and abscess of the brain, following that accidental blow on the head that he suffered in 1886.

The homicidal mania that Stephen later developed had a sexual basis, jealousy, but it is far more likely to have been post-traumatic than caused, as Stowell says, by syphilis.

'The effects of the blow', wrote Sir Leslie Stephen, 'were not perceived for some time'. But it was clear that all the promise of his pre-accident years had gone. Called to the Bar in 1884, and elected a Fellow of his College in 1885, nothing came of the promise which had so impressed his contemporaries. He obtained no briefs, though he kept chambers in Stone Buildings, Lincoln's Inn; he found no employment in Government, as so many other less brilliant members of his Trinity 'court' were to do. J. K. Stephen, in the strange lethargy which had overtaken him as a result of his accident, had not even his own house or flat—not even modest chambers in Jermyn-street or Half-moon-street. He lived with his parents in the family house at 32, De Vere Gardens, Kensington, opposite the Palace Gate of Kensington Gardens, and—a most important fact—only a five minute walk from High Street Kensington station.

I cannot help connecting the breakdown of both J.K.'s father, Sir James Fitzjames Stephen (in 1885), and the stroke that Sir William Gull suffered (in 1887), with the problems posed by the deterioration of J. K. Stephen's mind. That he did not, in the common phrase, 'go completely balmy', is evident from the fact that spurts of ambitious energy alternated with a lethargy which prevented his seeking, or getting, work, or even a place of his own.

Thus in the early part of 1888 he brought out a weekly journal called *The Reflector*, for which he wrote much of the copy. But this sold almost nothing, and, Sir James Stephen being left with the bill, folded within a few weeks.

All the same, as J.K. told his father, the Judge of the Queen's Bench, 'he now wished to dedicate himself entirely to literature.' The practical Sir James, who by now had recovered from the first instalment of his own illness, promptly appointed J.K. to the Clerkship of Assize on the South Wales Circuit. This was in

1888. In the following year, J.K.'s elder brother, Herbert, was to be appointed Clerk of Assize to the Northern Circuit, but with a record far different from that J.K. was to leave behind him.

It seems plain that, with all his growing oddity, J.K. had not, so far, shewn any signs of the more dangerous mental aberrations. I cannot believe that Sir James Fitzjames Stephen, successively Recorder of Newark-upon-Trent, Legal Member of the Council of the Governor-general of India, Professor of Common Law at the Inns of Court, and a Judge of the High Court of Justice since 1879, would appoint to any official position, far less one within the Justiciary, a son whose character might lead to scandal.

Even the cautious Memoir with which his elder brother introduces the 1898 edition of *Lapsus Calami and Other Verses* makes it plain that James Stephen treated his appointment on the South Wales Circuit as a sinecure, leaving the Deputy Clerk of Assize to do all the work.

'James,' wrote Sir Herbert Stephen, Bart, 'had for the time abandoned all professional work, but in the summer of 1888 his father appointed him Clerk of Assize for the South Wales Circuit, in the hope that in the intervals between circuits, when the official work of that post is comparatively light, he would be able either to resume his contributions to newspapers, or to acquire some practice at the bar. Of this, however, his health did not at any time permit. After vicissitudes of illness, and one period of leave of absence from his official duties which did, in fact, mean that he spent no time at all as Clerk, he resigned his Clerkship of Assize in 1890.'

When the records of the Circuit are examined, it will be seen that the few occasions on which Stephen was at his post were occasions whose dates fall between Ripper murders; and, in any case, he did not take up his Clerkship until the end of 1888. It is noteworthy that only one murder occurred in 1889, and none in 1890. Most of his time, when he was not under restraint (in 1890), Stephen spent at Cambridge.

The High Court Judge was soon to learn, with the frightful

episode which affected every member of it then alive, what an appalling mistake had been made. The discovery that J.K. was the Ripper so broke up Leslie that he himself collapsed in 1889, and even had to give up the editorship of *The Dictionary of National Biography* in 1891; Sir James conducted the trial of Mrs Maybrick, in 1889, with such incompetence that the Liverpool crowds hissed and booed him behind his strong police escort, and the Home Secretary had to commute Mrs Maybrick's death sentence to one of life-imprisonment.

The summing-up had been so biassed; the directions to the jury so irrelevant to the facts; that the trial Judge was bitterly criticized in the fullest detail afterwards by Sir Charles Russell, not only in that eminent advocate's capacity as defence counsel for Mrs Maybrick, but even after Sir Charles had become Lord Chief Justice of England, and Lord Russell of Killowen.

Only the wilful determination to protect 'the good name' of the Judicature prevented successive Home Secretaries from heeding Sir Charles's warmly argued condemnation of Sir James Fitzjames Stephen's many misdirections to the jury. That Mrs Maybrick, patently innocent of having caused her husband's death by the criminal administration of arsenic, was forced to serve the full term of her life-imprisonment (with the usual remission for good conduct) is yet another crime which must be fairly charged to the mental instability of the Stephens in general and of J. K. Stephen in particular.

On the death of Lord Russell of Killowen in 1900, the scandal of the Maybrick trial, against which the former Sir Charles Russell had never ceased to protest, was revived as a subject of outspoken comment by the newspapers, especially in view of Russell's recorded statement that 'if I was called upon to advise in my character as head of the Criminal Judicature of this country, I should advise you* that Florence Maybrick ought to be allowed to go free'.

Of the patent incapacity of Mr Justice Stephen to try Mrs Maybrick or anyone else, the Liverpool *Daily Post* had no doubts. In its issue of 13th August, 1900, it had this to say of

* I.e. the Home Secretary.

Stephen—without comment or contradiction from any other member of the ambitious Stephen family:

'In fancy one still hears the distant fanfare of the trumpets as the judges with quaint pageantry passed down the hall, and still with the mind's eye sees the stately crimson-clad figure of *the great mad judge** as he sat down to try his last case. A tragedy, indeed, was played upon the bench no less than in the dock.

'Few who looked upon the strong, square head can have suspected that the light of reason was burning very low within; yet as the days of the trial dragged by—days that must have been as terrible to the judge as to the prisoner—men began to nod at him, to wonder, and to whisper. Nothing more painful was ever seen in court than the proud old man's desperate struggle to control his failing faculties. But the struggle was un-availing. It was clear that the growing volume of facts was unassorted, undigested in his mind; that his judgment swayed backward and forward in the conflict of testimony; that his memory failed to grip the most salient features of the case for many minutes together. It was shocking to think that a human life depended upon the direction of this wreck of what was once a great judge.'

Let us pass over the fact that, despite this harsh but just condemnation of a trial judge—for which the Editor and proprietors of *The Post* were never prosecuted—Mrs Maybrick was to remain in prison for another four years, and that, since 1889, successive Home Secretaries of both political parties had maintained the verdict imposed on the fat-headed jury† by 'the mad judge'.

With politicians and 'established' civil servants, 'face' always took precedence over justice.

But it is important to notice the dates: they will give us a clue

* My italics.

† The jury was composed of three plumbers, two farmers, one milliner, one wood-turner, one provision-dealer, one grocer, one ironmonger, one house-painter and one baker. And this was a jury asked to find on evidence that only professional toxicologists might have comprehended!

to the 'triggering' of that so obvious madness of Mr Justice Stephen's. Of course, he was already stricken with the Stephen hereditary insanity; but what had brought on the climax too painfully evident at the trial of Mrs Maybrick?

The trial of Mrs Maybrick opened at St George's Hall, Liverpool, on 31st July, 1889. Exactly a fortnight earlier, on the night of 16th/17th July, Alice McKenzie had been brutally killed by Mr Justice Stephen's homicidal maniac son. It is not hard to understand how the judge came so scandalously to mishandle the case; it was Mrs Maybrick's misfortune, not only to have incurred the enmity of the Maybrick family and their servants—who all conspired, consciously or subconsciously, to accuse her of the murder—but also to be tried by a judge desperately grasping on to a disappearing sanity, his mind lost to him in the horror of contemplating what his own son was and had done.

Leslie Stephen, in his memoir, tactfully covers the period after J.K.'s committal to an asylum for his two years' 'cure': '[J. K. Stephen] gave up his place and resolved in October, 1890, to settle at Cambridge.' And it did seem as though Gull had cured him. 'He gave lectures, spoke at the Union, and was much beloved by his companions. In 1891, he wrote an able pamphlet, *Living Languages*, in defence of the compulsory study of Greek at the universities.'

'In the same year he published two little volumes of verse, *Lapsus Calami* and *Quo Musa Tendis*, chiefly collections of previous essays [i.e. poems]. The first went into two editions, and both were republished as *Lapsus Calami and Other Verses*, with a life by his brother Herbert, and one or two additions in 1896.

'In 1891, his disease suddenly took a dangerous form, and he died 3rd February, 1892.'

'He was buried at Kensal Green, where his parents and grandparents, Sir James and Lady Stephen, are also buried. A brass has been placed in King's College Chapel to his memory, and also in the chapel at Eton.'

I realized, when I read Dr Stowell's article in *The Criminologist*, that far too much hearsay had gone into the story, and that

Stowell, though he would have liked to name an Heir to the Throne as the Ripper, was not quite sure who the Ripper was. The inconsistencies were apparent even to Stowell.

However, I was struck by one curious fact: if Stowell was hinting that Eddy was the Ripper, why did he say: 'Now for my suspect. I prefer not to name him, but to call him "S".' Why 'S'?

Now in all deformations or perversions of an original truth, something of the original remains. It is this truism that, in embellishing a tale, the human mind clings on to one *fact*, which has enabled folklorists to retrieve, from the most fanciful of legends, that underlying truth that we call 'historical fact'. So with this choice of 'S'.

But let us return to Stowell for a moment. He writes that 'Jack the Ripper was obviously Sir William Gull's patient, and Mrs Acland told me that she had seen in her father's diary an entry, "informed Blank that his son was dying of syphilis of the brain".'

Would such an entry have been made in the diary of *any* physician in the year 1889? For it was not until 1913 that Hideyo Noguchi demonstrated that paresis is produced by the surviving spirochetes of syphilis.

As Howard Haggard explains in his *Devils, Drugs & Doctors*,* 'Prior to the demonstration that paresis was a form of syphilis, the connection between the two diseases was suspected; but since paresis could not be influenced by treatment with mercury or salvarsan, it was assumed that the insanity was in some way the result of syphilis, but not a manifestation of active syphilis. Noguchi, however, demonstrated the living spirochetes in the brain of paretics and thus shewed that the functional and anatomical changes in the brain, manifest as paresis, are directly due to their presence or action. He likewise demonstrated that locomotor ataxia is due to the action of spirochetes in the spinal cord. The only difference between this disease and paresis is the part of the nervous system that the spirochetes attack: in the one case the spinal cord, in the other the cerebrum.'

* New York: Harper & Brothers, 1929.

But let us take this suspicion of the Gull diary entry a step further. It was not until 1905, fifteen years after Sir William Gull's death, that Schaudinn and Hoffmann, working at the University of Berlin, saw, for the first time in human history, the organism of syphilis. If that entry was in Gull's diary, then Gull must have been possessed of prevision which enabled him to anticipate these later findings.

The fact is—the fact *must* be—that Mrs Acland, not herself a doctor, but merely connected with doctors, was 'remembering' for Dr Stowell in the light of knowledge acquired long after the death of her distinguished father in 1890. What she had seen was that initial 'S', but not the entire name, for then Stowell could not have hinted that Eddy was the Ripper. This 'S', in fact, was a constant in an otherwise developing story.

Taking my investigation in an orderly a manner as possible, I wrote down the qualifications or characteristics that 'S' was required to have:

a. 'S' must have been contemporary with Eddy, or at least near enough in age to have given the rumour-mongers an excuse for confusing 'S' with Eddy.

b. 'S' must have been close enough to Eddy in some important particular, again to excuse his being confused with Eddy.

c. 'S', quite apart from being intimately connected with Eddy or Eddy's family, must have been important in himself, to provide powerful motives for hushing up his crimes.

d. If, however, 'S' were not so important that the revelation of his crime(s) could threaten the social order, then perhaps his family or some other member of his family, might be of great importance in the State.

e. Assuming that 'S' was the Ripper, then an analysis of the Ripper's mentality, as revealed not merely by the murders, but by the vast exhibitionistic literature originating from this maniac, should help to disclose his identity.

f. Some link appeared to have been established between the Government in general and the Ripper, as a 'poem' of the Ripper's appears to contain an allusion to a letter that Queen

Victoria wrote to the Home Secretary. This could only have happened if the Ripper was either highly placed socially, or his family were in a position to discuss the Queen's letter.

Now, the only 'S' who fitted *all* these requirements was an 'S' who had been intimate with Eddy since the summer of 1883: Jim Stephen. It is clear also that, homosexual or not, an intimacy, jealously possessive on Stephen's side, and lazily tolerant on Eddy's, sprang up between these two in those 'golden weeks' whilst Stephen was endeavouring to fit Eddy for entrance to Trinity. Homosexual or not, this intimacy had an element in it perhaps even stronger than sexual attraction. The Stephens were all greatly ambitious, and, at Sandringham and Cambridge, Stephen persuaded himself to believe that he had 'captured' Eddy for himself. Eddy, as soon as he had left Cambridge for the Army, quite evidently made no serious efforts to sustain the emotional link with Jim Stephen. If Stephen had not received that accidental blow on the head in 1886, just as he was beginning the outstanding career that all prophesied for him, he would have accepted Eddy's 'ungrateful' falling away with no more than sulks, or at the worst, bitter reproaches. As it was, under the influences of his post-traumatic mania, his 'revenge' took a horribly worse form.

Obviously, to support this theory that the 'S' of Stowell's tale was Stephen, more convincing evidence is required. But the destruction of private papers means that the amount of *external* evidence must be small, even if available. What, then, of the *internal* evidence?

In *The Criminologist* of August 1968, Mr C. M. MacLeod published an article of great interest, 'Ripper Handwriting Analysis', in which the author argues that it is entirely possible to discern from handwriting the writer's attitudes towards sex and sexual violence. He went on to say that the two specimens of the Ripper's handwriting revealed a 'propensity to cruelly perverted sexuality to a degree that even the most casual amateur graphologist could hardly mistake'.

Without arguing the merits of the graphologist's science, I feel that, given the handwriting of one known to be a sadistical murderer, it would not be difficult to discern those characteristics of handwriting which indicate the homicidal maniac. Besides, with what was Mr MacLeod comparing his written texts?

Assuming that the 'S' of Stowell's tale was J. K. Stephen, we can make a much more practical analysis of the Ripper's handwriting, by comparing the known Ripper letters with the handwriting of J. K. Stephen.

Obviously, the Ripper took pains to alter the normal character of his handwriting, but there are some characteristics of Stephen's which plainly reproduce themselves in the Ripper letters. The most striking of these common features between the handwriting of the Ripper and that of J. K. Stephen is the letter 'K', and the reader is recommended to study the compared examples—see plates 15 and 17.

But there is another link between the Ripper and J. K. Stephen which has never been examined and given its due importance for the good reason that, until now, Stephen has never been identified as the Ripper.

The Ripper was a poet, although, as with his handwriting, he falsified his poetic skill to conceal his real identity. But there are tricks of versification which are so natural to a poet that he is unaware of them, and so reappear no matter how fundamentally he thinks that he is changing his style.

Now Stephen wrote two volumes of verse, *Quo Musa Tendis* and *Lapsus Calami*, which appeared in 1891, after the 'cure' which had freed him from the insane asylum.

There are two links which connect the verse of Stephen with that of the Ripper, a link of style, which will be examined first, and a link of sentiment. To make the linkage *clearer*, the passages are set side by side, and the relevant words italicized.

STEPHEN	THE RIPPER
But, Frank, I do assure you,	*Up and down the goddam town*
Whatever other little game	Policemen try to find me

STEPHEN	THE RIPPER
I chance to play from day to day—	But I ain't a chap yet to drown
(I hope I do not bore you?	In drink, or Thames or sea.
I'm aiming at a certain chat	
I had with you, and therefore	
You must attend, my worthy	
friend)—	
Will not effect the least neglect	
Of what I really care for.	

The Ripper verse contains, as McCormick comments, a reference to a newspaper's suggestion that the Ripper had committed suicide by jumping in the Thames. Note that unconscious trick of the 'internal rhyme': 'You must *attend*, my worthy *friend*/Will not *effect* the least *neglect*' (Stephen). Compare it with the Ripper's 'Up and *down* the goddam *town*', and the following lines from Stephen:

The work goes *on* till life be *gone*

I chance to *play* from day to *day*

. . . they bought The *Times*; a list of *crimes* . . .

Apart from similarities of style, there is much in the mentalities of both Stephen and the Ripper which seems to produce similar sentiments. Take a stanza of Stephen's for instance, remembering that it was written, not necessarily in 1890 but possibly even before the murders of 1888.

With the curious title, *The Malefactor's Plea*, it is a fairly long poem, of which the last stanza seems to echo something far more significant to Stephen than to the reader:

> When inoffensive people plant
> A dagger in your breast,
> Your good is what they really want:
> They do it for the best.

This is really extraordinary, for here is Stephen identifying himself both as victim, almost certainly of a 'tragic' love affair, and as the brutal 'executioner' of 'the harlots of Jerusalem'.

All these poems are in a secret language, full of allusions to what the author thinks will never be discovered. The following is an example.

A Paradox?

To F.C.H.

(*A Conversation Recapitulated*)

> To find out what you cannot do,
> And then go out and do it:
> There lies the golden rule: but few
> I ever found above the ground,
> Except myself, who knew it.
>
> You bid me do from day to day,
> The single thing I can do;
> I can't do what I can't, you say?
> Indeed I can; why, hang it, man!
> I solve it *ambulando*.

'Ambulando', in Latin, means 'in walking', or 'whilst walking', a gruesomely precise description of what the Ripper did on those grisly nights of murder.

> The small pursuits you undertake
> For innocent diversion,
> No earthly difference will make;
> The work goes on till life be gone;
> I stand by that assertion!
>
> Although a modest man, my friend,
> I'll make you this confession:
> I feel that I have got an 'End'—
> A *telos*,* eh? as you would say—
> My *métier*, my profession.

* Greek for 'end', or 'aim'.

Which is ——: well, never mind the name;
　But, Frank, I do assure you,
Whatever other little game
I chance to play from day to day—
　(I hope I do not bore you?

　　I'm aiming at a certain chat
　　I had with you, and therefore
You *must* attend, my worthy friend)—
Will not effect the least neglect
　Of what I really care for.

Pausing only to observe that there are no fewer than six 'internal' rhymes in the above quotation, we must note the paranoia and what seems to be the boasting confession of a secret life and secret 'duty' in these otherwise negligible verses.

So much for the link between the poetic style of J. K. Stephen and that of the Ripper. The link between their respective sentiments is even more striking.

That Stephen hated women is a fact that he made no attempt to conceal, and this hatred is so irrational that it would be impossible to believe that anyone could nurture it without some tremendous damage to his reason. In the very month in which Frances Coles was offered up as 'the final sacrifice'— 13th February, 1891—Stephen contributed this 'justification' to *Granta*:

A THOUGHT

If all the harm that women have done
Were put in a bundle and rolled into one,
　Earth would not hold it,
　The sky could not enfold it,
It could not be lighted nor warmed by the sun;
　Such masses of evil
　Would puzzle the devil
And keep him in fuel while Time's wheels run.

But if all the harm that's been done by men
Were doubled and doubled and doubled again,
And melted and fused into vapour and then
Were squared and raised to the power of ten,
There wouldn't be nearly enough, not near,
To keep a small girl for the tenth of a year.

Pausing only to note the recurrence of the 'ten' theme—
'the power of ten', 'the tenth of a year'—a theme which occurs
most frightfully in the Ripper killings, let us consider the
sentiments that this ungoverned and ungovernable detestation
of women could inspire—and inspire to the point that Stephen
makes no bones about exposing his detestation to the world.
Again it is significant that this second 'poem' appeared in
The Cambridge Review in the month in which Frances Coles was
killed—February, 1891.

IN THE BACKS

As I was strolling lonely in the Backs,
I met a woman whom I did not like.
I did not like the way the woman walked:
Loose-hipped, big-boned, disjointed, angular.
If her anatomy comprised a waist,
I did not notice it: she had a face
With eyes and lips adjusted thereunto,
But round her mouth no pleasing shadows stirred,
Nor did her eyes invite a second glance.
Her dress was absolutely colourless,
Devoid of taste or shape or character;
Her boots were rather old, and rather large,
And rather shabby, not precisely matched.
Her hair was very far from beautiful
And not abundant: she had such a hat
As neither merits nor expects remark,
She was not clever, I am very sure,
Nor witty nor amusing: well-informed
She may have been, and kind, perhaps, of heart;

But gossip was writ plain upon her face.
And so she stalked her dull unthinking way;
Or, if she thought of anything, it was
That such a one had got a second class,*
Or Mrs So-and-So a second child.
I do not want to see that girl again:
I did not like her: and I should not mind
If she were done away with, killed, or ploughed.
She did not seem to serve a useful end:
And certainly she was not beautiful.

Why the editor of *The Cambridge Review* should have accepted and printed this perfectly appalling poem it is hard to say. Its lunatic bias against women is so evident and so significant that the incidental snobbery of the writer—'Her boots were rather old, and rather large,/And rather shabby, not precisely matched/'—may be overlooked. The Stephens were desperately active parvenus, and in such one expects this rather laboured and exhibitionistic snobbery.

But what must be noticed is that, because she 'did not seem to serve a useful end', this woman, in J. K. Stephen's opinion, deserved to be 'done away with, killed, or ploughed†'. No plainer revelation of Stephen's murderous values could ever have been made public.

In the business of avenging wrongs done against him, Stephen was, as he must have thought, 'fair'. Even some small slight put upon him called for plenary punishment, and in the 'justice' of punishment, Stephen made no distinction between man or woman as the offender.

* Apart from its hatred of women in general, this poem reveals a strong personal antipathy towards a doubtless real woman. Though Stephen was in the First Class of the Historical Tripos, he got only a Second in the Law Tripos—a bitter disappointment, not only to the ambitious barrister-to-be, but also to his father, the judge of the Queen's Bench.

† 'Ploughed', here can have only the meaning 'subjected to sexual intercourse'. It is interesting, in view of the fact that the Ripper's victims had not (in the police and newspaper definition of the idea) been 'sexually assaulted', that Stephen, in this poem of hate, considers 'ploughing' a fate worse than death.

For instance, on 4th July, 1882, he was in a railway carriage at Malines, in Belgium. A fellow-passenger, a Belgian, in leaving the carriage, trod on Stephen's toes. This is an experience that most of us have had to endure, with more or less of patience. But, even though the shoes be completely ruined, it is not an experience which haunts us down the nights and down the days.

But listen to how Stephen records the happening:

4th July, 1882. MALINES. MIDNIGHT.

Belgian, with cumbrous tread and iron boots,
Who in the murky middle of the night,
Designing to renew the foul pursuits
In which thy life is passed, ill-favoured wight,
And wishing on the platform to alight
Where thou couldst mingle with thy fellow brutes,
Didst walk the carriage floor (a leprous sight),
As o'er the sky some baleful meteor shoots:
Upon my slippered foot thou didst descend,
Didst rouse me from my slumbers mad with pain,
And laughedst loud for several minutes' space.
Oh may'st thou suffer tortures without end:
May fiends with glowing pincers rend thy brain,
And beetles batten on thy blackened face!

The italics, in both poems, are mine. I find the 'poem' on the incident at Malines even more frightening than that on the hated woman; the former is more exact in its sadistical day-dreaming. And it is clear, from the date of this 'poem', that the 'accidental blow on the head' at the end of 1886 merely accelerated Stephen's progression towards that destructive madness which is already apparent in the Malines 'poem'. He must have been an actor of consummate skill to have impressed himself on the Prince and Princess of Wales as a serious, 'nice' young man.

And now we come back to something I mentioned earlier, Stephen's curious and so far inexplicable heading of an apparently innocent poem, 'Air: *Kaphoozelum*'.

Even by today's 'permissive' standards, *Kaphoozelum* was a dirty ballad, only proper to be sung at beery after-rugger sessions. No matter what the poem that this strange request headed, Stephen had *Kaphoozelum* in mind when he wrote it, and *Kaphoozelum* is about 'the Harlot of Jerusalem', a term which, without straining meaning, might well apply to any East End whore of the 1880s.

'I'm down on whores', wrote Jack the Ripper—and proceeded to demonstrate his objection in his own horrible manner. A man who had *Kaphoozelum* so much in mind that he set one of his Cambridge-published poems to its tune, must certainly have brooded on whores.

> In days of old there lived a maid;
> She was the mistress of her trade;
> A prostitute of high repute—
> The Harlot of Jerusalem.

> Hi ho, Kaphoozelum,
> Kaphoozelum, Kaphoozelum,
> Hi ho, Kaphoozelum,
> Harlot of Jerusalem!

There is no need to quote the twenty-four stanzas of this crude ballad, but the 'plot' is significant.

After Kaphoozelum is introduced, the next to appear is the Student, who lived in a hovel by the wall.

> One, night, returning from a spree,
> With customary whore-lust he
> Made up his mind to call and see
> The Harlot of Jerusalem.

The next stanza is immensely significant.

> It was for her no fortune good,
> That he should need to root his pud,
> And chose her out of all the brood
> Of Harlots of Jerusalem.

This is a sentiment which must have been echoed in their dying rattles by 'Polly' Nicholls, Annie Chapman, Elizabeth Stride, Katherine Eddowes and Mary Ann Kelly, in the autumn of 1888!

But the next stanza deserves our deepest attention:

> For though he paid his women well,
> This syphilitic spawn of hell,
> Struck down each year and tolled the bell
> For ten harlots of Jerusalem.

If the poem refers to 'ten harlots', why, then, does Jack the Ripper, in one of his thirty-four attested letters, talk of '*eight little whores*'?

> Eight little whores, with no hope of heaven,
> Gladstone may save one, then there'll be seven.
> Seven little whores, begging for a shilling
> One stays in Henage Court [*sic*], then there's a
> killing.

> Six little whores, glad to be alive,
> One sidles up to Jack, then there are five.
> Four and whore rhyme aright.
> So do three and me,
> I'll set the town alight,
> Ere there are two.

> Two little whores, shivering with fright,
> Seek a cosy doorway in the middle of the night.
> Jack's knife flashes, then there's but one,
> And the last one's the ripest for Jack's idea
> of fun.

Now there were two murders of women earlier in 1888 that most Ripper 'experts' deny as forming part of the Ripper series. Yet if we add these two murders to the five that all are agreed that the Ripper committed, and the three which came after, the last in 1891, thought by some to be Ripper murders, we do arrive at the figure of ten. Ronald Pearsall, in his *The Worm in the Bud*, states definitely that 'there were eight murders by Jack the Ripper in 1888 . . . 'the first murder was in April, but it did not receive wide publicity'.* This would make Jack's 'Eight little whores, with no hope of heaven' fit beautifully. But I feel that, however many may be attributed to the Ripper, the murders were initially planned to be ten, because that is the number of harlots that 'the syphilitic spawn of hell' struck down.

Another point is that the reference to Heneage Court implies knowledge which can have come to the Ripper only through an association with officialdom. For it was the whore in Heneage Court who was *not* murdered. Perhaps Rosy was not the only woman to escape, but she is the only woman, identified and named in the record, who went free—thanks to P. C. Spicer.

Spicer was on duty in Whitechapel on the night of 29/30th September. Like all the other police officers in the district, he had been specially warned to keep a lookout for the Ripper. On this night he decided to patrol his beat in a direction opposite to that of his usual walk, and at some time after 2 a.m. he walked down Brick Lane, entered Heneage Street and continued down a narrow alley known as Heneage Court. At the bottom of the alley was a small court in which was a brick dustbin.

The constable's bull's-eye lantern, flashing here and there, came to rest upon two pairs of legs, belonging to a couple seated on the dustbin. The woman, Rosy, was well known to P.C. Spicer as a common prostitute, but the man was an unknown. Yet he had blood on his cuffs, and carried the black bag which had already appeared in various 'witness' stories. As Rosy had two shillings in her hand, Spicer took both man and woman into custody. The man, however, was identified as 'a respectable doctor', and released.

* *The Annual Register* for 1891 notes of Coles's murder, on 13th February, 1891: 'Another murder, in many respects resembling those attributed to "Jack the Ripper," in a narrow thoroughfare running under a railway arch . . .' There was no doubt in contemporary minds that the series of murders began in early 1888 and continued until the murder of Coles in February 1891.

The last point to notice is perhaps the most sinister of all.

> Jack's knife flashes, then there's but one,
> And the last one's the ripest for Jack's idea of fun.

In the murder of Mary Ann Kelly, the Ripper excelled even his most bestial of preceding brutalities. So it is true that the last one of 1888 was certainly 'the ripest for Jack's idea of fun'.

This murder has been commented upon by many writers as being connected with the Lord Mayor's Show, traditionally held on 9th November. Kelly was killed and mutilated in the early hours of the night of 8/9th November, 1888, and some writers have even suggested that the Ripper, with his 'maniac's cunning', chose this date because the police were occupied with preparations for the show.

I suggest that the date of Kelly's horrible death was chosen by the Ripper for a very different reason: it was to be a 'birthday present' for the Prince of Wales, father of that Eddy whose 'jilting' of Stephen had finally turned a brain already ripe for post-traumatic mania.

A Ripper letter to Mr Lusk—prominent member of the Whitechapel anti-Ripper Vigilants—contains something of importance which has not been detected by the numerous writers who have aired their theories on Jack the Ripper.

'Say Boss, you seem rare frightened. Guess I like to give you fits, but can't stop long enough to let you *box of toys* play copper games with me, but hope to see you when I don't hurry too much. Goodbye, Boss.' [My italics.]

'Box of toys' is 1888 rhyming slang for 'boys'—today it's 'jumpfers', i.e. 'jump for joys'. As has been shewn earlier, such rhyming slang was very fashionable among the 'toffs'. Whether Stephen developed this use of rhyming slang at Cambridge or picked it up in the various 'East End Settlements', he certainly knew his way about the oddities of Cockney rhyming slang.

And that brings up the most important question: why should so much effort have been put into covering up Stephen's guilt? A maniac is not responsible for his actions, vile though they be, and there can be few families in this world in which *some* insanity has not made its disagreeable and inconvenient appearance. But there were important reasons why the Ripper's identity had to be suppressed:

1. He had been the tutor and was known to be a close friend of Prince Albert Victor, next-but-one in line for the Throne.
2. He was the second son of one of Britain's most famous judges, Sir James Fitzjames Stephen.
3. Though Stowell intended the words to convey a different meaning, he was right when he said that 'his suspect's' family 'for 50 years had earned the love and admiration of large numbers of people by its devotion to public service to all classes, particularly the poor, but as well to industry and the workers'. This is a true account of the Stephen family.

One would imagine what might have happened to the Crown and the Justiciary had a Stephen been shewn to be the Ripper.

We shall probably never know whether the murder of Frances Coles, on the night of 13th February, 1891, under the railway arch between Royal Mint Street and Chamber Street, was a Ripper killing. There was no extensive mutilation, the woman's throat having simply been cut, literally, from ear to ear. But against the theory that it was *not* a Ripper crime was the significant attempt at mutilation—an attempt which failed, presumably, only because the murderer was prevented from finishing his grisly task by the arrival on the scene of P.C. Thompson.

Frances Coles was found dying by P.C. Thompson, of H Division, with her throat cut, her clothing, in the delicate phraseology of the police, 'disarranged', and mutilations of what the same delicacy calls 'the lower part of the body'.

Within minutes, long before the police ambulance had arrived, a crowd was assembled about the bloody corpse of Frances Coles, or 'Carrotty Nell', as she was known 'in the trade'. Like all the other known or suspected Ripper victims, she was a prostitute on the night-prowling, lower-income bracket.

The fact that she was still alive meant that the murderous assault on her can have been made only minutes before the constable, flashing his bull's-eye lantern into the darkness of the railway arch, found the dying woman. But no-one had been seen by anyone leaving the scene of the crime. The very absence of a suspect made all think of the Ripper, that mysterious character who came and went between police patrols.

However, though there was no-one about, this time the police found a suspect, and this time he was charged with wilful murder. His name was Thomas Sadler, and he was ship's fireman on the S.S. *Fez*, then lying in St Katherine's Docks.

How Sadler was found was easy. Lying in the gutter by Coles's body was a new hat. The shopkeeper who had sold it was quickly traced, and he told how Coles, short of the money to buy it, had gone out into the street, and there 'borrowed' the necessary money from a man 'hanging about outside'.

The police had a description from the shopkeeper, and they also had a much more significant description from the keeper of a lodging-house in White's Row. A man, bleeding badly, because, he said, he had been knocked down and robbed by some roughs, had called at the lodging-house, stayed half-an-hour with Coles, and was heard to leave at about 1 a.m. After about half-an-hour, Coles went out, and was next seen dying by Constables Thompson and Leeson.

The police followed the trail of the man to the London Hospital, where they found that Coles's 'friend' had called at the Out-Patient's Department, complaining of an injury to his rib. However, the doctor on night-duty could find nothing wrong with the man beyond a cut over his eye, which was quickly treated. All the same, the doctor remembered that the man's clothing had been saturated in blood. Sadler was traced and arrested, and charged with the wilful murder of Frances Coles.

Poor Sadler, who protested his innocence, was pre-judged by the British press with a vigour and finality worthy of the finest traditions of French journalism. But though denied legal aid, Sadler managed to get a letter off to the secretary of his trades-union, complaining how ill the police had treated him.

The publicity proved Sadler's salvation, much as its irresponsible libelling angered him. For along came Mr Harry Wilson, a solicitor, to defend and, eventually, to clear him. McCormick says that Wilson was instructed by the Secretary of the Stokers' Union, but the fact that Wilson, the solicitor, was a cousin of Harry Wilson, the barrister-friend of Eddy's, is a remarkable coincidence. The police, by means of the old forensic trick of asking for remand after remand in the hope of finding the clinching evidence against Sadler, fought hard to secure a conviction. But Wilson's defence of Sadler at Bow Street was so convincing that the police abandoned the case.

It was the widespread rumour that Sadler was the Ripper which was the principal argument that Wilson used in saving his client. He proved that in every previous Ripper murder Sadler had been at sea. So anxious had the police been to find a Ripper that they had overloaded the case against Sadler.

Had he been accused of anything but that of being the Ripper, I doubt that the Establishment, in the person of Harry Wilson, would have exerted its power to save him, and so prevent the further spread of interest in the Ripper.

For a Wilson comes again into the story, though his true identity seems to have escaped the otherwise observant McCormick. The passage that I shall now quote from his *The Identity of Jack the Ripper* refers to the last *known* Ripper murder, that of Mary Kelly.

Kelly was buried in the Roman Catholic cemetery at Leytonstone after a service at Shoreditch church . . . A Shoreditch clerk, Mr Henry Wilson, offered to pay the cost of the interment, though there was no indication that he knew Kelly or was any relative of hers.

This 'clerk' was, in fact, a clerk in Holy Orders, the Reverend Harry (not Henry) Wilson, M.A., vicar of St Augustine, Stepney. A Cambridge man, he was uncle to both Henry Francis Wilson, the friend of Eddy, and Harry Wilson, the solicitor. Once again a Wilson, on behalf of that mad Ripper whose identity all the Wilsons seem to have known, stepped in to do what small thing he could to make amends for crimes that they could have done nothing to prevent and that, in all justice, they could not seek to punish.

A conviction for murder demands that the prosecution must shew that the accused had motive, means and opportunity. It would not have been difficult to demonstrate that the Ripper had the Means (a knife and adequate physical strength) and the Opportunity (the desperate need for money of the victims, and the physical circumstances which made a sudden murderous assault possible). But what could have been Stephen's motive?

If we return to that bawdy poem, *Kaphoozelum*, we may find a clue.

The reader will recall that

> . . . though he paid his women well,
> This syphilitic spawn of hell
> Struck down each year and tolled the bell
> For ten harlots of Jerusalem.

The 'poem' continues with the account of a rape:

> He leaned the whore against the slum,
> And tied her at the knee and bum.

It is true that there was no tying, no rape as such, of any of the Ripper victims, but, instead of rape with the *mentulum*, here was that more terrible thing, rape with the knife. And, as

179

Colin Wilson points out, there was a 'symbolic' tying of the body (though this excellent writer merely gives the facts, and does not express, save by implication, the idea inherent in this term):

'The killer,' says Wilson, 'was apparently not interested in [Mary Nicholls's] genitals. In most rape cases, the victim is left with her legs spread apart; Mary Nicholls's killer *placed hers tightly together, and pulled down her skirt . . .*' [My italics.]

Here is the analogue of that action performed by that 'syphilitic spawn of hell' in *Kaphoozelum*: the Ripper did not 'tie her at the knee and bum', but he composed the terribly mutilated body *as though it were so tied*.

Now in *Kaphoozelum*, as the student and the current Harlot of Jerusalem were fornicating, they were espied by an Onanite, whose generic name sufficiently explains his tastes. The latter objected to what he saw:

> So when he saw the grunting pair,
> With roars of rage he rent the air,
> And vowed that he would soon take care
> Of the Harlot of Jerusalem.

In the poem, the Onanite is worsted, in a manner which recalls one of the more earthy episodes in *The Miller's Tale*, and it concludes with what could be called a 'happy ending':

> As for the student and his lass,
> Many a playful night they'd pass,
> Until she joined the V.D.* class,
> For harlots in Jerusalem.

---

* There may be an 'in' pun here, since 'V.D.' stands for 'venereal disease' and 'Volunteer Detachment' and 'Volunteer Decoration'. Not only Eddy and J.K., but all the other members of the Stephen 'court', were members of the Cambridge Rifle Volunteer Corps (or Detachment).

This is pure hypothesis, but let us suppose that this is the sequence of what happened:

1. J.K. ('Jim'—'James'—'Jacques'—'Jack') is in love with Eddy, in a dominant fashion.
2. Events—*and* Eddy—enable the Prince to wriggle free of this dominant, demanding love.
3. Not in the army, Stephen cannot reassert his old dominance, and though he writes to Eddy regularly, Eddy 'brushes off' 'dear old Jim' as competently as he does 'dear old Harry'.
4. Frequenting, in all certainty, the same homosexual meeting-places in London and elsewhere (e.g. *The Crown* public-house in Charing Cross Road) used by Eddy and his less normal friends, Stephen's jealousy is roused to dangerous heights.
5. Either an accident (the family story) or syphilis (Stowell's story) or merely the hereditary 'taint' affects Stephen's brain, and insanity develops either paranoia or paresis.
6. The trauma of detecting Eddy with a woman may have been an actual experience or a symbolic one; the 'harlot' may have been a real harlot or she may have been a woman who stepped in between Eddy and Stephen: in all probability, the Princess of Wales. (The removal of the uterus from the slain woman is symbolical of an attack on women, not as whores or even as females, but as *mothers*.)
7. The 'trigger-word' which may have set Stephen's mind on eviscerating women (Harlots of Jerusalem—i.e. predominantly Jewish Whitechapel) was the ancient trade-self-introduction of the harlot: 'Coming with me, *dear*?' (or variants on that invitation—though always with the accent on the 'dear'). As Stephen in his Jack the Ripper aspect wrote: 'Four and whore rhyme aright/So do three and me/'—just so do 'dear' and 'deer'—and how many times had dominant Jim seen a *deer* gralloched, in the days when Eddy, completely under Jim's control, had invited him to those stag- and deer-stalkings about which Labouchere, in

Truth, was always complaining. This may sound somewhat far-fetched, but psychiatric studies have demonstrated even more implausible facts.

8. To avoid scandal, for the reasons given above, no charge was brought against Stephen, and 'the mental home in the Home Counties' that Stowell mentions can have been used only when Stephen shewed signs of violence. The probability is that a male nurse acted as Stephen's keeper whilst he lived with his family at 32, De Vere Gardens. All the family and their friends were alert to spring into action to save the Establishment from scandal. For instance, the solicitor, Harry Wilson, lived handily just around the corner at 9, Cambridge Place.

9. Determined at all costs to keep the secret of Jack the Ripper's identity quiet, Stephen's family and friends tried to present J. K. Stephen to the world in as normal a light as possible. He wrote his poems, had them published by the eminently respectable firm of Macmillan & Bowes, Cambridge, and saw edition after edition called for. Perhaps more readers than we think saw the sinister pun of the title, *Lapsus Calami*, usually translated as 'a slip of the pen', but perfectly well understandable as '(One who was) Lost by the Knife', or 'A slip of the Knife'.

10. With his patient treated more and more as 'normal', Stephen's keeper relaxed his vigilance until, one day in the bitter winter of 1890/1, J. K. Stephen slipped away to kill his last victim, Frances Coles. As in previous cases, he walked down De Vere Gardens, through St Alban's Grove and Kensington Square, and took a ticket from High Street Kensington (District) Station to Aldgate East. He cut her throat, *began* to mutilate her naked abdomen, and stopped only because, with the hyperaesthesia of insanity, he heard P.C. Thompson approaching. What triggered off this final outburst we shall consider later.

But the insanity was becoming too difficult to 'contain'. The shock of J.K.'s murderous actions, and, perhaps even more, the shock of having to conceal them; to act as accessories before, during and after the murder; had broken up the Stephens. Sir James Fitzjames Stephen collapsed physically and mentally, and 'on the advice of his physician', ended a brilliant legal career; Leslie gave up the first-editorship of *The Dictionary of National Biography*; Lushington went into a decline which pretty well ruined his chances as a barrister; he ended up as an Indian judge; and others in the family were no less grievously affected.

11. With Sir William Gull's death the family were forced to take sterner measures. Nearly senile with shock and what Leslie calls 'a disease which had been slowly developing (and which) began to affect his mental powers'. Sir James, though without the homicidal mania, was almost as mad as his son. Leslie, though not mad (he was to recover, become President of the London Library, and receive a K.C.B. in 1902), was so stricken down by the family scandal as to be momentarily useless. Of them all, only Herbert (later Sir Herbert) kept his head, and when, in the October of 1891, some more proof of Eddy's 'faithlessness' began to trigger off what, by now, Stephen's barrister brother, Herbert, recognized as the aura of the dangerous condition, he decided not to play about with private nursing homes. J.K. was packed off to St Andrew's, Northampton, and though from there he continued to write to Eddy and all his friends, he was kept under strict guard until he died.

Although I have assumed, 'with the best authorities', that there were five *established* Ripper murders, I have not felt compelled to go along with them to the point of affirming that there were *only* five such murders. The murder of Frances Coles on the early morning of 13th February, 1891, was, to my mind, a Ripper murder. But there is some further evidence to suggest that the Ripper might have succeeded in his intention of 'striking down each year and tolling the bell for ten harlots of Jerusalem'.

Despite Colin Wilson, Robin Odell, Donald McCormick and

others, there was a theory that there had been ten Ripper murders. I give them, with the dates:

Emma Smith	3rd April,	1888
Martha Turner	6/7th April,	1888
M. A. Nicholls	31st August,	1888
Annie Chapman	8th September,	1888
Stride & Eddowes	30th September,	1888
(*double, obviously counted as one*)		
Mary J. Kelly	9th November,	1888
Annie Farmer	21st November,	1888
Mellett (or Davis)	28th December,	1888
A. McKenzie	17th July,	1889
Frances Coles	13th February,	1891

—a total of ten.

> . . . this syphilitic spawn of hell
> Struck down each year and tolled the bell
> For *ten* harlots of Jerusalem.

When Jack wrote that there were 'eight little whores, with no hope of heaven', two—Emma Smith (3rd April) and Martha Turner (6/7th April) had already taken their fearful way out.

Now, all but the 'classic' five—Nicholls, Chapman, Stride, Eddowes and Kelly—have been excluded from the 'authenticated' Ripper list because, as it is said, their murder-pattern did not conform to the 'classic' Ripper design; that is, they were not fully eviscerated. But even the Ripper himself admits that being disturbed at his 'fun' would alter the pattern, as when he wrote to the Editor of the Central News Agency to say that the coppers had prevented his taking Eddowes' ears.

What inclines me now to think that there *were* ten, and what is more, that Jack set out to 'get' ten, is this new evidence which can hardly be coincidental. Earlier it was stated that those commentators were mistaken who had connected the killing of

Kelly with the Lord Mayor's Show on 9th November. More appropriately they should have connected it with the Prince of Wales's birthday that fell on the same day. That association, however, leads to an even more suggestive one:

Victim	Death-date	Royal or 'classical' occasion
Smith	3/4th April, 1888	Feast of Cybele, the Great Mother,
Turner	6/7th August, 1888	Birthday of Duke of Edinburgh. Eddy's *bon vivant* uncle and companion.
Nicholls	31st August, 1888	Birthday of Princess (afterwards Queen) Wilhelmina of the Netherlands (*then staying at Windsor*).
Chapman	8th September, 1888	...
Stride & Eddowes	30th September, 1888	...
Kelly	9th November, 1888	Birthday of Prince of Wales.
Farmer	21st November, 1888	Birthday of the Empress Frederick, the Prince of Wales's sister.
Mellett (or Davis)	28th December, 1888	The Feast of the Holy Innocents, especially observed by the religious Princess of Wales.
McKenzie	16/17th July, 1889	4th anniversary of the striking of the medal for Eddy to commemorate his receiving the Freedom of the City of London.
Coles	13th February, 1891	The Ides of February—the Roman Feast of Terminalia.

Now all this may be the merest coincidence, but if the Ripper believed that Eddy had withdrawn his affection because he had been 'got at' by some or all of the other members of the Royal Family, then the murders could have been some kind of maniac blood-sacrifice, whose significance could not have been lost on the distant, intentionally remote persons for whom the 'sacrifice' was offered up.

It does, indeed, seem likely that it was to the murder of 'ten harlots' that Stephen's maniac compulsion drove him. There is the fact that the first (Smith) was 'offered up' on the Feast of the Great Mother, a savage deity whose temples were served by castrated priests who, after their ritual castration, dressed as women. There is also the fact that the tenth and last 'offering'

(Coles) was made on the 13th February, the Ides of February, the Roman Feast of Terminalia in honour of Terminus, patron of limits, boundaries, treaties, and *endings*. It was customary, though forbidden by King Numa Pompilius, who had established the feast, *to offer blood sacrifices*—usually a young lamb or pig. Unless it is the wildest coincidence, the 'sacrifice' that the classical scholar, Stephen, offered to Terminus on the morning of the Ides of February, 1891, bore a name which made her markedly suitable as a victim—Coles: Latin *coleus*, from Greek *κολεός*, 'a sheath', which in Latin is 'vagina'. It was in this same year that J. K. Stephen published his very able pamphlet, *Living Languages*, in defence of the compulsory study of Greek at the universities.

But there is evidence, to which I shall return later, that Stephen's habits of thought did, in fact, support my hypothesis that he would have been unusually conscious of the date—of any date—*in strictly classical terms*. For a dedicatory poem prefacing his *Lapsus Calami* is dated a month only after his 'final' murder of Frances Coles, and Stephen has written the date in the Roman manner: *id. Mart. mdcccxci*—'The Ides [15th] March, 1891'.

It seems to me here that in his murderous symbolism J. K. Stephen was addressing his indignation to two types of person: the classical men, such as Oscar Browning, who would understand the significance of 3rd April and 13th February, and those with deficient Greek or Latin (Eddy and his interfering family) who needed reminders a great deal less subtle to spoil their birthday complacency and merry-making.

But what of the possibility of Stephen's being able to be in Whitechapel on the relevant dates?

To put the question more clearly: if Stephen, in virtue of his fellowship of King's College (since 1885), had returned to Cambridge on the collapse of his plans to practise on the South Wales Circuit, how had he managed to be on hand, *in London*, to commit the ten 'sacrifices'?

The contemporary reference books make it clear that, until 1889, Stephen was what was once called 'a proper gremial'—

that is, a permanent resident of the University; only in 1890 did he move to lodgings at 18, Trinity Street, next door to the *Blue Boar,* and only a door or two from both the Hawks Club and the Athenaeum Club.

A glance at the dates of the murders makes it clear that, out of eleven killings—nine singles and one double—only *one,* Farmer, took place during actual term-time, whilst two others, those of Kelly and Coles, though taking place during term, fell on half-term holidays. Here is the list:

1. Emma Smith.	3rd April, 1888. Easter Sunday fell on 1st April. Lent Term at Cambridge ended that year on 27th March; Easter Term began on 18th April.
2. Martha Turner.	6/7th July, 1888. Easter Term had ended on 24th June. This murder took place during the Long Vacation.
3. M. A. Nicholls.	31st August, 1888. Long Vacation.
4. Annie Chapman.	8th September, 1888. Long Vacation.
5. Stride & Eddowes.	30th September, 1888. Michaelmas Term began *on the following day* (1st October). ***Note that it was in the *Michaelmas* Term of 1880 that J. K. Stephen was President of the Union; and on the day before the Michaelmas Term of 1888 'celebrated' his Presidency with his only double 'sacrifice'.
6. Mary Kelly.	9th November, 1888. Half-term holiday, as Michaelmas Term divided; but the significance of the date, 'the Prince of Wales's birthday', would have drawn Stephen to London in any case. Cambridge is only 54 miles from London; the journey by rail took $1\frac{1}{2}$ hours in 1888. From Paddington to

	Aldgate by Metropolitan took rather less than half-an-hour.
7. Annie Farmer.	21st November. The Princess Royal's birthday. No holiday at Cambridge, but there would have been nothing to prevent Stephen's catching an evening train from Cambridge.
8. Mallet (or Davis).	28th December, 1888. Michaelmas Term had ended on 19th December. Lent Term would not begin until 8th January.
9. A. McKenzie.	17th July, 1889. Long Vacation.
10. Frances Coles.	13th February, 1891. Lent Term half-holiday fell on 14th February.

There would thus have been no difficulty at all in Stephen's visiting London, even though engaged principally in Cambridge. That Stephen, though living in college until 1889/90, considered 32, De Vere Gardens, his father's house, to be his 'permanent address' is evident from the entries for the years 1886–92 in *The Post Office London Directory*, where the three Stephen brothers are listed thus:

Harry Lushington Stephen, barrister, 3, King's Bench Walk, E.C.
Herbert Stephen, barrister, 4, Paper Buildings, Temple, E.C.
James Kenneth Stephen, barrister, 3, Stone Buildings, Lincoln's Inn, W.C.

—the private address, in all cases, being given as 32, De Vere Gardens.

In connection with J. K. Stephen's resuming University life, it should be noted that no fewer than *nine* Stephens graduated at Cambridge between 1852 (Sir James Fitzjames Stephen, J. K. Stephen's father) and 1889. And that no fewer than six Stephens—at the time of the Ripper murders—were members of the Senate; the six including J. K. Stephen. When one recalls that Sir James Fitzjames Stephen had become one of the University Counsel in 1872, and remembers that he and his brother Leslie, with four of the former's sons, were in the Senate, one may realize what influence this powerful Stephen corporation could—and did—exercise!

As Stephen, in his *persona* of Jack the Ripper, wrote:

> I've no time to tell you how
> I came to be a killer.
> But you should know, as time will show,
> That I'm society's pillar.

Dr Stowell is certainly correct in one of his conclusions:

'Sir Charles Warren, though he was the victim of bitter criticism and was forced to resign his appointment as Commissioner of Police for the Metropolitan area, handled a difficult and delicate problem with great skill.

'His chief responsibility was to prevent the murders and, subject to fulfilling this duty, he did his utmost to save from shame a much loved family by avoiding bringing one of its members before a criminal court. Justice could not have punished "S", for at the time of committing the murders he was a lunatic and could only have been sent to a lunatic asylum. This is precisely what Sir Charles Warren, Sir William Gull, and the young man's family endeavoured to achieve and actually did achieve. . . . I cannot conceive any other humane way of dealing with a sadly affected young man and preventing a continuation of the atrocities which he committed entirely irresponsibly.'

Except that Sir Charles, Sir William and the family did not succeed in saving the 'ten harlots' from destruction, Stowell is right.

7. The Breath of Scandal

Eddy himself was not directly involved in the Ripper murders, although his reputation would have suffered if it had been disclosed that the murderer was none other than his former tutor, J. K. Stephen. For this reason, careful steps were taken to ensure that the truth never leaked out. But the Cleveland Street affair was another matter, for in this case Eddy was the central participant. It is hardly surprising, therefore, that the Establishment conspired elaborately to conceal the truth, and that, until now, this process has not been fully recognized. On account of the publicity that the official enquiries had attracted, it was necessary to mount the whole pantomime performance of a criminal trial, with contracted judge, counsels, witnesses and plaintiff. The preliminary step that led to the exposure of this sordid affair was taken on 2nd July, 1889, when P.C. Hanks, on behalf of Inspector Abberline of the Yard, called at the General Post Office to question a delivery boy, Swinscow, concerning some recent thefts.

Swinscow did not have a police record. A 'boy' at the Marlborough Club, founded by the Prince of Wales, Swinscow, had been detected in theft, but had not been charged only on the intervention of Lord Henry Arthur George Somerset, son of the Duke of Beaufort, and Extra Equerry and Superintendent of the Stables to H.R.H. the Prince of Wales. To distinguish him from

191

another Lord Henry in the family, this eminent person was generally known as 'Lord Arthur'. Hanks's interrogation of Swinscow soon revealed what was, in those days, a far more serious crime.

For Swinscow confessed that another young post-office clerk, Newlove, had invited him to go to a certain house, 19 Cleveland Street, and there take part in 'offences' for which the recently passed Criminal Law Amendment Act had made ample provision.

Four days later, after the police had made some enquiries Newlove was questioned, and broke down with hardly more resistance than the younger Swinscow had shewn. Swinscow was then summoned, and the two youths were taken to the police-office, where both were asked to make sworn statements as to the reasons for their going to Cleveland Street and the actions that they had performed there.

On the following day, 7th July, Newlove was again taken to the police-office and on the following day, 8th July, Newlove 'gave a name' to Inspector Abberline, who had already achieved notoriety in the Ripper case by arresting no fewer than two innocent men.

The 'certain name' that Newlove gave to Abberline was that of a clerk in Holy Orders, Veck. On 9th July, P.C. Hanks took Newlove to the latter's mother's house, and there, concealed, heard Veck offer money to the youth to defend himself against 'any court actions'.

Not until 20th August was Veck arrested, and not until 27th August were he and Newlove charged at Marlborough-street Police Station with 'having committed unnatural offences with male persons, and with having induced others to do the same'. The case was heard on the same day, but not dealt with until 4th September. They both pleaded guilty and were committed to prison, Veck to four months imprisonment and Newlove to nine months. It is hard to see why Veck, who used Newlove, younger than himself, to collect and corrupt lads even younger than he, should have got off the more lightly. And neither did Ernest Parke, ambitious, 'leftish' editor of a newly founded 'campaigning' weekly, *The North London Press*, for whom there were two pertinent questions:

1. Why did Veck, a minister, get only four months, whilst a clergyman in the previous year had got 'life' for what seemed less heinous offences?
2. Why, if the information that 19 Cleveland Street was being used as a male brothel had come to the police on 2nd July, was the owner, Hammond, allowed to move out his furniture and depart for France on 6th July, *three days* before a constable had been assigned to watch the house?

What made the case complicated was that there were several interests involved.

The pattern evolves roughly as follows:

1. Telegraph-boys attract the attention of the police by obviously having more money to spend than their small wages would warrant.
2. Suspecting no more than simple peculation, the police interview a 'sample' over-spender in the normal way.
3. The police questioning reveals the source of the 'pocket money', and, in so doing, the existence of a male brothel at 19, Cleveland Street.
4. The police decide to obtain evidence enough to net a number of the wealthier/more aristocratic patrons of this establishment.

   BUT . . .

5. In the meanwhile, the news of Newlove's interrogation had got out. This not only alerted some homosexual 'toffs' to a possible danger of their being charged under the new Act, but it made it imperative that active steps be taken to silence all possible weak/treacherous witnesses.
6. Yet the identity of some of the brothel's customers made it necessary for the Government to involve itself, to prevent an Empire-rocking scandal. The Treasury was entrusted with the task of suppressing the facts, working independently of

Scotland Yard and of the private interests who had instructed a shady solicitor, Arthur Newton, to '*hush things up.*'

7. So that we have this situation:

   a. Inspector Abberline, working closely with Ernest Parke, editor of the *North London Press*, is all out for a conviction of the 'nobs'; the more exalted the better.

   b. Arthur Newton, richly fee'd by anxious customers of brothel, instructs his regular inquiry-agent, Adolphe de Gallo, of 39, Great Marlborough-street (same address as Newton's) to get the lads, the only witnesses to be feared, out of the way.

   c. The Treasury is anxious, *at all costs*, to hush this scandal up. In the course of its activities, it finds it easier to contract an uneasy alliance with the conscienceless Arthur Newton. Both the Treasury and Newton are after the boys, for the purpose of bribing or threatening them into silence.

Of course, the easiest solution would have been to buy Parke off—if any of the parties, save Inspector Abberline, had known that Parke was collecting information to expose Vice in High Places. Unfortunately, though Parke's reporters were exchanging information with Abberline's plain-clothes detectives, neither Newton nor the Treasury realized that the Press had got wind of the scandal—they thought that all that they had to do was to outwit the zealous Inspector Abberline.

The first achievement of the Treasury–Newton alliance was to get Hammond out of the way to France. As Hammond had not even been charged, the police could do nothing to prevent his departure.

In the meanwhile Arthur Newton had collected the seven lads likely to prove dangerous witnesses. Having threatened them sufficiently to make them pliable, Newton then installed each lad in lodgings, from which he was to emigrate to Australia, with a complete set of clothing, £20 in cash, and an assured income of £1 a week for the next three years. One of these lads, Algernon Alleys, recalled that Newton had told him: 'The

AT BOW STREET.

ing a Scapecoat for Treasury Sins.

HE PROSECUTION OF NEWTON.

Defence emphasise the fact hat for five months the Public Prosecutor took no action—Allegations against a police-constable—Mr. Gill's tough fight for his clients.

aring the whole of this week, Mr. Vaughan been engaged at Bow-street in hearing the ge of conspiracy to defeat the ends of ce which has been brought against Mr. r Newton, the well known solicitor at borough-street, Taylerson his clerk, and phus de Gallo interpreter. The case is g heard in the small court upstairs, and gh the room is generally full, few of the to find admittance, the audience being posed almost exclusively of legal gentlemen, nalists, artists, and police officers. Mr. ace Avory, instructed by Mr. Angus Lewis, s the attack for the Treasury, while Mr. another Treasury counsel, defends Newton ; Mr. St. John Wontner, who also frequently for the Treasury, appears for Taylerson de Gallo. The defendants were allowed a behind their legal representatives, and ently,

ESPECIALLY MR. NEWTON,

opted counsel in the conduct of the defence. dock, however, was not unoccupied, two or e prese-men regularly finding a seat there. h Mr. Vaughan on the bench was generally be seen Sir Augustus Stephenson, the citor to the Treasury and Director of Public ecutions, and two or three other gentlemen, found it an admirable platform for a display ignity that was positively overwhelming. first day was occupied mainly with the ence of a boy named Algernon Edward ys. He is a good-looking, curly-haired

ALLEYS.

th of twenty, who at one time was employed the Marlborough Club. He was convicted dishonesty, but was saved from imprisonment the interposition of a friend, and who afterrds turned out to be Lord Arthur Somerset. e intimate relations thus established between

THE PAGE BOY AND THE PEER

sequently became of a character that cannot particularised. Alleys for some months was resident at 19, Cleveland-street, but when the ak up of the establishment took place last y, he was living at home with his parents at sbury, in Suffolk. Here he was in the habit receiving letters from "Mr. Brown," who he I was Lord Arthur Somerset, but he destroyed se letters last August on receiving an onymous letter a king him to do so. The osecution sought to establish that an attempt d been made by the three defendants to get oys to leave the country. But in the course his cross-examination by Mr. Gill it was empted to be shown that Newton had acted the instance of Alleys' father in getting his a new start in life abroad, and that the boy ng a mere tool in the hands of Inspector berline and Constable Hanks had attempted ead Newton and the others into a trap. A ong point in the defence in regard to this particular witness was the production of a letter itten, the witness declared, out of his own

head, but which Mr. Gill suggested had been dictated by the police. Certainly the phrase-ology was far more finished than that of others admittedly the result of the boy's own unaided efforts.

The next witness was a boy named

THICKBLOOM

who gave a fresh turn to the case by importing into it the name of P. C. Sladden. Thickbloom is the officer who watched the house, 19, Cleve-land-street, for a week or so after Newlove was arrested on 4th July, in order to see what visitors went there. If Thickbroom's evidence in regard to Sladden goes uncontradicted it will not be difficult to understand why that officer's watching was productive of such meagre results in respect of the indentification of visitors to the house. Thickbroom, referring to an interview he had with Mr. Newton, said he thought he and the other boys were going to see Lord Arthur Somerset's father.

Who suggested you could see Lord Arthur Somerset's father ?—Two constables.

Do you know their names ?—I know one, Sladden. They never said it was Lord Arthur Somerset's father, but they spoke like that.

Where were you spoken to about this ?—Well, Perkins had a letter making an appoint-ment with Sladden outside his (Sladden's) house. We had met him the night before as well. We saw Abberline first, and then went and

SAW SLADDEN.

He was alone, but he met the other constable afterwards. We walked together towards the Tottenham Court-road police-station. We then followed a rank of policemen from the station till Sladden fell out on his beat, as Sladden had told us to do. We told Sladden we were dis-missed from the Post Office, and he said, " Go on, you aren't, are you? Well, I didn't think they would d.-hat dirty trick." Then Sladden went on : " I know somebody who wants to know when you are dismissed, and who asked me to tell him. I'll go and do so, and let you know." Sladden said he did not know whether it was

LORD ARTHUR SOMERSET'S FATHER

who was coming or his solicitor. Neither of those turned up, but another constable in plain clothes came up and spoke to Sladden, after which Sladden made another appointment for the following Monday. " You leave it in the hands of these toffs," said Sladden, " and you'll be all right. I know myself there's £1,000 down for you when you start." When witness came to swear the information against Newton, witness told Inspector Abberline that he did not want to mention Sladden's name, not wish-ing to

GET THE CONSTABLE INTO TROUBLE

Abberline remarked on Sladden's stupidity in having anything to do with the matter, but did not tell witness he need not say anything about Sladden.

Another line of the defence was disclosed, when a Marlborough street Police Court official was cross-examined by Mr. Gill, as to the names of the person who swore the informations on which a warrant granted on 12th November against Lord Arthur Somerset.

Mr. Avory objected to this line of cross-examination, and

Mr. Gill said that every word of that informa-tion was in possession of the authorities

MONTHS BEFORE.

Mr. Vaughan remarked that that was a question which he did not have to go into.

Mr. Gill responded that it was a question which would have to be very fully gone into.

Mr. Vaughan: But not on this issue before phase.

The proceedings on Tuesday closed with the evidence of another Post Office boy named Perkins, who told the story how De Gallo got the boys together in a coffee house in the Edgware-road, kept them there for a night in the expectation of being taken abroad, and then when one of their number had failed to turn up according to promise, sent them back to their homes. The line of cross-exami-nation showed that the defence wanted to prove that the suggestion about going abroad pro-ceeded from the boys, and that the interview with them was sought by De Gallo in order to extract for a client of Mr. Newton's information concerning the Cleveland-street case.

On Wednesday, the evidence took rather a sensational turn. Mr. Avory sprung upon the defence two witnesses from

BRUSSELS AND ANTWERP

who identified Newton and Taylerson as being in those cities assisting in the escape of Ham-mond to America. Taylerson it was stated accompanied him in the foreign steamer *Pennland,* which sailed from Antwerp on 5th October. On this day, Wednesday, first reference was made to the coming libel suit, the boy Perkins stating that he had seen Mr. Slater, Mr. Parke's solicitor, but—this in answer to Mr. Avory—he had given him no information. A third post-office messenger named

WRIGHT

was called, and he generally corroborated the evidence of the others.

The last of the messengers, Swinscow, was in the box nearly the whole of Thursday. He was subjected to a more searching cross-exami-nation than even the previous witnesses, and in this case the severity of Mr. Gill's catechism has been the most striking feature. Mr. Gill hitherto has conducted his case with consummate skill and minute care. He has missed not the very smallest opportunity of weakening the evidence of the boys, and of emphasising the extraordinary and inexplicable omission of the Treasury authorities to take any action against Lord Arthur Somerset and others during the five months that elapsed between the 5th July and 12th November.

Swinscow done with, Mr. Avory called upon Mr. Parke who had the day before been sub-poenaed by the Treasury to produce the six letters which

WERE POINTED IN THE NORTH LONDON PRESS

of 21st December, it being intimated in the same issue that they were at the service of the Public Prosecutor. Mr. Parke handed in the letters, and at the same time tendered a num-ber of other letters, cards, and photographs. Owing to the fact that he is defendant in the libel trial which should be held next week, no questions were asked him. Mr. Gill men-tioned that he presumed Mr. Parke would have no objection to the defence inspecting the letters he had handed in, to which he replied "certainly not." The evidence of the keeper of the coffee-house in the Edgware-road, where De Gallo had held interviews with the boys, closed the day's pro-ceedings. The case for the prosecution will probably close to-day (Friday) with the pro-duction of Inspector Abberline and Constable Hanks. The court will then adjourn till next week, to enable the defence to decide upon the line of action they will adopt.

The North London Press's account of the Cleveland-street trial.

reason we want to get you away is so you shouldn't give evidence against you know whom.'

Swinscow, however, wrote home, and described the situation to his mother, who took the letter to the police. Realizing that, if one had 'gone soft', there was little point in keeping the rest, Newton sent the lads away. Alleys, an obvious key-witness, since he had received compromising letters from a 'Mr Brown', who was none other than Lord Arthur Somerset, was about to be wafted off by the private detective when the lad was snatched away by the police.

In hasty response to an anonymous letter, Alleys had destroyed some compromising letters from 'Mr Brown' but enough of the letters remained for the police to identify the writer, 'Mr Brown', with Lord Arthur, and, after a considerable delay, issue a warrant for his lordship's arrest.

In the meanwhile, in a quite unprecedented manner, all six lads were taken to *the Treasury* without the knowledge of the police, and there, without legal representatives or blood relatives, were closely questioned.

All the commentators have represented Ernest Parke and his *North London Press* as a 'one-man' campaign against the tolerance of unnatural practices in high places. But in fact at least two other journals, *The Scottish Leader* and *Truth* (which means only Labouchere) were not only supplying Parke with ammunition, but had themselves begun a campaign against 'vice'.

What we had better here call 'the authorities' had come face to face with the fact that Inspector Abberline's men had been busy, and had collected the names of known frequenters of No. 19, Cleveland Street. 'The authorities' were most concerned with two of those names, that of the future Duke of Clarence and of Lord Arthur, Superintendent of the Stables to Eddy's father.

However, the zealous Inspector Abberline could not, or would not, be deflected from what this officious man thought the line of duty.

It was in the issue of Saturday, 28th September, 1889, that Ernest Parke first intimated to his readers that he had a Big

Story on its way, and on 16th November *The North London Press* named the men involved in the 'West End Scandals', as Lord Arthur Somerset, Hammond and Lord Euston, eldest son and heir of the Duke of Grafton.

As Pearsall rightly says, 'had Ernest Parke restricted his brief to Lord Arthur', nothing could have happened to him, but Parke had not only mentioned Lord Euston, he had even got an indifferent artist to draw his lordship, and that made matters not quite so simple. The outcome was that Lord Euston sued the editor of *The North London Press* for criminal libel.

The case now being *sub judice*, *The North London Press* could no longer comment on it. What its editor did, however, was to get his friends to organize a 'Fair Trial Fund', its list headed by the names of the 'Leftists' of the day, H. W. Massingham, T. P. O'Connor, and the like. However, before he went up for trial, Parke did mention sarcastically that the great 'revelatory' newspapers such as Stead's *Pall Mall Gazette*, *Lloyd's* and *Reynolds'*, were strangely silent. It is difficult to explain why *Lloyd's* and *Reynolds'* refrained from joining in, but perhaps it was the presence of Eddy's friend, Lionel Cust, now on the staff of the *Pall Mall*, that stopped Stead from joining in the witch-hunt.

Now, just as Wilde had no reasonable cause to bring an action for criminal libel against the Marquess of Queensbury, the Earl of Euston really had no *very* good case for prosecuting Ernest Parke for having said that the Earl had called at 19, Cleveland Street. For the Earl did not deny that he had done so. He said, in evidence before the magistrate's court, that he had been approached by a man in Piccadilly, who had given him a card offering that truly Victorian entertainment of *poses plastiques*, at 19, Cleveland Street.

Examined, Lord Euston seemed astonished that anyone should find his going to look at *poses plastiques* anything to his discredit.

He had arrived at 19, Cleveland Street, he said, paid off the cabby, knocked at the door, and had been admitted by a man. The man asked the Earl for a sovereign, which was handed over. But, instead of being conducted to a room full of personable young women in 'classic' poses, the Earl was shocked, he said, to be presented with 'an indecent proposal'. Indignantly, Lord Euston called the man 'an infernal scoundrel' and 'threatened to knock him down if he did not at once allow him to leave the house'.

And that, said Lord Euston, was the one and only time that he had ever visited what he now knew to be a house of decidedly ill-fame.

Between the police-court hearing and the trial at the Central Criminal Court, there was much activity. Pearsall says that 'just as [the police] had been over-enthusiastic in the Boulton and Park case,* so were they in their endeavours to staple Lord Euston to the mat. Witnesses of the goings-on in Cleveland-street were taken over London in cabs so that they could recognize Lord Euston at various sites. Captain Webb at Westminster Enquiry Office had shewed photographs of Lord Euston to witnesses, so that identification could be facilitated. Unfortunately, he had omitted to supply photographs of full length with a foot scale delineated thereon. The general consensus was that Lord Euston was a man of medium height, stout, face clean-shaven, dark moustache, thin on top (there was a variant—fair hair). Even Mrs Morgan, who kept a tobacco and sweet shop at 22, Cleveland Street, opposite number 19, agreed with this. Lord Euston, on his appearance in the witness stand, must have confounded many of them, for he was six feet four inches tall.'

The fact is that the witnesses were *led* to 'identify' Lord Euston, sitting in the court, as the gentleman who had so frequently visited No. 19. After having got all the witnesses to describe him as a man of medium height, Lord Euston's counsel then asked him to stand up. The implication was obvious—these witnesses could not have been as certain of their evidence as the defence would have had the Court believe.

A key witness for the defence was John Saul, a male prostitute

* A notorious transvestite scandal of 1870, in which a well-known nobleman was involved.

and pimp who admitted that he had led 'a grossly immoral life' for the past twenty years. Saul had to admit that, though he had done a little acting (as extra) at Drury Lane Theatre, his real vocation was what was so painfully obvious from his appearance and manner. Unable to stand up against the practised probing of counsel and judge, Saul confessed that the police had given him immunity only on condition that he bore witness against the plaintiff—Lord Euston. The chief points of his evidence may be briefly summarized:

1. He had met (the implication was that he had been 'picked up' by) Lord Euston in Piccadilly.
2. In *May, 1887*, he had taken Lord Euston (by the implications of the first statement, a practising homosexual) to 19, Cleveland Street, *proved a male brothel by the evidence given in the trial of Veck and Newlove in the preceding September (1889)*.
3. To Saul, Lord Euston was known as 'The Duke'.*
4. Thus, Saul having identified Lord Euston as a practiser of unnatural vice, whom Saul himself had taken to a male brothel, *as far back as May, 1887*, Saul confirmed the evidence of the other witness for the defence—Mrs Morgan, the confectioner and tobacconist, of 22, Cleveland Street, the two O'Loughlins, and the rest of the neighbours who had all testified on oath that they had seen Lord Euston frequent the male brothel.
5. BUT at no time, *explicitly*, did Saul testify that he had performed unnatural acts with 'The Duke'.

Pearsall's account represents a fair cross section of the general opinion on this subject:

'The witnesses and police had not taken account of Lord Euston's stature; the police and Parke had not realized the basic unreliability and bad image of their key witness [*Saul*].

* It is a common error to assume that *this* was the evidence against Eddy, as a visitor to Cleveland Street. Eddy was not created Duke of Clarence & Avondale until 24th May, 1890—his Grandmother's 71st birthday.

Now thoroughly alarmed, Parke intervened. He had other material, other sources that would prove he had been stating the truth, that Lord Euston had been in the habit of frequenting 19, Cleveland Street, but, when encouraged by Lord* Justice Hawkins to tell all, Parke said that he could not betray his sources.'

In his summing-up, Hawkins told the jury that Lord Euston was accused of 'heinous crimes revolting to one's common notions of all that was decent in human nature'. But he failed to point out to the jury that if the accusation had been made, it was by implication only. For the wretched Saul, Hawkins did not hide his disgust and contempt.

The jury took only half-an-hour to reach its opinion that Ernest Parke, as editor of *The North London Press,* was guilty of criminal libel. In a kindly manner, Hawkins asked Parke if he would like to reconsider his decision not to name his sources? No, said Parke; that was impossible. Hawkins then said that if a day would help Parke to reconsider his decision, the Judge would be happy to defer sentence. Parke thanked the Judge but said that, as his opinion was not likely to change by the following day, he would accept the Judge's sentence at once. Accordingly Hawkins pronounced sentence: one year's imprisonment.

With suspicious unanimity, the other editors turned on Parke. He had, said *The Saturday Review,* 'ministered to a foul taste with fouler lies; he deserves as much mercy as a pole-cat'; to *The People,* 'Lord Euston has earned the gratitude of society for enabling the law to stamp on a miscreant (*i.e. Parke*) who, if he had his deserts, should be whipped at the cart's tail from one end of London to the other.'

Pearsall, saying rightly that 'the Cleveland Street Scandal still has the power to intrigue', goes on to say that, 'if Saul was right, if Lord Euston was known as "The Duke," and had been at 19, Cleveland Street as early as 1887—Lord Euston steadfastly maintained that he had only been there on that one

* Then actually 'Mr Justice Hawkins'.

occasion in 1889 and then for a matter of five minutes—then Parke was right and his year's imprisonment was a gross miscarriage of justice. If Saul was lying—and there is every reason to suppose that he was, living as he was at the mercy of the law —why was he not immediately indicted for perjury?'

Well, in the first place, Saul *was* lying when he said that he had taken Lord Euston to the brothel at Cleveland Street as early as May, 1887, a fact which must have been known, not only to the police, but to the prosecution also. But so many other people were lying in this case that the *sworn* evidence can have been given only with the connivance of both prosecution and defence.

If one consult the record of the rates and other levies paid on 19, Cleveland Street, from 1886 to 1890 one begins to understand the complexity of the plot to 'take the heat' off Eddy and some other notable and notorious frequenters of 19, Cleveland Street. For this record shows that Hammond was not even the tenant at the time when Lord Euston was supposed to have committed the offences. In fact, the tenant was Michael O'Loughlin, one of the defence witnesses!

It is, indeed, the presence of Michael O'Loughlin amongst the defence witnesses, no less than the evidence given by him under oath, which proves the completely fraudulent nature of the 'trial' of Parke.

For with months of 'patient undercover work' by Metropolitan and Post Office police, Captain Webb's private eyes and —presumably—'enquiry agents' employed by the Treasury, no-one had done what I was able to do within half-an-hour: consult the rate-books of that London district containing 19 Cleveland Street.

Michael Loughlin (or O'Loughlin), described in court as 'an unemployed waiter' had been called as a key witness to identify Lord Euston as a man whom (O')Loughlin had seen entering and leaving 19, Cleveland Street.

(O')Loughlin said that he had attended the Ascot Hunt Cup two years previously; had had Lord Euston pointed out to him; and had seen him in Cleveland Street, entering and leaving

No. 19 'more precisely about three times at the end of May and the beginning of June (1889)'.

And nobody in either of the courts—or nobody reading the detailed accounts of the case—stood up or sent a message by the usher of the court or wrote to the police and said: 'But if Lord Euston went to No. 19, Cleveland Street at the beginning of May or beginning of June, he wasn't visiting Charles Richard Hammond's house, he was visiting that of *Michael O'Loughlin!*'

The easily-consulted extract from the rate-books makes this clear:

Midsummer 1887–Midsummer 1888	Ephraim Tysall
Midsummer 1888–Midsummer 1889	Michael Loughlin
Midsummer 1889–	Charles Richard Hammond

(three quarters of a year's rates unpaid)

In other words, if the rate-books speak correctly, Hammond, the mâle-brothel-keeper, had been a tenant of No. 19 *only one fortnight* when a 'tip' caused him hurriedly to leave for France. And if Parke's enquiries had led him to believe—as he claimed —that he had witnesses to testify that on at least five occasions Lord Euston had visited No. 19 with either John Saul or Frank Hewitt 'for improper purposes' (Lord Euston said that he had never heard of such persons), who was running the brothel between 1887 and 1889? If it wasn't Hammond—who was certainly not the tenant—then it can have been only Ephraim Tysall (who was not mentioned in the case) or Michael (O')Loughlin, the 'unemployed barman', called with his father, the dealer in greens and coal, as a witness to testify to the improper nature of No. 19—a reputation that, said (O')Loughlin, he had gathered from rumour!

The truth is that once the affair had come into the open, it could not be swept under the carpet. However much of a travesty of justice subsequent proceedings would prove themselves, the public had at least to *see* that justice was done. And

Labouchere was almost certainly right when, in *Truth* of 16th November, before the 'prosecution' of Parke, but after Parke had printed his first scare, Labby claimed that Monro, Chief Commissioner of Metropolitan Police, threatened to resign if the case were further 'hushed up' by the Treasury and the Home Office.

Of course, the case *was* hushed up. Even the royalty-hating Labby and the truth-at-all-costs Inspector Abberline were quietened, and by promises of promotion, threats, bribes and all the other traditional inducements to keep silence or speak to the brief, everybody went through with this judicial farce. The credit of an Empire was at stake; and where appeals to patriotism failed, other methods of persuasion were obviously successful. It was extremely well managed; and if the lacy texture of the 'story' is apparent to us now, it was not so obvious at the time.

Parke, of course, consented to become a victim; he took his year like a man. But it was obvious that Hawkins, in 'punishing' Parke for 'this very atrocious libel', was unhappy to have acted out the charade, even in the best of causes. His words to Parke might have been severe; his manner most certainly was not.

Frank Harris, who knew the whole story, kept his mouth shut, but permitted his indignation to boil over in the pages of *The Fortnightly Review*. Harris did not believe that Euston was guilty of any homosexual offences, but he did believe that Parke, who had been 'permitted to see the substance of a statement made to a police inspector', had been trapped into the victim's position before the necessity of his becoming 'the victim of duty' had been explained to him. Harris was justly indignant. But, like all the others, he kept mum.

All that he permitted himself to say in *The Fortnightly* was this:

'Every judge's wife wants to be a Lady and her husband gets ennobled the quicker the more he contrives to please his superiors in the hierarchy. If Lord Euston had been Mr Euston of Clerkenwell, his libeller would have been given a small fine, but not imprisoned, though the imputation even of ordinary immorality would have injured him in purse and public esteem generally, whereas it could not damage Lord Euston in any way.'

This was plain speaking for those who could read between the lines—and those who could knew that Harris was right. Lord Euston, because his reputation as a heterosexual could not be disputed in even a 'real' trial, was never in any danger of loss of reputation. But this, of course, was why he had been chosen to act the part of the libelled man.

And again, of course, Harris was right in saying that 'every judge's wife wants to be a Lady, and her husband as a rule gets ennobled the quicker the more he contrives to please his superiors in the hierarchy'. Hawkins got his peerage, as Baron Brampton, in 1899, and in that year he was also made a member of the Privy Council.

Sir Charles Russell, Q.C., who had conducted the 'brilliant' prosecution of Parke, had not to wait so long. In 1894 he was appointed a Lord of Appeal in Ordinary, with the title of Baron Russell of Killowen, and in the July of that year became Lord Chief Justice of England, the first Roman Catholic to have occupied that exalted legal position since the Reformation.

There were other rewards to come, but not until the Prince of Wales had become King. It made it easier for Lord Euston to 'help out' in protecting Eddy's good name from truly deplorable scandal that Euston was Provincial Grand Master of Northamptonshire and Huntingdonshire Freemasonry, whilst Eddy was preparing to be installed as Pro-Grand Master of Berkshire Freemasonry.

Nearly the last word in this extraordinary case belongs to the Prince of Wales, when he was told 'beyond the shadow of a doubt' that his Superintendent of the Stables and Extra Equerry, Lord Arthur Somerset, was 'one of Those'. The story goes that, even when the 'proofs' of 'Podge's' homosexuality were laid before the Prince, he exclaimed, 'I won't believe it, any more than I should if they accused the Archbishop of

Canterbury.' The Prince added that any man 'addicted to such a filthy vice' must be regarded as 'an unfortunate lunatic'.

Convinced—at least, so says Montgomery Hyde and Sir Philip Magnus—of the truth of the matter, the Prince wrote to Lord Salisbury, then Prime Minister, expressing his satisfaction that 'Podge' had been allowed to dodge the warrant, but asking that, should 'Podge' 'ever dare to shew his face in England again', he should be allowed to visit his parents quietly in the country, 'without fear of being apprehended on this awful charge'.

There was homosexuality, and worse, far too near the Prince's own private life that he should have failed to be tender towards 'Podge'. But was 'Podge' any more guilty than Euston? The Prince's letter is tantamount to ordering Salisbury to order the Director of Public Prosecutions to quash the warrant. It is impossible to believe that the elaborate plot, designed to protect his elder son and heir from one of the worst of his follies, should have been carried out without Court approval and Court connivance.

8. *Exile to India*

'The year 1891 was the unhappiest in the Prince of Wales's life,' writes Philip Magnus in his *Edward the Seventh*. It is not easy to see on what this opinion is based, for the preceding year would seem to deserve to be recalled with more horror than was 1891.

It was, for one thing, the year of two big scandals, both involving the Prince of Wales and not, for a change, his pleasure-seeking, completely irresponsible elder son.

The first scandal, the now notorious Tranby Croft scandal, not only convicted Lieutenant-colonel Sir William Gordon-Cumming, Bart, of the Scots Guards, of cheating whilst playing baccarat (an illegal game) with the Prince of Wales and other guests of a wealthy shipowner, Arthur Wilson, but it also compelled the Prince, and not for the first time, to enter the witness-box to testify. But on the first occasion in which he had appeared in the witness-box during the Mordaunt divorce case, the Prince had been treated with every courtesy by the Judge, Lord Penzance, and by 'both sides', and he had been cheered by the mob when leaving the Law Courts.

Gordon-Cumming had been forced to sign a paper, to which the Prince of Wales and other guests put their signatures, bearing the following most ambiguous wording:—

'In consideration of the promise, made by the gentlemen whose names are subscribed, to preserve silence with reference to an accusation made in regard to my conduct at baccarat on the nights of Monday and Tuesday, 8th and 9th September, 1890, at Tranby Croft, I will on my part solemnly undertake never to play cards again as long as I live'.

Perhaps if only 'gentlemen' had been in the know, that promised silence might have been kept; but there were ladies in the house-party. When, on the following day, the Prince left Tranby Croft to watch the last day of the Doncaster races with Eddy, staying the night with the 10th Hussars, someone from Tranby Croft began to talk.

There was only one thing for Gordon-Cumming to do now that the secret was out, and that was to bring an action for libel against his original accusers, Mr and Mrs Arthur Wilson, Mr and Mrs Lycett Green and Berkeley Levett, one of Gordon-Cummings's own subalterns.

Gordon-Cumming lost the case, but the jury's verdict did nothing to improve the Prince's image. The Solicitor-general, Sir Edward Clarke, 'leading' for Gordon-Cumming, treated the Prince, as witness, with hardly veiled insolence, and the mob hissed the Prince as he drove away to Marlborough House.

Although the other scandal never 'broke', save as exciting gossip amongst those 'in the know', it could have done even more harm to the Prince's image than the Tranby Croft affair. This scandal just avoided was the sudden and venomous turning on the Prince of his old boon companion, Lord Charles Beresford, sharer, with the Prince, of the favours of Lady Brooke, the future 'socialist' Lady Warwick, and blackmailer of the future George V.

Reconciled to his wife, Lord Charles was sent a letter of bitter reproach by Lady Brooke, a letter which, like so many others of its kind, fell into the hands of Lady Charles, who took it to the Jewish *éminence grise* of the day, the solicitor George Lewis.

Lady Brooke had no sooner written the letter than she regretted it, and asked her lover, the Prince of Wales, to recover it for her. Lewis permitted the letter to be read by the Prince, but would not permit him to have it. The Prince insisted that the letter be destroyed, but Lewis 'explained' that he could not do that without the consent of Lady Charles. The Prince twice called on Lady Charles to ask her to give up the letter, but on each occasion she refused.

Faced with such obduracy, the Prince punished Lady Charles by ceasing to invite her to Marlborough House, where, to her chagrin, Lady Brooke was still welcome. Lord Charles's Irish temper boiled up at 'the affront' put upon his wife. Before leaving to take command of H.M.S. *Undaunted*, he called on the Prince—it was 12th January, 1890, just three days before the Cleveland Street trial opened at the Old Bailey—to complain of the treatment that his wife had received and was receiving. In the heat of temper, Lord Charles called his former royal friend 'a blackguard and a coward', and left the royal presence in the most insolent manner imaginable, vowing that he would have his revenge.

By the middle of the next year, 'Society', following the Prince's lead, had cold-shouldered Lady Charles to such an extent that she announced that she would be selling her London house, and living abroad. In a fury, her husband, Beresford, proposed to call what today we term a 'press conference', and to give the 'rights and wrongs of the case' to the newspapers and agencies of the world. To make sure that his threat would be treated in all seriousness, Beresford sent a threatening letter, not to the Prince, but to Lady Charles, with instructions to shew it to the Prime Minister, Lord Salisbury, and then to despatch it to the Prince.

Through the tact of Salisbury and Sir Edward Clarke, whom Lady Charles had consulted professionally, the letter was not sent, and grudgingly, the Prince, on the insistence of his trusted advisers, agreed to submit to Lord and Lady Charles Beresford's blackmail, and once more to receive them at Marlborough House. The Princess of Wales was so upset by this averted scandal, coming so soon after the successfully managed Cleveland Street scandal and the very badly managed Tranby Croft scandal, that she stayed away from Sandringham for the

Prince's fiftieth birthday, preferring to spend that day with her sister at Livadia, where the Tsar and Tsaritza were celebrating their Silver Wedding.

Eddy, rescued from *open* scandal by that conspiracy of good-will called the Cleveland Street case, admitted no need to alter the *privately* scandalous character of his behaviour. For all the self-indulgence of the 'corpulent voluptuary', his father, Edward, was at his wits' end to know how to curb the misbehaviour of his son.

Whilst police, Ernest Parke, Lord Euston and all the other *dramatis personae* of the Cleveland Street farce were being prepared for their parts, Eddy was bundled out of England to get him out of the public eye at a time when his name, in connection with the goings-on at the male brothel, was common gossip at the higher level of society.

At the end of October, 1889, European royalty collected at Athens for the wedding of Constantine, Duke of Sparta, heir to the Greek throne, and a nephew of the Prince of Wales, with Princess Sophie of Prussia and Germany, the Kaiser's sister. The festivities over, the Princess of Wales returned with her parents to Copenhagen, whilst the Prince of Wales and Eddy revisited Egypt in H.M.S. *Osborne*.

On 31st October the Prince of Wales took his farewell of Eddy at Port Said, and Eddy was introduced to the man who was to be his companion, or, at least, an important member of his suite, throughout his forthcoming tour of India, Sir Edward Bradford, V.C., later Chief Commissioner of the Metropolitan Police. The intention to keep Eddy out of serious trouble or to clean up trouble if it came is so obvious in the appointment of Bradford to the suite that it is surprising that it has not been pointed out before. For with Eddy's Equerry, Captain Holford, and Captain Harvey, Bradford was in immediate attendance on Eddy. There was also Captain the Honourable Alwyne Greville, who had been Eddy's constant companion since he first joined the Service, and had been Equerry-in-Waiting to Eddy before Holford succeeded him.

Only two accounts survive of this Indian tour of Eddy's,

which so resembled that of his father, both in origin (to get the Prince of Wales out of the public eye following a series of public scandals) and in detail.

The first is the highly condensed version in James Edmund Vincent's officially authorized *Memoir* and the other is J. D. Rees's *H.R.H. the Duke of Clarence and Avondale in Southern India.* Both are extensively indebted to the heavily censored articles which appeared in such Indian journals as *The Asiatic Quarterly* and such British journals as *Macmillan's Magazine*, whilst Rees's book is heavily padded out, as was Dalton's *Cruise of the "Bacchante"*, with boring and, in the context, irrelevant 'reflections on the social and financial conditions of India'.

For the rest, Rees and Vincent give merely a 'Court Circular' type account of Eddy's progress through India. 'At ten o'clock the Duke of Connaught, Lord Reay (the Governor of Bombay), and Captain Hext (Director of Marine), came on board; and when the Prince went ashore there were addresses, streets lined with troops, and so forth; but all this was not for long, for the stay in Bombay extended over but a couple of hours, and then the Royal party left for Ganesh Khind, where, after a full dress dinner, sundry native Princes were received, amongst them being the Rajah of Kolapore ... At Poona, the Prince stayed for four days as the guest of the Duke and Duchess of Connaught at Magdala House. On the first of these days, the Prince saw tent-pegging by the bodyguard, held a Durbar at half-past two, rode with the Duke and Duchess of Connaught to see a temple (the steed being an elephant which took fright and stopped) and "afterwards drove for two hours through the town of Poona, which was illuminated, and arrived at Magdala House, the Duke of Connaught's, about seven, after having been covered with garlands about a dozen times. Big dinner in mess dress at 8.30." '*

Such summaries as 'the next day there was polo in the morning, and in the evening, the party, including Lord and Lady Claud Hamilton, Captain the Hon. and Mrs Alwyne Greville, Mr Caton Woodville [*The Illustrated London News*

* Quoted from a no-longer existent letter of Eddy.

artist, who was so greatly admired by Van Gogh], Captain Edwards and Surgeon Jones, went to Hyderabad, where the splendour of the reception accorded by the Nizam was beyond description,' make one realize just what has vanished from the lives of the British aristocracy and upper-classes, especially from those of the men and women who formed the intrusive ruling classes of India.

But, Vincent points out, 'life at Calcutta was not, however, purely a life of ceremonial. Time after time the Prince played polo, and at Kanchrapara, on the 11th of January, he and the Duke of Connaught, accompanied by Messrs Hamilton, Gladstone and Captain Holford, got a day's snipe-shooting, which produced sixty-eight couple, in spite of rather poor shooting in the morning, which was frightfully hot.'

Through all this artificial and heavily censored prose, something human occasionally breaks through to give a glimpse of Eddy as he must have been, rather than as Court historians wished posterity to see him.

'The reader can hardly fail to realise the dark Indian night, the long lines of soft lights rising tier upon tier against the dark background of the trees, the swarthy conjurers with their weird deceits, the barbaric music, the rhythmical swaying of the Nautch girls, the tempestuous frenzy of the kuttak dance—and in the midst of it our soldier and sailor Prince, hardly past his boyhood, in the guise of an eager and animated spectator.'

Eddy 'did' all the tourist sights, including the prison in which Tippoo Sahib had imprisoned the British soldiers, the Residency at Lucknow, the memorial at Cawnpore, Akbar's Fort, the Taj Mahal, and the Moti Musjid.

That Eddy enjoyed himself goes without saying. Like most of the Royal Family, he was an excellent shot:

'After a mile and a half of tracking we came upon the bull in some thick jungle. I saw him about thirty yards off before H.R.H. did, and covered him with my rifle. H.R.H. fired, and the bull fell. He fired again and so did Bensley. The bull plunged on his head towards us. I put a .500 bullet into his head, and we then fired about six more shots into him, until he was quite dead. Magnificent bull, 19 hands high; 6 ft 2 in measured to halfway between the hump of the neck and the high ribs of the back. Span of horns 34½ inches.' *

This little expedition ended 'in drenching rain'. It is pleasant to record that, on the following day, after Eddy had visited the Christian school at Tinnevelly, he saw Nautch girls and jugglers in the evening.

'On Monday, the 16th of December, the Prince and his suite embarked upon the *Kistna* for Rangoon. The weather in the Bay of Bengal was abominable, and Captain Holford records its effects with much humour, complaining bitterly of the "French cook on board, who will send up nothing but the richest of made dishes," which must have been aggravating when the vessel was in the middle of a bursting monsoon, and touched the tail of a typhoon.

'Both at Rangoon and Mandalay the Prince was received with full honour and high enthusiasm; and it is pleasant† to think of him, with his suite, attending Divine service on Christmas Day, in the palace which had been King Theebaw's where the communion-table "covers the king's throne, which is surmounted by a pinnacle, and is called the centre of the universe".'

The non-religious aspect of Christmas quickly reasserted itself, and on Boxing Day 'there was snipe-shooting in the morning (twenty-six couple), a garden-party, at which the entertainment consisted of boat-races and tugs-of-war by men and women, and a dinner-party'.

* Holford.
† 'Pleasant' for Vincent and similar toadies, but not, one imagines, for King Theebaw, who had been kicked off his throne by the British less than five years before.

Two days later Eddy attended the Thayetmyo Royal Visit Races, where oddly named horses and jockeys competed for the blue ribbon of the Burmese turf.

Eddy visited the Khyber Pass, Peshawar, Rawalpindi, Lahore, Chunga Minga, Kapurthala, Amritsar and Delhi. 'Two days of undisturbed sight-seeing followed, and on the next the Prince and one other gun went snipe-shooting, bagging forty snipe, ten brace of partridges (sic), and about ten head of miscellaneous game.' *

Eddy laid the foundation stone of a leper hospital at Junagad, after having seen the Nawab, and then returned to Calcutta, where, says Vincent, certainly without exaggeration 'the splendour of the reception was remarkable'. On 20th March, after a dinner at the Bycalla Club, with Sir L. H. Bayley in the chair, Eddy left India on the S.S. *Assam*, 'leaving behind the city of Bombay glowing with a beautiful sunset. This was the last we saw of India, after an almost unparalleled tour of almost five months.' †

'On his arrival home from India in May, 1890,' writes Georgina Battiscombe, 'Prince Eddy was created Duke of Clarence and Avondale. He had returned looking wretchedly ill; it was clear that his dissipations were beginning to undermine his health.'

He certainly might have returned looking a great deal healthier had he not stopped off at Cairo, this time without even his fairly easy-going father to put a dampener on his excesses. What the Khedive Tewfik had been unable to offer the Prince of Wales in the censorious presence of some of the more prudish members of his suite, Tewfik, always eager to give a guest the utmost in Oriental hospitality, offered to the Prince of Wales's son.

The presence of Sir Evelyn Baring, his self-confidence perhaps a little lessened by what he knew privately of his family's bank's impending collapse, General Sir Francis Grenfell,

* Vincent. When, according to Stowell's implications, he was in the last torpor of syphilis of the brain!

† Holford.

214

General Dormer, Lord and Lady Abingdon, Lady Sykes, Prince Louis of Battenberg and the Duke and Duchess of Sutherland, did nothing to impede Tewfik's hospitable plans.

'The quail-shooting was also of the best, 248 couple one day —"when we ran out of cartridges; I believe if we had worked hard we could have got five hundred couple"—and 204 couple later on the same ground.' *

But it had not been the quail-shooting which had sent Eddy back to England in May, 1890, 'looking wretchedly ill'.

* Vincent, quoting Holford.

9. *Eddy falls in love*

When, in talking of Eddy's 'dissipations', Mrs Battiscombe goes on to declare that 'the obvious solution would seem to be marriage', she means to say that the traditional thinking of Victorian parents led them to believe that a son would 'settle down' in marriage, after he had sown his wild oats. It is a *parental* point of view by no means dead even today.

Eddy, once the Cleveland Street scandal had been swept under the carpet, gave up none of his dangerous 'feasting with panthers'. If Hammond had had to 'levant', some of the older and more established male-brothel-keepers were still in business. The anonymous-sounding 'W. Jones' still kept his house of ill-fame at 13, Little College-street, to which Wilde was a frequent visitor; and Mrs Truman maintained hers next to the Albany Barracks, in Albany-street. The queer pubs, *The Crown* in Charing-cross-road, *The Windsor Castle* in the Strand, *The Pakenham*, in Knightsbridge Green, were all doing roaring business. And in all of them, not least the ultra-queer *Hundred Guineas Club*, where members and their guests assumed feminine names (Eddy was 'Victoria'), the future King of England was a regular and popular guest.

Although there is no evidence that Eddy met Stephen, after he was 'let out as cured', it seems that Jim Stephen was writing to Eddy.

'The affairs of Prince Eddy . . .' says Magnus, 'caused his

217

parents increasing anxiety. Because he was dissipated and unstable, an early marriage was obviously necessary. . . .'

The serious hunt for a wife for Eddy had, in fact, begun whilst Eddy was still in India, chasing buffalo or boys or Nautch girls, as the mood took him.

After opening the Forth Bridge, rebuilt after the terrible collapse of 1878, the Prince of Wales paid a State visit to Berlin, at the invitation of his nephew Kaiser Wilhelm II. With him, the Prince took his 'good' son, George, and a list, compiled by Queen Victoria, of princesses eligible for marriage to Eddy.

The first name on the list, it may well be understood, was that of the Kaiser's youngest sister, Margaret ('Mossy'). Being 'not regularly pretty', she was not to Eddy's taste, and the princess whom he would have married, 'Alicky', Princess of Hesse, his most attractive cousin, found the Prince not to *her* taste.

Eddy had a mind of his own, and all that he really lacked to make him fit perfectly into the society of his time was a sense of responsibility. He was now about to demonstrate both his obstinacy and his complete lack of responsibility by falling in love with the most unsuitable princess in all Europe, Hélène of Orléans.

On the death of the Comte de Chambord in 1883, he leaving no heir, her father, the Comte de Paris, had become the head of the House of Bourbon, and been accepted by the very powerful Royalist Party as France's rightful King. Still keeping up their splendid establishments in England, to which the Prince of Wales and his friends were constant visitors, the Orléans princes sued for, and obtained, the return to their family of the royal châteaux which had been 'nationalized' by the Republic.

But the Republicans were waiting, and matters of enmity came to a head in 1886, when the Comte de Paris married his daughter, Marie Amélie, to Dom Carlos, Duque de Braganza, heir to the Portuguese throne.

The marriage was celebrated with so much splendour, so much open defiance of Republican prejudice, that the Repub-

licans in both Chambers got to work immediately to expel the
'dangerous' royalist element from France.

Only five days after the wedding, bills were introduced, asking for disciplinary powers to expel both the Orléans and
Bonaparte princes, and for powers to confiscate their property
'for the nation'.

On 23rd June, the Bonapartes left France, and on the following day, the Comte de Paris and his family returned into exile.
Only with much difficulty had 'the authorities' been persuaded
to permit both families time to arrange their affairs in France.
At Dover, on landing from the cross-Channel steamer, the
Comte de Paris issued a public protest, in which he declared his
belief that a monarchy was the most suitable form of government for France, and in this protest he placed himself at the
head of the Royalist movement and its 'shadow government'.

The one serious aim of Bertie, whether as Prince of Wales or
as King, was to forge an unbreakable bond of understanding
between France and Great Britain. His friendship for France
and the French was so open that he was able to make friends
with Frenchmen of every social class and of every shade of
political opinion. No-one in France, or in Germany, for that
matter, doubted the sincerity of his wish for that *Entente Cordiale*
that he was, to his own happiness, to see effected before he
died.

It was an ambition which, whilst securing him a permanent
place in the affections of the French, earned him the mistrust
and enmity of the German people in general and of his nephew,
Kaiser Wilhelm II, in particular.

For all the Orléans princes Bertie had a great affection, and
especially for the Duc d'Aumale, whom the British Royal
Family always called 'Cousin Aumale'. Aumale had found
that certain way to the hearts of the English common people,
active patronage of the Turf. He had, in fact, created at Chantilly
another Ascot or Goodwood, as full of English horses, English
jockeys and British persons of distinction as the English courses
themselves.

As touchy in power as they had been when out of power, the

French Republicans saw danger everywhere. Only the infinite tact of the almost childish Bertie could overcome Republican suspicion. And now his elder son had to fall in love with the daughter of the openly declared Pretender to the Throne of France!

As Mrs Battiscombe says, 'nothing could be said against Princess Hélène personally; she was both good and attractive, and she would have made Prince Eddy an admirable wife had she not been a Roman Catholic and the daughter of the Comte de Paris, a pretender to the French throne'. The political difficulty, in the contemporary political context, formed the insuperable obstacle.

But to Motherdear, shaken by the touch-and-go escape of the Cleveland Street affair, by the Tranby Croft scandal and by the threat of Lord Charles Beresford's blackmailing tactics, there were no obstacles to a marriage between her darling Eddy and Hélène. Motherdear, from whom Eddy had inherited his quiet, stonewalling obstinacy, now set herself to triumph over every prejudice, personal or political, so as to 'cure' Eddy of his sexual failings by finding him a good wife.

That Eddy loved Hélène, there can be no doubt. It is also certain that she loved him more than he loved her—perhaps a rather too masculine mother had given this delightful girl an inclination towards softish, rather effeminate men.

Those scandals which were now the least pleasant of family gossip—Stephen the Ripper was out again—united the Family behind this projected marriage in a way which would be astonishing did we not know how eagerly the Family hoped to see Eddy 'settle down'.

Eddy's sisters were all for the marriage. His aunt Louise, now married to the foul-mouthed favourite of Queen Victoria, the Duke of Fife, played 'fairy godmother' to the two lovers, arranging that they should meet at her house, East Sheen Lodge, which was a few hundred yards from the Orléans house at Richmond, and making clear her benevolent view of the possible marriage by inviting both Princess Hélène and Eddy to stay at Mar Lodge, her house in Braemar.

The next 'insuperable' obstacle was Queen Victoria. Here again, the charm and, when she wished to use it, the cold intelligence, of Alix prevailed. At first, Queen Victoria 'would not hear of it', so Alix, with the advantage of understanding all the people concerned in this curious project, urged the young couple to go straight to Balmoral, only a short distance from Mar Lodge, and appeal to the very warm heart of the old Queen.

'The Princess would listen to no protests from her reluctant son, but, ordering a carriage, she pushed the pair into it, at the last moment thrusting a picnic lunch in after them to sustain their fainting spirits. All went as she had hoped and predicted; the Queen, taken by storm in this fashion, capitulated at once to the appeal of young love, and gave the couple her blessing.' *

Queen Victoria's change of mind, though 'predicted' by the Princess of Wales, was still surprising. On 19th May, the Queen had written a letter to her grandson warning him of the danger of falling in love with Princess Hélène. It is just possible that Queen Victoria had written the admonitory letter so as to bring the indolent Eddy's obstinacy into play. As her whole history shews, Queen Victoria had a very soft spot for Roman Catholics, and Princess Hélène's faith would not have seemed, to the religiously tolerant Queen, any objection to her becoming her granddaughter-in-law. That the Queen must have expressed her consent *formally* is evident from the fact that Bertie, no less than Alix, warmly welcomed the proposed marriage. Thus in August, 1890, whilst still at Mar Lodge, Eddy and Hélène became engaged. Motherdear was at Mar Lodge, too, but Bertie, though professedly delighted to hear of the engagement, would not break off his stay at Homburg, where he was taking the 'cure'. The day after the young couple had seen the Queen, A. J. Balfour, the minister-in-attendance at Balmoral, wrote to his uncle, the Prime Minister, Lord Salisbury.

'We shall have a great deal of trouble over it all, but it is impossible not to see the humorous side of the business. Will it be

* *Queen Alexandra*, by Georgina Battiscombe.

believed that neither the Queen, nor the young Prince, nor Princess Hélène, see anything which is not romantic, interesting, touching and praiseworthy in the young lady giving up a religion, to which *she still professes devoted attachment*, in order to marry the man on whom she has set her heart! They are moved even to tears by the magnitude of the sacrifice, without it, apparently, occurring to them that at the best it is a sacrifice of religion for love, whilst at the worst it is a sacrifice of religion for a throne—a singular inversion of the ordinary views on martyrdom . . .'

The Comte de Paris, however, refused to allow his daughter to become a Protestant, to the undisguised relief of the Prime Minister and of the Lord Chancellor, Lord Halsbury, who composed elaborate memoranda upon the political and legal aspects of the affair.

Ambitious though he was, the Comte de Paris was also deeply religious. Not very far in the past was his ancestor, the infamous Philippe Egalité, who had voted for the death of his cousin, Louis XVI, on the guillotine. The Count had, in our modern jargon, a 'guilt complex', that he sought to assuage with good works, an unquestioning faith in *his* branch of the Holy Catholic Church, and a life of such self-sacrifice as was compatible with his high social standing.

Both Philip Magnus and Georgina Battiscombe assert that the Comte de Paris was opposed to the marriage on religious grounds. But it seems far more likely that his opposition was on moral grounds. Although he did not frequent the company of the Prince of Wales, the other Orléans princes did, and Eddy's oddities were common gossip amongst the upper-classes.

The real facts of the situation are these:

1. The Act of Settlement, by which William and Mary succeeded to the throne, abdicated by James II, forbade any British sovereign to have a Roman Catholic as consort. In other words, both the Sovereign and the Sovereign's consort must belong to the Established Church.

2. Eddy was not the Heir to the Throne. He was no more than the Heir Presumptive to his father, who was the Heir Apparent. There was nothing in the Act of Settlement which would have forbidden Eddy to marry Hélène, even though she had stayed a Roman Catholic, though, before Eddy's eventual coronation, she would have needed to be confirmed in the Anglican faith.

3. Until the Papal decree *Ne Temere* of 1907, the Pope professed no authority over the marriage of Roman Catholic to non-Roman Catholic. A Catholic could be married in any church of any denomination, or even in a registry-office, without offending against the laws of the Roman Church, though, of course, the consent of the two Houses of Parliament would be needed to ratify this particular marriage.

4. Princess Hélène, born in England during her father's first exile, was *ipso facto* a member of the Church of England. It is not necessary to be confirmed in the Church of England to be a member of it—even English-born Jews and Muslims are members.

Alix found a cynically unwilling 'father confessor' in Lord Salisbury, who was inclined to pooh-pooh the 'gravity' of the situation, and to laugh when, in Magnus's phrase, the Princess of Wales 'argued that apostasy ought to be accepted as conclusive proof of [Hélène's] disinterested love'. However, the Prime Minister warned the Prince of Wales in the most serious manner not to air the view that the Princess Hélène might remain a Roman Catholic if she gave an undertaking that any children of the marriage should be brought up as members of the Church of England. In his distress, the Prince wrote to Ponsonby that 'The Lord Chancellor is now being consulted, but till the Ct. de P. consents to the change of Religion, one might just as well consult the Great Mogul.' To his son, Georgy, the Prince wrote dolefully, on 12th October, 1890, 'What the ultimate result may be, God only knows . . . I am not very sanguine.'

A month later, the Prince of Wales wrote to Georgy that

Eddy's prospects were 'in a deplorable state, as Hélène went to see the Pope (!), he naturally pointed out the iniquity she would commit if she changed her religion. This brings everything to a deadlock; and it is a sad state of things and makes poor Eddy quite wretched.'

The fact is that Hélène went to the Pope for reassurance and to see whether or not his Holiness could find a solution to the *impasse* created by the Comte de Paris's setting his face against the marriage. There was not, as some writers have claimed, any question of the Pope's giving a dispensation to allow the marriage to take place. According to Papal law at that time, no dispensation was necessary.

All that Hélène got from Leo XIII was a lecture, and this not so much on religious grounds as because the Pope was then sulking over the 'snub' that he had received from the British Government.

After the forcible unification of Italy, which culminated in 1870 with the 'invasion' of Rome by the troops of Victor Emmanual II, Great Britain had 'recognized' the unification, and thus the new Kingdom of Italy, but had decided also to continue to 'recognize' the Roman States, of which the Pope was the reigning sovereign, even though only the Vatican palace remained of the once extensive Papal temporal dominions. To give weight to this legal diplomatic fiction, the Papal consulates at Valetta and Gibraltar continued to be accorded, by Her Britannic Majesty's Government, full diplomatic status.

However, in 1884, 'realism' prevailed, and, it being obvious that the Pope was no longer the ruler of a sovereign independent state, the British Government withdrew their diplomatic status from the Papal consuls in Malta and Gibraltar. Five years later, Leo XIII could still not forgive the heretics' affront to the Vicar of Christ. There wasn't much that the Pope could do to get his revenge, but the affair of Princess Hélène and Eddy provided him with what we may suppose that His Holiness considered a literally God-sent opportunity. He warned her of the *certain* eternal damnation awaiting an apostate from the One True Faith and told her plainly that she must never marry the heretic, Eddy.

Having done his duty, His Holiness gave her his pontifical blessing, and sent Hélène back to England.

'All we can do now,' Alix wrote to Georgy, 'is to wait and see what time can do for us and trust in God to help us. In the meantime, they go on corresponding and loving one another from a distance.'

Nearer at hand, Eddy was extending the range of his affection. Though 'corresponding with and loving' Hélène from a distance, he was also corresponding with and loving from a distance Lady Sybil St Clair-Erskine, sister both of the unorthodox 5th Earl of Rosslyn and of the Duchess of Sutherland, whose husband was the companion-in-arms of Eddy's father. 'His mother, however,' says Mrs Battiscombe, 'knew nothing of this development; to her he was simply her lovesick boy over whom her heart constantly grieved.'

Like many another affair at lower levels of society, social pressures were too strong on both sides for the lovers to stay together. Later, Hélène was to become the beautiful Duchess of Aosta, and Sybil, too, was to go her own way, marrying the 13th Earl of Westmoreland in the year that Eddy died.

And because there was really nothing to engage his more serious attentions, Eddy once more took up the tarts and nancy-boys of which no age in the world's history has had a shortage.

The Ides of February, 1891, came around, and Jack the Ripper made his final blood-sacrifice, Frances Coles.

He had promised, and now delivered 'ten harlots of Jerusalem'. Frances Coles was the last, and the homicidal maniac returned to defending the use of Greek in the universities.

The murder of Coles—incomplete (because interrupted) though it had been—which ended the promised series of sacrifices, had given Stephen that necessary catharsis which enabled him to return to comparative sanity.

It was to be his last 'sane' year; and 1891 is marked, not only with the last murder in the Ripper series, but also with the publication of his book of poems, *Lapsus Calami* (the Latin dedication to his College's Founder being dated significantly, '*id. Mart. mdcccxci*'—making it more than likely that Coles's death on '*id. Feb. mdcccxci*' was no coincidence!).

But the year was also notable for his production of a most competent defence of compulsory Greek in the Universities. Beginning as a successful lecture given at Cambridge, *Living Languages* is that lecture expanded and reinforced with new arguments.

There was also another paper, of an entirely different nature, which was found in the surviving medical records of James Kenneth Stephen. Though this three-page pamphlet, dated 'Cambridge, *May*, 1891', is anonymous, there is no doubt that it was the work of Stephen, and was printed for confidential circulation (it is headed '*Private and Confidential*') among those Cambridge circles where rumours of Stephen's insanity were, he knew, being discussed.

The paper is printed in full as an Appendix; here it will be necessary only to say that it is a curious defence of his own sanity, in a manner which makes it apparent, even to the layman, that the writer is more than a little unbalanced. Never was paranoia so clearly proclaimed.

The pamphlet opens with this:

'About the end of October last [i.e. 1890—a year in which there was no Ripper killing], Dr G. H. Savage, formerly Principal of Bedlam,* formed the opinion that the gentleman hereinafter referred to was not in a state of perfect mental health, but was suffering from morbid excitement or cerebral exaltation. Dr Savage had some personal acquaintance with the gentleman in question and his past career; but the opinion in question was formed without personal examination, and indeed without seeing the patient.

---

* Despite Stephen's 'polite' references to Dr Savage, the underlying bitter antagonism of the paranoiac is seen in the use of the word, 'Bedlam'. The correct name of the institution was—and still is—'The Royal Bethlehem Hospital'.

'The opinion of Dr Savage became known to many relations, friends and acquaintances of the object of his suspicion, and to the members of his club, with results of a damaging, if not disastrous, character.'

The pamphlet then goes on to explain that Stephen had himself been examined by three leading British physicians, and that, in January, 1891, 'the patient was examined at Paris by two eminent French doctors, who certified in writing that he was free from brain disease'.

In the previous December, the pamphlet explains, 'Dr Savage expressed the opinion that the patient ought to be put under restraint; and that, failing this, he ought to go to some quiet and distant place for several months, if possible, under the close superintendence of a medical attendant. If this were not done he anticipated *an outbreak of a serious, and probably violent, character*. [My italics.] He especially deprecated staying in London, visiting Paris, or going to Cambridge.

'In defiance of Dr Savage's advice his patient stayed in London, visited Paris, and went to Cambridge.

'No serious or violent attack took place.'

Only the murderous attack on Frances Coles on the following Ides of February!

After explaining how the patient has been living quietly in London and Cambridge, 'reading, writing, speaking at public debates and political meetings, lecturing on law and coaching in history . . . ,' Stephen then mentions that 'in November, 1890, Dr Savage wrote the following letter, which was sealed up and endorsed "not to be opened till May 1891". On the first of May the patient opened the letter, which ran as follows:

'3, HENRIETTA STREET,
CAVENDISH SQUARE, W.
November 21, 1890.

'DEAR
According to promise I write my opinion as to the next 6 months of your life.

'For some weeks to come there will be waste of money, buying useless things, i.e. things for which you have no real need.

'You will borrow money right and left. You will dress in unconventional ways and cause worry to your relations.

'You will discover that you have incurred debts which of yourself you cannot pay and will feel it a grievance that you have to fall in with the conditions which are imposed.

'You will then take to bed and spend much of the spring in reading in bed and doing nothing of any good, not earning a living. The period will be one rather of exhaustion than of depression, and so the circle will be completed.

'I am,

'Yours truly,

G. H. SAVAGE.'

The pamphlet ends:

'. . . it is submitted that the opinion of Dr Savage on this case is absolutely worthless; and that there is no ground to suppose that the person referred to ever suffered from morbid excitement or exaltation.

'This suggestion is made in the interest of a person who has been gravely prejudiced, if not irreparably damaged, by an opinion formed in good faith, but, as he believes, on wholly erroneous grounds. It is not intended to depreciate Dr Savage's deservedly high reputation: but merely to imply that he has, in this case, made one of those mistakes from which the most eminent physicians cannot be wholly exempt.'

Exactly one year after this letter of Dr Savage's had been written—that is, on 21st November, 1891—James Kenneth Stephen, still wholly sane, in his opinion, was committed to St Andrew's Hospital, Northampton, from which he was never to emerge alive.

And what had triggered off that 'morbid excitement or cerebral exaltation' that Dr Savage, the leading alienist of his

day, had uncomfortably in mind when he penned his letter on
21st November, 1890, a little after he had seen Stephen? This:
that the day was exactly two years after the maniac murder of
Farmer on 21st November 1888—the birthday of the Empress
Frederick, sister of the Prince of Wales. On the third anniversary of this evidently troubling matter, the liberty of J. K.
Stephen was to end for ever.

Writing to me, a leading modern specialist in morbid psychology refers to 'the famous Stephen family, which included
Virginia Woolf who, I understand, suffered from chronic
depressive illnesses and eventually committed suicide. From
what you say it would seem, therefore, that there was a clear-cut
family history of manic-depressive psychosis—an illness which
many psychiatrists consider to be primarily genetically determined and may be associated with intellectual brilliance.'

Of the unhappy Stephen's intellectual brilliance there can
be no doubt. Nor, indeed, can there be of his certain insanity.

Eddy, like all other members of the Royal Family, was
allocated, and effectively performed, his share of all that
monotonous round of public duty which must always make the
reflective mind thank God that it was not born royal.

The Court Circulars of *The Times* and other newspapers, of
The Illustrated London News, *The Graphic*, *Black and White*, and
many another weekly journal, faithfully record the openly busy
life that Eddy led. Though he had become engaged to Princess
Hélène on 20th August, 1890, no word of this engagement had
ever reached even the most irresponsible sheets.

Vincent says, 'He did not, indeed, entirely desert his regiment, but for the remainder of his life the time which he could
spend with his comrades in arms became less and less and the
demands upon his time more pressing.'

This is true, but he was with the Tenth in York in April,
1891, and after that with his regiment at Marlboro' Barracks,
Dublin.

Three plans regarding Eddy's future presented themselves

for consideration—it would have sounded too optimistic to call them 'solutions'.

1. To let Eddy stay in Dublin with the Tenth. This was the proposal preferred by the Princess of Wales, who thought that the nearer Eddy was, the easier it would be to keep an eye on him.
2. To travel in Europe, which was Queen Victoria's plan.
3. To send him 'as a punishment and a precaution', to the furthest bounds of the Empire. This was the Prince of Wales's plan.

The discussion of Eddy's future provoked an active, lively and, at times, somewhat acrimonious correspondence among the principal members of the Royal Family.

Queen Victoria, in putting forward her plan that Eddy should travel in Europe, complained that he was 'too English', and suggested that meeting persons of his rank on the Continent might do much to cure him of this 'Englishness'.

The Prince of Wales responded briskly in Eddy's defence:

'If you think Eddy too English, it is a good fault in these days and will make him much more popular . . . His remaining in the Army is simply a waste of time . . . His education and future have been a matter of some considerable anxiety to us, and the difficulty of rousing him is very great. A good sensible wife with some considerable character is what he needs most, but where is she to be found? (*5th August, 1891*)'

At private secretary level, discussion was more outspoken. Writing to Lord Salisbury's private secretary, Sir Francis Knollys explained the situation thus:

'As you are aware, the Queen strongly advocates Prince Eddy travelling in Europe, instead of visiting the Cape of Good Hope (or, rather, South Africa), New Zealand, Canada, etc.

'Unfortunately, her views on *certain social* subjects are so strong that the Prince of Wales does not like to tell her his real reason for sending Prince Eddy away, which is intended as a *punishment*, and as a means of keeping him out of harm's way; and I am afraid that neither of these objects would be attained by his simply travelling about Europe. She is therefore giving her advice in the dark.'

Magnus suggests, probably rightly, that 'Queen Victoria was fairly well-informed, in fact, about the life that Prince Eddy was leading'. Since her correspondence shews her to have been singularly well informed about the scandalous behaviour of other members of her family, there is no reason to suppose that she was ignorant of those habits which had been causing 'considerable anxiety' to his parents.

The Queen stuck to her guns. There were, she admitted in a letter to the Prince of Wales (15th August, 1891), as many 'designing pretty women in the Colonies' as anywhere else, but Eddy would acquire more polish in his visiting European courts. 'A Prince', she said firmly, 'ought to be cosmopolitan,' and she gave it as her opinion that Wilhelm II was what he was 'to a great extent, owing to his having never travelled':

'You speak of [Eddy's] apathy and want of application. *You* disliked your lessons very much, and it was very difficult to make you apply. But you travelled a great deal, and with good people, and you profited immensely by what you saw, and by the number of interesting and clever people you got to know. 'No doubt you were much more lively than Eddy . . .

But in the end it was Alix who got her way. By the common consent of all the parties concerned, the courtship of Princess Hélène was abandoned, and a new bride found for Eddy, Princess Victoria Mary ('May') of Teck. Eddy would remain all the winter with his regiment in Dublin, and the marriage with Princess 'May' would take place in the following spring.

'I think (*Knollys wrote to Ponsonby on 19th August, 1891, almost a year, to the day, after Eddy's unpublicized engagement to Princess*

Hélène) the preliminaries are pretty well settled, but do you suppose Princess May will make any resistance? I do not anticipate any real opposition on Prince Eddy's part if he is properly managed and is told he *must* do it—that it is for the good of the country, etc., etc.'

Princess May made no resistance. The Tecks were not only poor, they were also morganatic, and the Duke himself had all the social disadvantages of the man who adventures outside his social position without the money to get back to his proper state in life. Handsome rather than pretty, but of ravishing beauty under the influence of deep emotion; clever, controlled, dominating, self-disciplined Princess May did what many another Victorian girl did: sacrificed herself for a father whom she loved and of whom she was more than half ashamed.

Eddy was promoted to lieutenant-colonel, and on 3rd December, 1891, whilst staying at Luton Hoo with Herr de Falbe, the Danish Minister, Eddy proposed to Princess May, and was accepted. The highly efficient Victorian publicity-machine went into its traditionally vigorous action, so that, in Vincent's words, 'all England rejoiced to hear that the Duke of Clarence and Avondale and Princess Victoria Mary of Teck were betrothed'.

The proposal and its acceptance were not only expected, they had been rehearsed. In the middle of November Eddy had written to Jim Stephen to tell him of the engagement which had been arranged. Jim answered some days later, but it was not from 18, Trinity-street, Cambridge, where he had been living since his last 'cure', but from the 'violent' ward of St Andrew's Hospital, Northampton, from which he was never to emerge alive. Stephen's unstable 'sanity' had been unable to withstand the trauma of sudden and violent sexual jealousy.

Though Ponsonby, some weeks earlier, had written of Eddy that 'I am told he don't care for Princess May of Teck, and she appears to be too proud to take the trouble of running after him, for which I rather admire her', the affianced pair did seem to like each other.

In her happiness, not only for the prospect of Eddy's wedding, fixed for 27th February, 1892, but for all that reparation and reconstruction that she hoped for from the marriage, Mother-dear wrote to the Queen:

'Beloved Mama,—this time I do hope that dear Eddy has found the *right bride* . . .'

'May,' she said, 'will be one of us at once, and the fact of her being English will make all the difference and carry the whole nation with them.' But Motherdear's kind heart couldn't forget at what cost this new prospect of happiness had been bought: 'the sad tragedy and blighted life of that sweet dear Hélène.'

10. 'I loved him so much . . . he was so wonderful!'

Too angry and humiliated over the Beresford blackmail affair to wish to be with Bertie, Alix let him spend his fiftieth birthday—9th November, 1891—alone. But the news, three days later, that Prince George had caught typhoid fever brought her hurrying back from Livadia, and in the face of a common peril the Prince and Princess of Wales forgot their momentary differences and became united once more at the bedside of their sick son.

George recovered, but nearly two months later, as the many guests, including the Tecks, were moving in on Sandringham for Eddy's twenty-eighth birthday celebrations, Eddy fell ill himself.

On 7th January, though he had complained of feeling unwell, Eddy insisted on attending a local shoot. As he left, he chanced to turn around, and, seeing his mother looking at him through a window, took off his hat and waved a smiling farewell. For many years that hat hung in Alix's bedroom.

He returned from the shoot looking ill and suffering from a bad headache. On the following day he collapsed with influenza, which had reached epidemic proportions throughout Europe.

His natural kindness forced him to rouse himself the next

day, so as to receive his presents and to thank the donors; but it was obvious that he was too ill to stay up. He went upstairs to bed, and was never to leave it.

' "I still see him before my eyes," wrote Motherdear, "as he went up the stairs for the last time in his life and turned his head to give me his friendly nod, which I must do without for ever now." '

The specialists, summoned from London, could do nothing, and the influenza turned to 'inflammation of the lungs', and then to pneumonia. As the family gathered around him, he raved in his delirium, and at 8 a.m. on 13th January, 1892, Alix told Bertie that they must face the fact that Eddy was dying. At a little after midnight, the doctors persuaded Alix to take a little rest. Hardly had she lain down on the sofa in the adjoining room, when she was hastily summoned to Eddy's bedside. Eddy, at last, was dying.

'It was as if I myself must die at that moment, and yet I had to master my tears and my deep, deep despair, and be calm. Although the tears were running down I spoke to him, but, Oh, he no longer heard me, and yet he was still talking, but only with great difficulty and effort and with that terrible rattle in his throat.

'All we could hear were the sounds of terrible agony in his throat and chest and our own sobs . . .'

Eddy seemed to rally again and again, so that the stricken watchers were advised to go and rest. Each rally 'was only for a few minutes, as a candle flares up once or twice and at length slowly dies out . . . it is hard, so hard, and Our Lord's ways are past understanding'.

And then a curious thing happened. The ghastly death-rattle stopped, and in a sweet, clear voice, the dying Prince said, 'Something too awful has happened—my darling brother George is dead.'

Seven hours after the family had gathered about his bedside, he suddenly asked, 'Who is that?'—and murmuring it again and again, ever more slowly and faintly, he dropped at length into the last sleep of all.

From the purely practical point of view, Philip Magnus is right when he states: 'The promotion of Prince George to the position of heir presumptive was a merciful act of providence. Prince George, who possessed a strong and exemplary character as well as a robust constitution, had early given promise of becoming the embodiment of all those domestic and public virtues which the British peoples cherish.'

There was even a rumour current for many years that, loved as he was, Eddy had been the victim of a judicial killing; that it was the knowledge that he had to die, to make way for one better suited to be King and Emperor, which plunged his parents into such paroxysms of grief.

The grief was real. The Prince of Wales sobbed openly at the funeral service at Windsor, when Eddy's coffin was carried in by officers and men of his old regiment. The Queen wrote to the Empress Frederick on 16th January, 1892, that her son 'is broken down', and as for 'poor dear Alix, though bearing up wonderfully, she does nothing but cry'. As the Prince of Wales had written to the Queen two days before, 'Gladly would I have given my life for his, as I put no value on mine . . . Such a tragedy has never before occurred in the annals of our family, and it is hard that poor little May should virtually become a widow before she is a wife.'

A paper-covered booklet, containing a sermon preached in Sandringham Church on the Sunday after Eddy's funeral, bears this inscription in his father's hand: 'To my dearest Wife, in remembrance of our beloved Eddy who was taken from us. "He is not dead but sleepeth." From her devoted but broken-hearted husband, Bertie.'

The morning papers of 14th January, 1892, carried the news in the 'Stop Press'—Eddy had died in the dawn, too late to catch the last edition.

In a lunatic aylum in Northampton, a patient, who had

written regularly to Eddy throughout his illness,* read the news, and pushed his breakfast tray aside.

For twenty days he refused all food and drink, nor did the hospital authorities consider that their duty lay in preventing this slow suicide. They knew his history.

The death certificate of James Kenneth Stephen, Male, 33 years, Barrister-at-law, of 18, Trinity-street, Cambridge, gives 'Cause of Death' as 'Mania, 2½ months. Persistent refusal of food 20 days. Exhaustion.'

He died on 3rd February, 1892. If one subtracts twenty days from 3rd February, one finds oneself at 14th January, 1892, the day on which the news of Eddy's death was broken to the world. There can be here no question of coincidence. Once Eddy had gone, Jim Stephen had no more wish to stay, and with the starved, exhausted body went the Ripper.

They buried Eddy with all the pomp and circumstance of that impressive ritual designed for those who were born to be kings and emperors. But when all the military splendour, no less than the tears, had passed away, and Eddy lay within his white marble sarcophagus, there rested, on that splendid tomb, almost until yesterday, a wreath of *immortelles*, bearing a card with the simple inscription, *Hélène.*

Later in that year, when George, in the ancient Biblical fashion 'had gone unto his brother's widow', and a new wedding was being planned, the Queen, who had loved Eddy dearly, was talking to another who had loved him well; Princess Hélène d'Orléans. '*Oui,*' said the Princess, '*je l'aimais tant. Il était si bon . . .*', 'Yes I loved him so much. He was so wonderful . . .'

Perhaps Mrs Battiscombe is right when she says that Eddy was 'lethargic, dissipated, impervious to education and manifestly unfitted to the high position for which he was apparently destined'. It is also true that he was a kindly man. He had remembered Captain Holford, his Equerry-in-Waiting, and had written to him from his death-bed, and surely those letters from poor Jim Stephen had not gone unanswered?

* Vincent, though he, of course, does not mention the lunatic asylum.

Sandringham Church.

But Eddy had one great gift which, in the opinion of some, outweighs in importance every other with which many may be blessed. He had the gift of inspiring affection.

May he rest in peace . . .

Appendix

The pamphlet written by J. K. Stephen and
privately circulated by him in Cambridge
and London after May, 1891.

About the end of October last Dr G. H. Savage, of 3, Henrietta Street, formerly Principal of Bedlam, formed the opinion
that the gentleman hereinafter referred to was not in a state of
perfect mental health, but was suffering from morbid excitement or cerebral exaltation. Dr Savage had some personal
acquaintance with the gentleman in question and his past
career; but the opinion in question was formed without personal
examination, and indeed without seeing the patient.

The opinion of Dr Savage became known to many relations,
friends and acquaintances of the object of his suspicion, and
to the members of his club, with results of a damaging, if not
disastrous, character.

The gentleman was never medically examined by Dr Savage;
but he was separately examined by Sir Andrew Clark, Dr
Hughlings Jackson and Dr Hack Tuke in October, November
and December.

Sir Andrew Clark declared that he was in perfect physical

health, and would continue so if he adopted certain regulations as to diet, clothing, &c., which he practically did.

Dr Hughlings Jackson was of opinion that his nervous system was in perfect order; he would give no opinion as to his brain.

Dr Hack Tuke, after a very prolonged and minute examination, could find no trace of brain disease; but was of opinion that Dr Savage was unlikely to go wrong on such a matter.

Early in January, 1891, the patient was examined at Paris by two eminent French doctors, who certified in writing that he was free from brain disease.

In December Dr Savage expressed the opinion that the patient ought to be put under restraint; and that, failing this he ought to go to some quiet and distant place for several months, if possible under the close superintendence of a medical attendant. If this were not done he anticipated an outbreak of a serious, and probably violent, character. He especially deprecated staying in London, visiting Paris, or going to Cambridge.

In defiance of Dr Savage's advice his patient stayed in London, visited Paris and went to Cambridge.

No serious or violent attack took place.

Dr Savage's patient has been, since January, at Cambridge and London. In the former place he has lived a busy and active life, seeing old friends, and making new ones; dispensing and receiving hospitality; reading, writing, speaking at public debates and political meetings, lecturing on law and coaching in history. He has contributed to newspapers, begun two books, and published a third. He has taken no advice, and subjected himself to no restraint.

During this time he has corresponded with Dr Savage, and has seen him when in London. At an interview in February Dr Savage expressed the opinion that he was much better, if not entirely recovered (despite his neglect of advice). Subsequently, after consultation with a friend of both parties resident at Cambridge, Dr Savage and Dr Hack Tuke wrote a joint opinion advising him to stay at Cambridge and go on with his work as a teacher.

In April Dr Savage, at an interview, admitted that his expectations had not come true; and that the defiance of his advice had not produced the expected evils. Upon the patient declaring that he believed he had never suffered from excitement or exaltation, or done anything he had cause to regret, Dr Savage said that this belief was a symptom of dormant disease, and a proof that the recovery was not perfect.

In November, 1890, Dr Savage wrote the following letter, which was sealed up and endorsed 'not to be opened till May 1891'. On the first of May the patient opened the letter, which ran as follows:

> 3, HENRIETTA STREET,
> CAVENDISH SQUARE, W.
> *November* 21, 1890.

DEAR

According to promise I write my opinion as to the next 6 months of your life.

For some weeks to come there will be waste of money, buying useless things, i.e. things for which you have no real need.

You will borrow money right and left. You will dress in unconventional ways and cause worry to your relations.

You will discover that you have incurred debts which of yourself you cannot pay and will feel it a grievance that you have to fall in with the conditions which are imposed.

You will then take to bed and spend much of the spring in reading in bed and doing nothing of any good, not earning a living. The period will be one rather of exhaustion than of depression, and so the circle will be completed.

> I am,
> Yours truly,
> G. H. SAVAGE.

During the first weeks above referred to, the patient bought nothing, borrowed nothing, and dressed conventionally. During the whole of the six months he rose early, worked hard, and earned a fair income. He never made any discovery of debts which he could not pay.

Dr Savage has often expressed the opinion that his patient would not recover without first going through a prolonged period of depression or exhaustion. It is common ground between him and the patient that no such period has taken place.

Dr Savage says that owing to peculiar circumstances for which he did not make allowance, his prophecy was not fulfilled: but he declares that his patient's present good health is temporary and that the prophecy will be fulfilled some day.

Dr Savage's opinions as to the future course of the disease were expressed, in November, in unqualified terms and with unbounded confidence.

Under these circumstances it is submitted that the opinion of Dr Savage on this case is absolutely worthless: and that there is no ground to suppose that the person referred to ever suffered from morbid excitement or exaltation.

This suggestion is made, in the interest of a person who has been gravely prejudiced, if not irreparably damaged, by an opinion formed in good faith, but, as he believes, on wholly erroneous grounds. It is not intended to depreciate Dr Savage's deservedly high reputation: but merely to imply that he has, in this case, made one of those mistakes from which the most eminent physicians cannot be wholly exempt.

CAMBRIDGE,
  May, 1891.

Note. Before J. K. Stephen was committed to St Andrew's Hospital, on 21st November, 1891, his manner had become so offensively eccentric that he had been expelled from his club.

Bibliography

Below are listed the *principal* works consulted in the preparation of this book. Works which have yielded merely a casual reference are not included here, though they are consistently mentioned in the text.

All the standard works of reference—*The Complete Peerage*, *The Army List*, *The Navy List*, *The Annual Register*, *The Dictionary of National Biography*, *The Cambridge University Calendar*, *Debrett*, *Burke*, *Dodd*, *Who's Who*, *Haydn's Dictionary of Dates*, *The Post Office London Directory*, *Kelly's* and other Directories, etc.—have been, as usual, of invaluable assistance.

The resources of the Westminster City Libraries, at St Martin's Street (Central Reference), Buckingham Palace Road (Westminster Collection) and Marylebone Road, as well as those of the British Museum and the Mile End and Whitechapel Road branches of the Tower Hamlets Public Libraries, have been, once again, essential to the collecting of necessary information; whilst, in the case of this particular book, the Rate-books of St Marylebone Vestry have proved of great value.

A LOUNGER IN SOCIETY. *The Glass of Fashion*. London: John Hogg, 1881.

ARCHER, FRED. *Ghost Detectives: Crime and the Psychic World*. London: W. H. Allen, 1970.

ARTHUR, SIR GEORGE. *Queen Alexandra*. London: Chapman & Hall, 1934.

BATTISCOMBE, GEORGINA. *Queen Alexandra*. London: Constable, 1969.

CROFT-COOKE, RUPERT. *Feasting with Panthers: A New Consideration of Some Late Victorian Writers*. London: W. H. Allen, 1969.

DALTON, D. D., JOHN. *The Cruise of Her Majesty's Ship "Bacchante", 1879–1882*. London: Macmillan, 1882.

FIELD, JULIAN OSGOOD. (*Published as 'Anon.'*) *Uncensored Recollections*. London: Eveleigh Nash, 1922.

— *More Uncensored Recollections*. London: Eveleigh Nash, 1924.

— *Things I Shouldn't Tell*. London: Eveleigh Nash & Grayson, 1924.

HARRISON, MICHAEL. *Fanfare of Strumpets*. London: W. H. Allen, 1971.

— *Painful Details: Twelve Victorian Scandals*. London: Max Parrish, 1962.

HARRISON, MICHAEL. *London by Gaslight*. London: Peter Davies, 1962.

HYDE, H. MONTGOMERY. *Their Good Names: Twelve Cases of Libel and Slander with Some Introductory Reflections on the Law*. London: Hamish Hamilton, 1970.

LEE, SIR SIDNEY. *Life of King Edward VII: A Biography*. London: Macmillan, 1925, 1927.

McCORMICK, DONALD. *The Identity of Jack the Ripper*. London: Jarrolds, 1959.

MAGNUS, PHILIP. *King Edward the Seventh*. London: John Murray, 1964.

MAYBRICK, FLORENCE. *My Fifteen Lost Years: Mrs Maybrick's Own Story*. New York and London. Funk & Wagnall's Company, 1905.

ODELL, ROBIN. *Jack the Ripper in Fact and Fiction*. London: George G. Harrap & Co., 1965.

PEARSALL, RONALD. *The Worm in the Bud: The World of Victorian Sexuality*. Weidenfeld & Nicholson, 1969.

'POT' AND 'SWEARS'. *The Scarlet City*. London: Sands & Co., 1899.

REES, J. D. *H.R.H. the Duke of Clarence and Avondale in Southern India*. London: Kegan Paul, Trench, Trübner & Co., 1891.

ST AUBYN, GILES. *The Royal George: The Life of H.R.H. Prince George, Duke of Cambridge, 1819–1904*. London: Constable, 1963.

STEPHEN, J. K. *Quo Musa Tendis*. Cambridge: Bowes and Macmillan, 1888.

— *Lapsus Calami*. Cambridge: Bowes and Macmillan, 1896.

TANNER, J. R. (*Ed.*) *The Historical Register of the University of Cambridge to 1910*. Cambridge: The University Press, 1917.

VINCENT, JAMES E. *His Royal Highness the Duke of Clarence and Avondale: A Memoir (Written by Authority)*. London: John Murray, 1893.

WILSON, COLIN. *A Casebook of Murder*. London: Arthur Barker 1962.

— *Ritual in the Dark*. London: Gollancz, 1960.

WILSON, COLIN and PITMAN, PATRICIA. *Encyclopaedia of Murder*. London: Arthur Barker, 1961.

Periodical publications

The Cambridge University Calendar
The Criminologist
The Daily Telegraph
The Field
The Graphic
The Leicester Chronicle
The Liverpool Post
Lloyds Sunday Newspaper
The Morning Post
The North London Press
The Pall-Mall Gazette
The Penny Illustrated Newspaper
The Police Gazette
The Queen
Reynolds' News

BIBLIOGRAPHY

The Saturday Review
The Scottish Leader
Spalding's Street and General Directory of Cambridge
The Times
Truth

Index

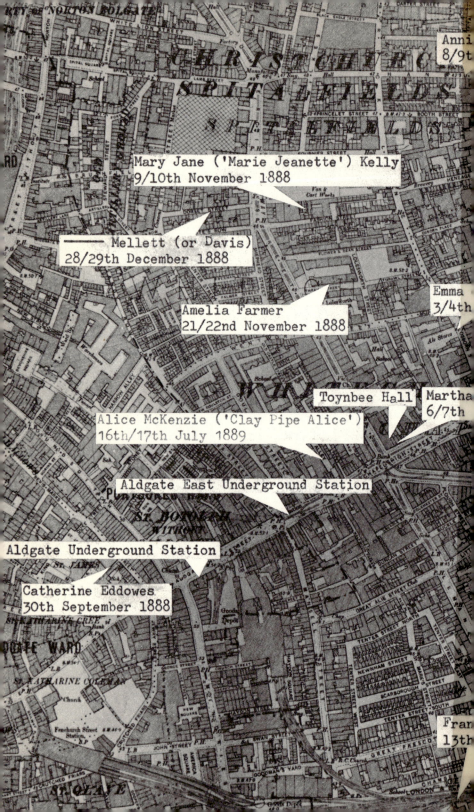

Anni
8/9t

CHRISTCHURC
SPITALFIELDS
SPITALFIELDS

Mary Jane ('Marie Jeanette') Kelly
9/10th November 1888

Mellett (or Davis)
28/29th December 1888

Amelia Farmer
21/22nd November 1888

Emma
3/4th

Toynbee Hall

Martha
6/7th

Alice McKenzie ('Clay Pipe Alice')
16th/17th July 1889

Aldgate East Underground Station

Aldgate Underground Station

Catherine Eddowes
30th September 1888

Fran
13th